Speaker's Handbook of Humor

Speaker's Handbook of Humor

Robert Orben

Merriam-Webster, Incorporated
Springfield, Massachusetts

A GENUINE MERRIAM-WEBSTER

The name *Webster* alone is no guarantee of excellence. It is used by a number of publishers and may serve mainly to mislead an unwary buyer.

Merriam-Webster™ is the name you should look for when you consider the purchase of dictionaries or other fine reference books. It carries the reputation of a company that has been publishing since 1831 and is your assurance of quality and authority.

Library of Congress Cataloging-in-Publication Data

Orben, Robert
  Speaker's handbook of humor / Robert Orben.
      p. cm.
  ISBN 0-87779-629-7
  1.Public speaking. 2. American wit and humor. I. Title.

PN4193.I5 O76 2000
808.5'1'0207—dc21

                                        00-038677

Printed and bound in the United States of America

123456BW:RRD020100

Introduction

So you're asking yourself: Who could use a handbook of speaker's humor? Speakers, sure. Professional speakers, certainly. But you're not either of those. You're in business, education, publishing or politics. You're an executive, a teacher, or in sales. But surely you haven't forgotten all those times when you've been asked to "stand up and say a few words."

We're living in an age of information technology, but regardless of the technology, words convey the information and the message. So whatever we can do to enhance the effectiveness of those words is the key to the success of the message. Enter humor.

Humor has morphed its way from show business into every aspect of modern life. TV commercials that make you laugh also make you buy. Studies have shown that students learn faster and retain more if the facts, figures and concepts are delivered with a dollop of laughter. Job applicants and officeholders are judged in many ways, but a sense of humor ranks high on the list.

In this new millennium, we have all become communicators. More and more, humor is the necessary key to making it all work. This transition of humor from the main stage to the mainstream is reflected in the time line of my half-century of comedy writing.

In the forties, fifties and sixties, I turned out books of professional-level comedy material. These books became the basic resource and starting point for many comedy performers of the time.

In the early seventies, the uses and users of humor were a-changing, and I carried laughter into a new area—corporate humor. National publications described me as a humor consultant to business—a bizarre concept to many at the time. Today using humor in business communication, advertising and employee relationships is an accepted practice.

In 1974, my writing took an even more high-visibility leap into a new area. I became a speechwriter for Gerald R. Ford. My unusual resume for a White House speechwriter got worldwide media attention. For many months, any reference to me was always preceded by "former comedy writer for Red Skelton and Jack Paar."

In 1976 I was appointed a Special Assistant to the President and Director of the White House Speechwriting Department, but interest in my humor writing continued strong, and television provided the clear indication of just how much the public had come to accept humor as a vital part of the political landscape.

In 1976, *All's Fair* was a new TV situation comedy set in Washington, D.C., with a political theme. It starred Richard Crenna and Bernadette Peters. A third character in the show was a fast-talking aide described as joke-writer to the President. The actor who played this Orben-inspired character later starred in such blockbuster films as *Batman*—Michael Keaton.

Now I'm not suggesting that political candidates should be chosen in joke-filled rooms. But every political figure today knows the importance of humor in shaping image and message. Political pundits and officeholders alike regularly monitor the monologues of Jay Leno and David Letterman. Are the jokes benign or harmful? Should they be ignored or countered? In political discourse and in every other form of communication, humor is a not-to-be-underrated ingredient.

The question I am most often asked is, "Can anyone do it?" A common lament is, "I enjoy a joke but I can't tell one." Not so.

Obviously, humor has to fit the style, sensibilities and situation of the user. I think back to what I was writing in 1964. I had just begun a six-year stint as a writer on the Red Skelton TV show. I was responsible for the monologue that opened the show. I was also sending jokes to Dick Gregory—and I was also sending a page a day of speech humor to Senator Barry Goldwater, who was running against Lyndon Johnson for President of the United States.

This array of comedic uses answers another frequently asked question: "Is humor interchangeable? Can a one-size joke fit all?" Hardly.

Nevertheless, anyone—everyone—can tell an effective joke, providing it's the right joke for them and the right joke for their audience. Even the most fearful of joke-tellers should take courage from the wisdom of Charlie Chaplin. Chaplin was quoted as saying, "If what you're doing is funny, you don't have to be funny doing it."

In this book you will find ways to determine what type of humor matches your personality and speaking style. You're taken step-by-step through the maze of situations, events and occasions that can challenge even experienced speakers. Even more important, you are given the material and know-how to turn challenges into triumphs.

The *Speaker's Handbook of Humor* is just that—a handbook to provide you with the expertise and material to get you through any speaking situation. The focus is on humor, but it is also a hands-on approach to writing, researching, rehearsing and delivering effective speeches.

The *Speaker's Handbook of Humor* is a lifetime of experience packed up into an easy-to-use humor tool kit.

You won't want to leave home without it.

Bob Orben

Using the *Speaker's Handbook of Humor*

This is a handbook in the true sense of the word—a reference to be carried from place to place by anyone engaged in the perilous and often nerve-wracking act of speaking in public.

Its premise is that no matter how small or large one's audience and no matter what we are speaking about, celebrating or selling, we are much better served if we deliver our message with humor, wit and style.

To this end, we have created an A-Z compendium of practical advice, reflection, jokes and one-liners aimed at the man or woman on the verge of standing up and speaking, whether it be an academic convocation or a retirement roast.

It is not meant to be read from front to back but consulted for the occasion, challenge or dilemma which presents itself to the speaker.

The jokes in this handbook are limited to those that target situations in which speakers often find themselves, ranging from humorous introductions to dealing with interrupters and hecklers.

It is arranged from A-Z with three forms of entry:

Major Articles or references to them are listed in capital letters.

ADVICE—AND HOW TO IGNORE IT

Jokes, gags, comic reactions and one-liners or references to them are listed under headings in upper- and lowercase letters.

Acknowledging a Gag Gift or Award

Some entries of this type include many jokes and are divided into sections by subheadings in italic type.

Audience

At a Black Tie Event

Cross-references to either kind of entry are listed at entry words that are in upper- and lowercase letters. The name of the entry being referred to is shown in all capitals if it is a major article and in upper- and lowercase letters if it is for jokes.

Audacious Behavior —See MISTAKES

Acknowledging Applause —See Applause

Major Articles

ADVICE—AND HOW TO IGNORE IT
ALWAYS LEAD THEM LAUGHING
ASSESSING YOUR AUDIENCE
CONTROLLING YOUR AUDIENCE
DON'TS . . . IF YOU WANT TO GET LAUGHS
HARD WORK OF HUMOR, THE
HOW TO SUCCEED IN HUMOR BY REALLY TRYING
KINDER, GENTLER COMEDY
LESSONS I LEARNED FROM LOWELL THOMAS
MISTAKES
MONEY AND SPEECHWRITING
OPENER: THE FIRST TWO MINUTES OF YOUR
    SPEECH
PREPARING FOR YOUR SPEECH
REHEARSING YOUR SPEECH
ROASTS:
    Preparing the Roast
    Delivering the Roast
    Serving the Roast
    Jokes for the Roast
    Responding to the Roast
SPEECHWRITERS: The Care and Heeding of Speech-
    writers
SPICING UP THOSE DULL SPEECHES
STAGE FRIGHT AND HOW TO DEAL WITH IT
STARTING YOUR SPEECH A WINNER
STORIES: WHERE DO THEY COME FROM?
TAPING: After the Applause Has Ended
TOPICAL HUMOR: THE CUTTING EDGE
USES AND LIMITS OF HUMOR, THE
USING HUMOR WHEN YOU'RE AFRAID TO USE
    HUMOR
"WHY HUMOR?"
WRITER'S BLOCK AND HOW TO GET AROUND IT

Speaker's Handbook of Humor

A

Accuracy —See *Don't Neglect the Facts* at DON'TS . . . IF YOU WANT TO GET LAUGHS

Acknowledging a Gag Gift or Award

First, I want to thank you all for this rare, thoughtful and obviously expensive gift. I can't imagine where you found it. *(Hold it up to your nose and sniff it.)* Hmmmm—Crackerjacks.

All of my life I've wanted something like this— which will give you some idea what kind of a life I've had.

As you can see, I am pleased, honored and deeply touched by this most thoughtful and valuable gift. And to let you know just how moved I am, let me just say that it will serve two very useful purposes: It is the last award in our program tonight—and it will be the first item in my garage sale this weekend.

First, I want to thank you all for this token of your depreciation.

Acknowledging an Introduction —See Introductions

Acknowledging Applause —See Applause

1

Adjourning —See Ending an Evening/Program

Ad-Libbing / Ad-Libs —See (1) THE HARD WORK OF HUMOR; (2) STARTING YOUR SPEECH A WINNER; (3) STORIES: WHERE DO THEY COME FROM?

ADVICE—AND HOW TO IGNORE IT

I.

A few years ago I was at a seminar for public speakers. A presentation on vocal technique was being given, At one point the expert said that there was never any reason for speakers to audibly clear their throats. If you felt a tickle or congestion, all you had to do was go through the physical motion of clearing your throat—but without sound—and it would have the same effect. He demonstrated the motion. So far, so good.

But a few minutes later, it was as if the gods had thought over this bit of advice and said, "Oh, yeah?" The speaker developed a frog in his throat. It was evident to the audience that he was applying his silent technique to the problem—unsuccessfully. The speaker continued with his presentation, and his throat continued to congest. Suppressed gurgles and rumblings from his larynx were now being carried over the sound system. But the expert gamely carried on as his face began to turn from a Renoir rouge to a fire engine red. Then the aural dam burst and the room was filled with the sound of grinding, gut-wrenching throat-clearing as listeners rushed to his aid with glasses of water.

This endeth the first reading on Advice.

***

Advice. If you're a speaker it comes at you in torrents. You get it in newsletters, magazines, cassettes, books, seminars, workshops, and conventions. And the advice is never tentative. It's always presented with absolute certitude—as if it just missed the trip down from Mount Sinai.

This advice is also curiously repetitive. You hear and read the same admonitions, suggestions, and rules to the point where you can lip-synch them with the pontificators. They become tradition. They become ritual. They become the scripture of the speaking profession—unchallenged and unquestioned.

Maybe the Question Period should begin.

Let's start with one of the most common bits of speaking advice you will ever encounter: A speaker should never, ever say to an audience, "Can everyone hear me?" To do so is the mark of the amateur, the unprofessional, the inept. On the other hand, no one has ever explained to me what is so ept about doing a minute of opening joke or premise before finding out that half the audience can't hear you.

Of course you check out the sound equipment, the microphone, and do a voice check before the audience comes into the room. But so much can happen during a program. Speakers before you readjust the microphone. Cords are pulled loose. The leg of a chair flattens a cable. Amplifiers go on vacation. What was perfect at 6:15 can be a shambles at 8:00.

If I'm on a program and I have any suspicion that the audience isn't comfortably hearing what is going on, I have no problem starting off with the scintillating line, "Before we begin, can you hear me in the back?" I believe in starting a speech with your best joke or story, and if only 60% of the audience is hearing it, a sizable amount of an audience's goodwill and attention are lost. By asking, "Can you hear me in the back?"—you know immediately if there is a problem, and can solve it. And while you're solving it, there's nothing wrong with saying, "Don't complain. You could be the lucky ones."

How many times have you heard or read advice on

3

public speaking that could more properly be called "Grooming and Posture 101"? The dogma here is that speakers should dress for success. They should be dynamic, forceful, have clean fingernails, blow-dried hair, never cling to the sides of the lectern, and—perish the thought—if they're of the male persuasion, never appear before an audience with their suit jackets unbuttoned. Good stuff!

Then I attend an event where a speaker is introduced and he casually stands up and strolls over to the lectern wearing a rumpled sport jacket and a pair of designer slacks. When he gets to the lectern, he doesn't unbutton his jacket because it was never buttoned to begin with. What he does do for the next 30 minutes is absolutely captivate his audience. He's funny, he's clever, he's informative, he's sensational. And rumpled sport coat notwithstanding, he gets almost $20,000 a speech for being so.

Moral: Words are the cake—delivery is the icing—wardrobe is the platter.

***

Every speaker, every performer, every artist, every individual has to find his or her own style. We unconsciously, more often than consciously, adopt patterns of speech, dress, and behavior that make us feel comfortable. We add to and alter these styles in the course of a lifetime, but what we end up with is usually not materially different from what we began with. There are very few Picassos in public speaking.

What this means is that, sometimes, the right advice is the wrong advice. A friend of mine, for many years a very successful variety performer always began his act with a very mild joke. One time I asked him why he did this as the joke wasn't all that great and it never got much of an audience reaction. He said he did it because he liked it and it made him feel good.

In essence, this "wrong" joke gave him the right comfort level to proceed with the rest of his act. Immediately following this slow opening, he went into some very effective material that grabbed his audience and never let go. The mild start did not hurt his performance. Its elimination might have. The right advice would have been the wrong advice.

Most advice offered to speakers is well-meaning. Which doesn't keep it from being misguided. This is particularly true when it comes to humor. In books and articles on public speaking, you frequently see the admonition that business and political communicators are not comedians and it is not necessary to use humor in speeches. True. It is also not necessary to wear shoes—but they help us get to where we want to go.

And so, let me offer one more bit of advice on advice: check to see who is giving it. The mind-set, experience, and limitations of the "expert" might very well skew the direction and content of the advice being given. For instance, I have rarely heard a warning against the use of humor by speech coaches and counselors who feel comfortable with humor. The cautioning is generated by those who are personally afraid of humor and pass on their fear. To the earthbound, flight is often threatening. Humor is not for everyone or every occasion, but there are few successful speakers who leave home without it.

II.

Perhaps the most often repeated well-meaning suggestion concerning speech humor is to try out the jokes on friends, neighbors, associates, and family. Why not? Test-marketing is a time-honored concept in merchandising. Plays are assessed and rewritten based on out-of-town tryouts and preview performances. Movies are given sneak previews and sometimes endings are changed, scenes are cut and characters modified, based on audience response. Why shouldn't your speech jokes benefit from the same procedure?

There would be nothing wrong with test-marketing jokes if you could do it to an audience that closely approximates that of the actual event. The suggestion, however, is that you try out the jokes on a few individuals. It is extremely unlikely that family, friends, even associates—can ever achieve in the abstract, the same awareness of an audience's experience, emotions, and group point-of-view necessary to judge the kind of speech humor that works.

The humor that works best and gets the biggest reaction in speeches, is frequently the "you had to be there" type of joke. In most instances, no one is better able than the speaker to understand the dynamics of an audience and an event that leads to the creation or adaptation of such a joke.

In my speeches and workshops on the uses of humor in business and political communication, I give the case history of a wildly successful speech joke. I describe the circumstances of the event, the nature of the audience, and I read the joke created for the speech. I then pause and look around for the reaction. There are always a few polite smiles mixed in with a majority of puzzled looks. The joke is perceived to be a loser.

Then I play a tape of this joke being delivered to its intended audience. Pandemonium! It gets 28 seconds of uproarious audience reaction as the laughter goes on and on and on. My immediate audience listens to this reaction with even more puzzlement until I explain what this joke meant to this particular audience, how it was researched, how it was written, and the principles involved in creating other jokes like it. But the point that I'm making is: If this joke had been tried out on friends, neighbors or associates—they would have reacted in the same unimpressed, puzzled manner as my immediate audience—and the joke-teller might have had second thoughts about using it.

***

It's obvious that we can and do learn from others. We also learn from our mistakes—but nobody lives long enough to make that many mistakes. And so, we read, listen, and observe—and try to learn from and profit by the experience of the "experts." But my advice on advice is that it should always be taken with a shaker full of salt. If it works for you—fine. But as you would when buying a car, road-test it first. However, when it comes to the total picture—your basic approach to speaking and/or performing—my strong suggestion is: Don't seek advice. And when it's offered, don't let it snuff out your dream.

When you ask for advice, the response usually falls into two categories. Your friends will offer unalloyed praise and blind acceptance. Others equate advice with finding fault and will dwell on what they perceive to be "wrong" with what you are doing. The danger here is that such criticism, such advice, usually echoes the tried and true, the establishment view. If you are marching to a different drummer, advice will quite often criticize the beat.

And since most advice tends to be a reflection of the status quo, the traditional, the earthbound, whenever I suggest that speakers and performers pursue their personal vision and pay scant attention to the "experts," I offer this case history.

In 1962, I was in Chicago to shoot some film of Dick

Gregory for the Jack Paar TV show. Dick Gregory had achieved overnight stardom in 1961, and his success was opening doors for black comedians in clubs and in television. During this trip, a press agent for a Chicago nightclub, who knew of my writing for Dick Gregory, told me about a young black performer who was trying to get a foothold in show business. Would I be able to help him? I told her I could only offer some advice and suggestions and said I would try to see his act when he played New York City.

A few weeks later, this young black comedian was playing a small nightclub in New York's Greenwich Village. Without contacting him beforehand, I went down to catch his act. It was different. Parts of it were very imaginative. The act had some unusual touches of warmth and whimsy. But the good elements were overwhelmed by loose construction, disorganized routining, and material that ran hot and cold. The audience reaction was mild. While I recognized the spark that was there, I felt that he was so far from having a commercial act, I didn't want to go backstage and offer the conventional lies that masquerade as praise when we want to protect feelings. I quietly paid the check, left the club, and never contacted him.

It wasn't more than a few months later that this same comedian made his first appearance on television. An instant hit! In a very short time he skyrocketed to the top as one of the funniest and most innovative new comedians in years. This potential advice-giver, this "expert," had only seen the performer for what he wasn't—not what he was.

The performer? Some of you may have heard of him. Bill Cosby.

Advice for Overcoming Writer's Block —See WRITER'S BLOCK AND HOW TO GET AROUND IT

Advice to the Verbose

When speaking keep in mind
These words or you'll be friendless;
Make your wisdom ageless—
Instead of merely endless.

Boy! For someone who isn't a weather forecaster,
you sure can talk up a storm!

After Applause —See Applause

After a Bad Joke

Sir, I think you've just become the Lightwit
Champion of the World.

After a Gag Gift or Award —See Acknowledging a Gag
Gift or Award

After a Glowing or Flattering Introduction —See
(1) A Flattering or Glowing Introduction, Responding
to; (2) Introductions

After a Humorous Introduction —See *Acknowledging
a Humorous Introduction* at Introductions

After a Lengthy Speaker —See (1) Long Speeches,
Comments and Harangues; (2) Previous Speaker(s)

After a Long Business Meeting —See (1) Long
Speeches, Comments and Harangues; (2) Meet-
ings/Conventions

After a Long Introduction —See Introductions

After a Long Question During the Q.&A. —See Long Question/er

After a Loud Singer

Now that's what I call a voice. I understand she has a range of four octaves and five miles.

You know something? It's really a shame to waste a voice like that on popular music. He could make a fortune calling out Bingo numbers!

After a Needling Introduction

I'd like to just say one thing about that introduction: They say that humor is a gift—and I guess _____ just hasn't gotten around to unwrapping his.

You have to admit that _____ never lies. First he said I was a speaker who needed no introduction—and then he gave me an introduction I certainly didn't need.

First, let me thank you for that kind introduction. I won't say what kind.

To start off, I want you all to know I'm firmly in favor of trade talks. And the first talk I'd like to trade is that last one.

First, I want _____ to know that he will certainly be remembered in my Thanksgiving prayer. When I thank the Lord for surviving this year's disasters, that introduction will be included.

I'd call that a postage stamp introduction. You're licked before you start.

It's at a moment like this that I wish I were one of those people who need no introduction.

After an Off-Color Joke / Cursing

After Someone Tells an Off-Color Joke

Well, those were certainly words to be remembered. Not repeated. Just remembered.

It's okay. I'll just fill in until the Vice Squad arrives.

When Someone Curses

Sir, I'm at a loss for words—and it's a shame you weren't.

After a Too-Long Talk —See Long Speeches, Comments and Harangues

After Light Applause —See Applause

After Opening Remarks —See Opening an Ad-Lib or Informal Talk

After Something Goes Wrong —See Mistakes and Misspeaking

After the Applause Has Ended —See TAPING

After You Forget Something —See Forgetting

After You Sip From a Glass

After Sipping From a Glass of Water

(Hold up the glass, examine it, and comment:) My favorite drink—Lake Erie Lite.

After Sipping a Drink

Just the way I like it. Any stronger and you'd need a prescription.

I'm one of those people who drink to forget—and it must work because I can't remember my next line.

After You Sneeze —See Sneezing

After Your First Big Laugh (following a slow start)

Thank you. I'm one of those timed-release speakers. I get better as I go along.

Age and Audience —See ASSESSING YOUR AUDIENCE

Air Travel and Humor —See THE USES AND LIMITS OF HUMOR

Alcohol and Public Speaking —See STAGE FRIGHT AND HOW TO DEAL WITH IT

Altering a Speech in Mid-Course —See ASSESSING YOUR AUDIENCE

ALWAYS LEAD THEM LAUGHING

When people learn that I was a speechwriter for President Ford during his campaign to retain the White House in 1976, they frequently comment, "It must have been fun." "Fun" isn't a word that usually comes to my

mind when discussing political campaigns; try unre-
lenting stress, impossible deadlines, missed meals, and
no sleep. But many years later, some of the fun has
emerged from more painful memories.

I think of the Western movie actor who wished President Ford well by saying, "May the chaw in your mouth
never turn dry."

I remember the winter of 1976. Our speechwriting
offices in the old Executive Office Building had steam
heat that could not be adjusted. It was either ON or
OFF. ON made the rooms Equatorial. OFF was Arctic
Circle. And so we ran the window air-conditioners to
bring the steam heat down to bearable—while we wrote
speeches on energy conservation.

***

We were always interested in the media coverage
of the campaign. While the president's motorcade was
going through a small town, I listened on our car radio to a local station reporting the event. The station announcer said something like: "You know, this is
the first time a President of the United States has ever
come to *our* city. So to give a moment-by-moment, eye-
witness account of this historic occasion, our roving
reporter, Buzz Bumper [or some such highly fictitious
name] is right square on the parade route ready to give
you his on-the-spot coverage. Take it away, Buzz!"

The next voice was Buzz Bumper himself. With
mounting excitement he said, "Yes, I can see President
Ford's motorcade approaching. It's just three blocks
away from the traffic light. Now it's passing the bank.
It's passing the gas station. In another fifty yards the
president—the President of the United States will be
here." Then came twenty seconds of total silence—
followed by "And there he goes!" Back to the station
announcer exulting, "Thank you Buzz Bumper for that

unforgettable eye-witness account of President Ford's visit!" Unforgettable. Well, he got that right.

Local media were usually courteous and somewhat in awe of a presidential visit. National media were more interested in a scoop, things going wrong, any sort of "gotcha." A few weeks before Election Day, President Ford gave a speech at Iowa State University. He began by saying, "It's great to be in Ohio." He immediately corrected it to "Iowa State" and joined with the audience in laughing. Then he explained, "You know how we Michiganders have Ohio State on our mind." It was the afternoon of the Ohio State-Michigan football game. As captain of the 1934 Michigan team, Ford had an understandable interest in the outcome of this contest between traditional rivals.

Nevertheless, we knew that media coverage of the speech would include a reference to the mistake, even though Ford immediately made the correction. A few hours later, as I was walking past a group of people watching a TV network reporter do a stand-up for the evening news, I became aware of the fact that in doing a piece about President Ford's misspeaking, he was having some troubles of his own. I worked my way up to the front of the group and watched.

The stand-up went something like this: "President Ford began his peach—CUT! President Ford began his speech with an insurrect, incorrect—CUT! President Fard began—CUT!" By now, a bit of sadism made me move a little closer to him. Seeing and recognizing me, he lost whatever composure he started with. I counted nine takes before he was able to report President Ford's misspeaking once. He avoided me for the rest of the campaign.

Misspeaking is something all communicators strive to avoid, but sometimes the reason for it isn't evident. One time President Ford was rehearsing a speech to be given on television. The speech was read using a TelePrompTer, and it went very well until the last sentence. Instead of "May God bless America," Ford said, "My God bless America." Noting the mistake, the President said, "Let's do it once more," Perfect except, once again, it was, "My God bless America."

Now all speakers come up with mental blocks that can be easily overcome by rearranging words. So I suggested changing the last line. Ford said, "Don't change the line. Change the prompter!" We all looked and saw what the president was reading from the prompter: "My God bless America." The next run-through was faultless.

***

Well, notwithstanding an incredible home-stretch finish, we lost the election. President Ford, down more than 30 points at the start of the campaign, closed the gap to less than two percentage points in the popular vote. He had campaigned so intensively that his voice had given out during the last few days, but his sense of humor had not.

In January of 1977, he gave his final address to the Congress. He began by saying, "In accordance with the Constitution, I come before you once again to report on the state of the Union. This report will be my last." Then he paused and with a sly smile added, "Maybe." It probably gave quite a few people something to think about.

On the morning of January 20, 1977, the senior staff met in the Roosevelt Room to say farewell to President Ford. It was an occasion for lumps in throats, but it also had a moment of laughter. On behalf of the senior staff, Vice President Rockefeller was to present the president with a large silver tray. It was a heavy tray and Rockefeller dropped it. It hit the floor with a clatter, and as Rockefeller stooped to retrieve it, Secretary of

Transportation William T. Coleman, Jr., said, "It's obvious the Vice President hasn't had much experience carrying trays."

For me, the last laugh came that night. My wife and I had gone out shopping. Dressed in our casual clothes, we returned through the lobby of our building as other couples, dressed in evening clothes, were leaving to attend Inaugural Balls. The desk clerk assessed the scene and observed, "It looks like the outs are coming in—and the ins are going out."

Funny, yes. Fun, no.

—See also (1) MISTAKES; (2) *Don't Neglect the Facts* at DON'TS . . . IF YOU WANT TO GET LAUGHS; (3) Dealing with a Faux Pas

Anecdotes —See STORIES: WHERE DO THEY COME FROM?

Anger and Comedy —See (1) KINDER, GENTLER COMEDY; (2) THE USES AND LIMITS OF HUMOR

Anniversary Celebrations

There's a very good reason why their marriage has lasted so long. Commitment! He promised they'd never part until the birds stopped singing, the Mississippi River stopped flowing, and the sun stopped rising. And she promised they'd never part until she completed her silver pattern.

They just celebrated their 25th wedding anniversary. Or, to be completely accurate—he celebrated, she repented.

Golden wedding anniversaries are always occasions for nostalgia and reminiscing. In fact, during dinner *(wife)* was telling me how she often thinks back fifty years to that dashing, handsome and virile young man who pursued her—and wonders what her life would have been like if she had married him instead.

A Golden Wedding anniversary is when your bride pours the champagne and no longer says, "Say when." She says, "Say if."

Scientists have now discovered a definite link between marriage, sex and astrology. If you've been married 25 years—it happens once in a blue moon.

Annual Reports

You can always tell when spring has arrived by the brilliant colors—on the covers of annual reports.

Annual reports are four color, 48 page booklets printed on 28 pound coated stock with die-cut vellum covers—that tell you how management is fighting to keep down costs.

You can learn a lot about a company just by looking at its annual report. For instance, the more pictures, the less profits.

An annual report is almost religious in its format. It's where the Report from the Chairman of the Board giveth—and the Notes to Financial Statements taketh away.

I love to read that opening letter from the Chairman of the Board. I mean, it's amazing they can write so well with their fingers crossed.

I don't want to cast any aspersions on the veracity of annual reports, but what Wall Street really needs is a polygraph printing press.

But if you really know how to read annual reports, you can always tell when a company is in trouble. It's when the auditor signs it under an assumed name.

Apologies for Poor Speaking —See THE HARD WORK OF HUMOR

Applause

Acknowledging Applause

Thank you. If there's one thing I appreciate in an audience, it's good taste.

Incidentally, feel free to applaud if the mood strikes you. Or, for that matter, even if it just nudges you.

What can I say? Applaud in my ear and I'll follow you anywhere.

I love applause. I really do. In fact, if there's one thing that would make my life perfect, it would be a doggie bag to take home any applause that's left over.

Thank you, very, very much. Applause is music to a speaker's ears and that's as close to hearing a symphony as I've ever come.

After Light Applause

I want to thank you for that thunderous ovation. Did you ever feel like a doctor in a Christian Science Reading Room?

Thank you. I'm not too proud to accept charity.

After Scattered Applause

First, let me thank you for that burst of spontaneous uncertainty.

After Weak Applause

Thank you for that wonderful round of restraint.

First, I want to thank you for that thunderous ovation. I've had more applause from a trained seal with arthritis.

Applicability of Humor —See SPICING UP THOSE DULL SPEECHES

Appropriate / Inappropriate Subject of a Roast —See *Preparing the Roast* at ROASTS

Apt Material for Speeches —See SPICING UP THOSE DULL SPEECHES

ASSESSING YOUR AUDIENCE

I.

I try to have a Q.&A. period after my speeches on the use of humor in business and political communication. During a recent Q.&A. period, I was asked a question that I answered with an anecdote about Jack Benny.

But as I proceeded through the story, I couldn't help but notice a slightly glazed look come over the eyes of some of the younger listeners. And so, when I finished the anecdote, I asked how many in the audience were unfamiliar with the name "Jack Benny"? About 10% of the group raised their hands.

Shock is too mild a word to describe my reaction. Here was an audience of bright, knowledgeable junior executives. Jack Benny had been a superstar of show business. His shows were consistently in the Top Ten of radio and television ratings throughout the Thirties, Forties, Fifties and Sixties. His death was as recent as 1974—and already the memory of this outstanding performer was receding into the cobwebs of time.

On my flight home, mulling over the audience response, I thought about a similar occurrence that had happened a few years back. I was a consultant to a corporate writing team putting together a conference. The writers ranged in age from the late twenties to the middle thirties. Again, all were bright, aware, informed people.

We needed the name of a child star for one of the elements of a presentation. I immediately opted for the preeminent child star of this century—Shirley Temple. Not so fast, Orben! A couple of the writers who were in their twenties had never heard of Shirley Temple. NEVER HEARD OF SHIRLEY TEMPLE??? SHIRLEY TEMPLE????? And the writers in their thirties who recognized the name and knew she had been a child star, had no other factual or emotional identification with her. We eliminated the reference.

Upon reflection, I realized that there was no real reason to think that this now-generation writing team would be aware of Shirley Temple. She was the darling of America before any of them had been born. Except for the late, late movies and show business histories, there would be no likelihood that they would be aware of her. Certainly, they could not have the instant recognition of—or share the affection for—the adorable little charmer that Shirley Temple was.

Neither would there be a reason for a younger audience to be aware of Jack Benny without ever having enjoyed the weekly identification his radio and TV shows provided to older Americans.

***

So what does all this mean? Is there a lesson to be learned for speakers and performers?

Except in the areas of our specific expertise, we tend to unconsciously proceed on the belief that our listeners have just about the same body of experience and awareness of history, current events, and language that we do. This is a dangerous assumption for any speaker and may become more of a problem as we grow older and our lifestyles, interests and pools of information diverge and differ from those of substantial numbers in our audiences.

Our use of language is a prime example of this. Have you noticed that many, if not most, of the slang expressions you use are the slang words of your youth and formative years? Slang is the fast food of language. It's fun, colorful, easy-to-use, and constantly changing. We don't necessarily adapt to the change. Quite often we tend to hold onto and use the slang of our earlier years, and in so doing, we sometimes date our approach and confuse our listeners.

President Reagan once used the word *keister* for his backside. The word was unknown to all but older generations. *Keister* was slang from the early past of the 20th Century. The use of such outdated slang got a lot of media attention that did not convey the image of a speaker tuned in to the moment.

President Reagan frequently drew from his memory

bank of pet phrases, anecdotes, and stories—assuming the subject matter was shared by all. Sometimes it wasn't. At a press conference, he claimed that Congress had reneged on an agreement to cut $3 in spending for each dollar of increased taxes he had approved. Reagan said, "I never got the $3. So I'm like the fellow in the story. I'm still yelling, 'Pay the $2!'—only three, in my case."

After the press conference ended, reporters asked the White House press office what the President meant by the "pay the $2" reference. None of them seemed to have heard the expression before. Actually, it was the running gag and blackout line from a sketch Willie Howard did in a Broadway show in the Thirties. The essence of Willie's sketch was eventually condensed into an often told joke that was heard for many years after. But, very clearly, the joke had not made it to the present time.

There's a classic story about the inmates of a prison who had so often told the same jokes to each other that they no longer had to tell the entire joke. They assigned a number to each joke and when they wanted to tell it, they'd just say, "34!"—and the other inmates would remember the story and laugh. Well, President Reagan, in just doing the $2 punch line—the equivalent of "34" also assumed his listeners knew the story. They didn't.

At one time or another, we all fall into this trap. Consider some of these items, subjects and phrases: "Taint funny, McGee!" . . . "Lucky Strike Green has gone to war!" . . . Amelia Earhart . . . Judge Crater . . . "Pucker up!" . . . "He knows his onions." . . . Sex-change operations in Denmark . . . Zoot suits . . . Leisure suits . . . Nehru jackets . . . Nehru.

At varying times during the last seventy years, all of these subjects and expressions have drawn our national attention. When used in a joke or as part of a reference, most Americans would have instantaneously recognized them. Depending upon the age of the listener, some or most of these items would not be recognizable or understood today.

If speakers and performers are to be effective, their words and message must be clear and understandable. If they use verbal antiquities or dip into information that presumes prior knowledge on the part of the audience—it's all over.

***

Now let's broaden the scope of this concept. So far we've been concentrating on catch-phrases, slang, and awareness of pop culture. What about the total knowledge and awareness of listeners? To paraphrase a popular Washington question: What do members of an audience know and how thoroughly do they know it?

Jay Leno, was quoted in *Rolling Stone* as saying, "There isn't any political humor anymore because people don't know enough. That's the way it goes. The attention span is so short. You can't do anymore what Mort Sahl could do with words."

Pat Oliphant, a Pulitzer Prize-winning political cartoonist, referred in a *Washington Post* interview to the many times he has used Michelangelo's "Creation" as a peg for a topical cartoon. He then went on to say, "The problem is, as education becomes more and more of a mess in this country, and people learn less and less about the arts and history, the possibility of using those sorts of metaphors is disappearing. It will get to a stage where eventually you won't be able to use the classics at all, or allusions to historical events."

Perhaps the ultimate view of this problem was cataloged by Ben Stein. In an article published in *Public Opinion* magazine, Stein surveys some California teenagers and their knowledge of recent history. He writes about a student at USC who "did not have any clear idea when World War II was fought. She believed it was some time in this century. (She is a journalism major.) She also had no clear notion of what had begun the war for the United States. ('Pearl Harbor? Was that when the United States dropped the atom bomb on Hiroshima?') Even more astounding, she was not sure which side Russia was on and whether Germany was on our side or against us."

This does not mean that we are experiencing the dimming of America. Young people today are as bright and quick and potentially teachable as ever. The problem is they are no longer readers. They are watchers. Their most influential classroom is the TV screen. With each passing year they know less and less about more and more. They acquire a vast and superficial and mostly visual awareness of contemporary life. The net effect is perhaps best summed up by R. Emmett Tyrrell, Jr., who wrote "Television communicates with pictures, as did the caveman."

***

A lot is claimed for television as an educational force. The potential may be there, but so far the negative impact of TV is more apparent. It represents a sometimes entertaining but slow and inefficient vehicle for conveying information.

We watch news programs and quite frequently the file footage or beauty shots that accompany the commentary bear no relation to what is being said. How many times have you watched TV news with other people and asked, "What did he/she just say?" And your fellow watchers can't answer because they were mesmerized by the irrelevant visual images—paying scant attention to the verbal content.

With jump cuts, 10-second bites, and a never-ending assault of images, TV provides an ocean-wide array of recognition but a wading pool of knowledge. This visual bombardment leaves no time to consider what is being presented, so the informational staying power and educational impact of TV are limited.

But for better or worse—positive or negative—television is shaping the audiences you will have to face in the years ahead. There are lessons to be learned.

Television is best at conveying emotions, impressions and perceptions—weakest at communicating facts, figures and concepts. In the future, warmer and more anecdotal speeches will be the winners.

Much of television is hyper—stimulating the nervous system and shrinking the attention span. Your speeches will have to be shorter and punchier—relying more on the bullet approach to presenting subject matter than on more leisurely developed exposition.

Television is visual, continuously dangling bright and shiny objects in front of our eyes. Colorful language, verbal pictures and brighter delivery can provide the same appeal.

But most important of all, television has created new audiences—more sophisticated in many respects and with different attitudes, interests and stores of information from those of the past. More than ever before, the ability to analyze and respond to the needs, concerns and capacities of these audiences, will dictate success or failure.

To lead the parade, you have to know the marchers.

II.

Fortune-telling is one of the world's oldest professions. From the soothsayers of antiquity to crystal ball gazers peddling their omniscience at carnivals, knowing the unknowable has always captured the public's attention. "Madame Nostrashamus—she knows all, sees all, tells all." How does she do it?

The technique is a rather simple and fairly obvious one. Sherlock Holmes amazed Dr. Watson with it. In the trade it's known as a "cold reading." The fortune-teller, without being obvious about it, studies every aspect of the client's physical appearance, speech, clothing and jewelry. In casual conversation before the future is peered into, further insights are gleaned from chance remarks.

Madame Nostrashamus will then, with a great deal of histrionics and metaphysical mumbo-jumbo, feed back to the client what she has already observed, deduced, and been told. When this is done adroitly, a level of credibility is established.

The Madame will then very carefully venture into new territory using her existing database as her guide. She will make a somewhat vague or tentative assumption. She looks for a flicker of acknowledgment, the hint of a nod—or, if she has guessed wrong, the shadow of a frown. If the thrust is right and she senses a reactive green light, she drives right on through the intersection and onto a safe road. If her analysis has been incorrect, she quickly and deftly turns to another direction—and her client is soon diverted and disarmed by new and, perhaps, more germane scenery.

It is an art form. It draws on intuition, observation, intelligence, and chutzpah. These are attributes that make a good fortune-teller. These are attributes that make a good speaker.

The success of Madame Nostrashamus depends on how well she reads her audience of one. Most speakers feel their assessment of an audience ends when they have completed the research and writing of their speech. To some extent, they go into the event on automatic pilot. The work has been done. The audience is in place. Now get the words out and go home. Madame Nostrashamus would never approve.

We tend to think of an audience as a vast homogeneous sea of faces without much considering the tides, currents, and whirlpools within that sea. No two audiences are alike. People have moods—audiences have moods. People have likes and dislikes—audiences do, too, and they frequently vary substantially from audience to audience.

That's why there is no such thing as a 100% guaranteed, foolproof, can't miss joke—or story—or comedy act. The great classic comedy acts and comedians have all occasionally bombed because there is no such thing as consistency in audiences. But the closer you come to reading the temper and mood of an audience, the better your chance of avoiding disaster. And I don't just mean the analysis of your audience that is done before the event—but also your reading of the actual audience sitting in front of you.

Madame Nostrashamus and stand-up comedians do this all the time. The savvy stand-up comedian studies each new audience before going on. Age, dress, conduct, size of audience, and how they are reacting to other acts—all go into determining the material to be used and the sequence of its use.

This testing and divining of what is right for the audience continues when the comedian is on stage. The first joke in a political bit goes quietly. An internal alarm goes off, and without the audience ever knowing, the rest of the bit is dropped, and the first joke of a dating routine is told. The performer is continually testing the comedic waters and adjusts course to make sure the listeners are tuned in and responsive.

Speakers rarely do this. They arrive at an event with a prepared speech and they do it—regardless of circumstances or conditions that may dictate a change. But the alert speaker should also learn from the response given earlier speakers. Coughing, program shuffling, the scratching and scraping of chair legs, eyes not focused on the dais, are all good and clear indications that an audience is less than enthralled by what is being said. And so, consider what *is* being said. Is your approach similar? Can your speech be cut or altered? Do it.

Written speeches need not be cast in concrete or delivered as scripture. It is rarely done, but there is no reason why a prepared text shouldn't have optional inclusions and/or deletions. Appropriate tabs can allow a speaker to easily turn to a standby piece of material— or delete a section no longer applicable or suitable. In this way, a speech can be delivered with the same flexibility and sensitivity to the audience as would be achieved by an ad-lib performance.

***

There is one area, more than any other, in which speeches have failed to address the needs and wishes of an audience. It is a problem that has been with us through the ages. Just one small illustration of it can be seen in a painting by George Catlin which is part of the Paul Mellon Collection at the Virginia Museum of Fine Arts. Catlin was a 19th-century American artist who is best remembered for his realistic depictions of the everyday life of American Indians.

The painting I'm referring to was done more than 100 years ago. In the background are a few teepees with some women and children standing in front of them. It is snowing, and they are stolidly watching a lone Indian who is in the foreground and standing in the middle of a circle of individual mounds of snow. A bit of feather headdress can be seen emerging from the top of each of these mounds of snow. The painting is called "A Long Speech."

Feel for the snow-covered listeners and be aware that at one time or another, we have all given audiences a tad more than they wanted to hear. A too-long speech may very well be the most common and most easily rectified failing in public speaking. Comedy clubs have an easy solution when an act is bombing or on too long. They either blink the lights, cut the sound, gently lead the comic off—or all three. Somehow, this approach, however justified, doesn't seem quite right for a CEO or political figure. And so, determining when to stop becomes an exercise in self-regulation.

To some extent, the running time of a speech can be determined when it is written and rehearsed. The length should be appropriate to the event, the subject, and the audience. Show business gives us two important axioms: "Always leave them laughing" and "Always leave them wanting more." Of the two, the second is more important.

Your speech may fit all the pre-event requirements as to length and approach, but sometimes, in performance, the audience tells you when it's time to quit. The alert speaker has to take heed. It may be just a slight increase in movement or a slight decrease in attention—but it's an unmistakable signal to pull the plug. A speaker should be able to do this by gracefully cutting to a prepared finish—and speeches should be written and hard copy tabbed to allow for this kind of smooth transition.

Yes, but what about the important facts and figures and viewpoints that won't be heard? They won't be heard even if you do them. A tired audience tunes out.

***

What are the consequences of not correctly assessing your audience? Disaster!

All speakers have their favorite war stories of jokes that bombed and speeches that crashed. They're fun to talk about years later. At the time, they're like a kick in the stomach. An example of what happens when a speaker doesn't know the territory might provide incentive.

President Reagan rarely missed in his reading of an audience. But when he did make the wrong call, he joined the rest of us on the speaking-disasters Titanic.

President Reagan spoke at a ceremony in the Rose Garden of the White House honoring the 207th birthday of the Marine Corps. A contingent of Marines were standing at attention, and their commandant, General Robert Barrow, was standing beside the President.

As reported by the Associated Press, "Reagan tried to warm up the audience with a story about a group of gung-ho Marines sent to an Army camp for airborne training. An Army lieutenant told them they would jump out of a plane flying at 800 feet.

"The Marines huddled, then sent a spokesman to ask the lieutenant if the plane could fly lower, perhaps at 500 feet, Reagan said. 'Well, he explained that, no, it couldn't because the parachutes wouldn't have time to open,' Reagan said. 'Oh, they said, Oh, we're wearing parachutes?' "

The Marine audience then did what they are supposed to do when standing at attention before their general and the Commander-in-Chief of all of our armed forces. They stood at attention. No laughs. No chuckles. No applause. Spit and polish silence.

President Reagan tried to cover the stillness by saying, "I think you have heard it." But I'm certain that presidents have no special immunity against the slightly queasy feeling of mortification we have all experienced, that starts in the pit of our stomachs and rushes outward in a crimson blush of embarrassment to the very tips of our ears, fingers and toes—after we've built to a funny that wasn't.

Know your material, but above all, know your audience.

III.

"You gotta know the territory!"

That thought, expressed in the opening scene of Meredith Willson's classic musical *The Music Man*, is also the key to speaking and speechwriting success.

You gotta know your subject matter. Sure. You gotta have an acceptable delivery. Sure. But, in addition, you gotta know the territory—and the territory is your audience. You have to know where it's coming from, where it's going to, and what information, attitudes and feelings it has picked up along the way. And so, you find out as much as possible about each individual audience you face.

But you also have to be aware of major trends and sea changes in what audiences will accept or reject. What worked twenty years ago, ten years ago, or last February—isn't necessarily right today. Any speakers, humorous or otherwise, who put themselves on automatic pilot will inevitably face a day of reckoning.

Let me describe one such day. The event took place just a few years ago and only the names have been deleted to protect the embarrassed. It happened at a banquet. The audience was big-city sophisticated. The featured speaker/entertainer was an established performer. He did an act that had worked for him for many, many years. But the times, they were a-changing.

The performer started off with a sequence of family jokes that focused on his wife's alleged deficiencies—in cooking, in shopping, in bed, etc. It was a sequence that had obviously worked for him in the past but was now sadly out of step with this audience. The laughter was strained and sparse. Women were turning to other women and saying, "Can you believe this?" The murmurs at each table rose up and joined together in a buzz of disapproval.

31

The comedian, no fool, sensed something was going wrong. But he didn't know what. He just knew he had to take another approach. So now he slid into another chunk of material that had always been surefire. He did some well-crafted, well-told ethnic stories. Now the buzz from the audience went into high gear. Heads were shaking, eyes were rolling upward, and members of various minorities were getting up and stomping out. The exit doors opened and slammed shut with ever-increasing frequency. Perhaps "catastrophic" is too strong a word to describe a performance—but this one came close to earning it.

As all nightmares do, this one ended. The performer still didn't have a clue as to what the problem was. Here he had done his top-drawer, never-miss bits, and he wound up emceeing a riot. Visibly shaken, he was taken to a reception following the banquet. A reporter came over to ask a few questions and the comedian, angry and confused, put the blast on him. An associate pulled the plug on this attack by saying to the comedian, "Shut up. We're lucky we got out with our lives." All of this, of course, was duly reported in the next morning's paper.

Now, unless getting out with your life is the goal, there are lessons to be learned. What *did* go wrong? Was the problem misreading a single audience or was the performer marching to yesterday's drummer?

In this case it was a little of both. It should have been apparent to anyone in show business that a sophisticated metropolitan audience would be sensitive to—and supportive of—the social, political and economic changes we have seen in the last thirty years. But the realization and acceptance of these changes is reflected in virtually every audience today. Sexist jokes don't work. Ethnic jokes don't work. Racist jokes don't work. When told, they not only don't work, but they frequently are met with the same high-visibility negative response awarded our performer.

This comedian hadn't seen the pages turning on the calendar. What was right thirty years ago, he believed, would be right forever. Wrong! Each generation brings its own beliefs, attitudes and social conditioning into play when it reacts to jokes, speeches and speakers. You gotta know the territory—the emotional and psychological territory occupied by your audience.

***

Humor is the ultimate test of whether you are in tune with your audience and the times. If your listeners think a particular person, place or party is just great— and you're doing put-down jokes about that person, place or party—you're in trouble. And if not only your immediate listeners, but a majority of *all* listeners think the person, place or party is just dandy—you're in even greater trouble.

Much of today's humor is half laughing, half voting. Quite often we express via laughter our support for—or disapproval of—people, policies and positions. And so, humorists and all communicators must not only know where their immediate audience is coming from—but where *most* audiences are coming from. And even more important—where they are headed next.

This sort of divination is always difficult. It is most difficult during times of transition. We are in such a time.

For the last thirty years there has been a refreshing freedom of approach available to those who do comedy. There have been few, if any, restrictions on subject matter and how to present it. This is the bright side. Excess has been the dark side. In the last decade humor has experienced a free fall of taste.

In the comedy clubs, the showrooms of Las Vegas,

and on cable television—we get a steady succession of the screamers, the scratchers, and the mindless chanters of foul language. In a major concert hall, I heard one of them use the same four-letter word four times in one sentence. I couldn't help but wonder if there shouldn't be a thesaurus of obscenities to help such a sadly uncreative performer.

If you listen to this kind of comedian often enough, you realize it isn't clever, it isn't innovative, it isn't a statement—it's just verbal exhibitionism. Overwhelmingly, the four-letter words are used to give a punch to jokes that don't have one.

The pendulum of what is acceptable on a public stage has swung a long way to the left in the last half century. Years ago burlesque was always considered the home of sexual humor. Today the sketches and monologues of burlesque would almost qualify for Sesame Street. A four-letter word uttered by any burlesque top banana or nightclub comedian in those days would have been grounds for instant dismissal. Sex was implied. Today it comes with blueprints.

I've spent a good part of my lifetime in show business—writing for performers in variety, nightclubs, radio and television. There is very little I haven't heard or seen. I'm beyond being shocked—but I'm not beyond being offended.

***

Now what has all this to do with speakers who use humor? No business executive or political figure is going to sprinkle an opening joke with four-letter words. But an almost imperceptible change of attitude regarding what is acceptable or not acceptable sometimes takes place.

The unzipped approach to comedy on cable television encourages the network sitcoms and talk shows to become more explicit. Each show vies with the others. "Well, if they got away with it, we can too. Maybe take it a step further." A climate of acceptability is created. It affects what appears on television, what is heard on radio, what appears in print—and, eventually, although in a very diluted form, what is found in speeches.

And so, while a four-letter word may not find its way into a joke or a reference, maybe a five- or seven-letter word might. A blatantly tasteless joke wouldn't be considered—a borderline story may be.

Special situations can lead to faulty judgments. An all-male or all-female event—a roast—an informal just-between-us type gathering—are often situations in which the bounds of prudence and good taste are overstepped. Is it worth it? Rarely.

It comes down to this: How much of an audience can you afford to offend? 20%? 10%? 5%? What if only one listener is turned off—but that one listener is key to your success or your future? There are risks galore in making any speech. The risks are compounded and guaranteed when you venture into questionable language or territory. Ask yourself: "Would you want to read the joke or reference credited to you in tomorrow's newspaper—or hear it repeated, also with credit, in casual conversation?" Because, if it's pungent enough, it will be.

Further, I feel we are now in a period of comedic transition. The humor of hostility, of conflict, of shouting, of X-rated language and subject matter, has been with us a long time. It has appealed mostly to younger audiences—giving voice to rebellion—against family, authority, society, the system, you name it. Speech humor is always geared to the older, more conservative, establishment listener.

But that is now the direction in which America is heading. We're growing older. We're growing families. We're growing more conservative. We're growing more concerned that we may have lost something precious when we began to lose sight of what used to be called "middle-class values."

We see this rethinking process going on in humor—an awareness of the more innocent laughter found in small-town America. Even in the comedy clubs, some of the more perceptive newcomers are beginning to sense that audiences have had enough of the mean-spirited, the noise, and the language. There is a hesitant, but encouraging, trend back to humor that is both funny and repeatable.

I've found that the comedians who last—the humorists people have honored and loved for many, many years—are those you would feel comfortable to have come as a guest to your Thanksgiving dinner. Low-key, funny, friendly, who give you the feeling of being "just folks."

Next Thanksgiving, would you, your manner, your delivery, your humor and your speech, be welcome? Think about it. The invitations are being written.

Assuaging Anger, Confusion, Fear through Humor —See USES AND LIMITS OF HUMOR

Assumptions about Audiences —See ASSESSING YOUR AUDIENCE

Attack Humor —See (1) *Preparing the Roast* at ROASTS; (2) KINDER, GENTLER COMEDY

Attention-Grabbing —See OPENER: THE FIRST TWO MINUTES OF YOUR SPEECH

Attire for Speakers —See ADVICE—AND HOW TO IGNORE IT

Audacious Behavior —See MISTAKES

Audience

I like to speak to audiences at a vacation resort like this because you're miles and miles away from the cares of home and as a result, you're always relaxed, at ease and worry free. So tell me—what makes you so sure you locked the front door?

How come audiences never have to audition?

The problem with speaking in *(name of town)* is, the people are very conservative. Very conservative. If you're a big hit, they give you a nodding ovation.

Audiences in *(name of town)* are like any other audience except they don't have coffee breaks. Every ninety minutes you just hold a mirror up to their lips.

Speakers, keep one thing in mind,
Be your subject sex or widgets;
Go straight to your conclusion—
The minute your audience fidgets.

What speakers fear most is a poorly coordinated audience. People who can't sleep and applaud at the same time.

The interest rate is coming down,
Of this there is no doubt.
You know it when your audience—
Is slowly walking out.

I feel pretty relaxed up here because I asked the bartender what kind of a group you were. He said you're real middle-of-the-road. I said, "What do you mean—middle-of-the-road?" He said you drink liberally and tip conservatively.

It's always a pleasure to speak to an audience like this—accomplished, distinguished, loaded— a group that always knows which side its cracker is caviared on.

The audiences at most business meetings are made up of people who are busy, involved, industrious and who have far better things to do with their time—listening to speakers who don't.

I'm a firm believer in the Laffer Curve. The worst curve an audience can throw you is no laughers.

No, Virginia, Winkin', Blinkin' and Nod is not an audience listening to _____.

You can always tell an audience that's spent a little too much time at the Happy Hour. When they try to clap—they miss.

Believe me, it's not easy to electrify a group that's already gassed.

It's very easy to spot the mothers in an audience. They have polish on top of their fingernails—and peanut butter and jelly under them.

At a Black Tie Event

As I look about this very distinguished audience—the women in gowns—the men in Republican leisure suits. . . .

To an Audience of Doctors

This is the first time I've ever spoken to an audience of doctors, so I've tried to do all the things my mother told me to do when going to a doctor: Put on clean underwear. . . . Try to look poor. . . .

To a Quiet Audience

Just my luck to be in a building that isn't zoned for laughs.

Audience Assessment —See (1) ASSESSING YOUR AUDIENCE; (2) USING HUMOR WHEN YOU'RE AFRAID TO USE HUMOR

Audience, Noisy —See Noisy Audience

Audience Preparation —See (1) STARTING YOUR SPEECH A WINNER; (2) CONTROLLING YOUR AUDIENCE

Audience Reaction —See (1) *Don't Step on Your Laughs* at DON'TS . . . IF YOU WANT TO GET LAUGHS; (2) LESSONS I LEARNED FROM LOWELL THOMAS

Audiences —See MISTAKES (for assertion that audiences love both the unexpected and the audacious)

Audience Testing —See TAPING

Audience Viewed as Friends —See STAGE FRIGHT AND HOW TO DEAL WITH IT

Audio / Acoustic Problems —See Equipment

Audiotapes —See TAPING

Avoiding Humor (and the risks thereof) —See USING
HUMOR WHEN YOU'RE AFRAID TO USE HUMOR

Awards / Awards Ceremonies

I'm kinda embarrassed getting this honor because I really am a very modest person. An extremely modest person. A tremendously talented
and wonderfully deserving modest person.

Frankly, I'm not used to getting awards. Up till
now I've always taken great pride in my humility.

And finally, I want to thank the one person above
all others who has worked and slaved and sacri-
ficed for so many years to bring this moment
about . . . me. *(And if you want to carry the
thought one more step, begin kissing your hands
and arms.)*

B

A Baby Is Crying

I just read that the minute you're born, your share of the national debt is $67,000. So you can understand why that child is crying.

Bad Joke —See After a Bad Joke

Bald Speaker

There are a lot of inequities in life. For example, this hotel has the nerve to charge me full rate for my room, bath and what's in it—a bottle of shampoo and a hair-dryer.

The Good Book says the very hairs on our head are numbered. All I can say is, I'm getting mighty sick of deficits.

Frankly, I never considered myself bald until I went to a formal dinner and bent over to pick up a napkin. The woman next to me looked down at my head, turned to the waiter and said, "No melon, thank you."

I don't want to seem conceited, but I always knew I'd come out on top. I just never figured it would be one comb full at a time.

If You're Bald and Make an Outrageous State-ment: And if you believe that, I've got something else I'd like to sell you—hair tonic.

You might have noticed I have Democratic hair. It's gone from the majority to the minority.

I try to maintain a positive attitude toward all things. For instance, there are some who might say I'm bald. On the other hand, I have a natu-rally curly scalp.

If You're Balding: They say that talking to your plants will help make them grow. This morning I started talking to my hair.

I don't want to brag, but did you ever see such a full head of sideburn?

Before the Speech —See STARTING YOUR SPEECH A WINNER

Beta Blockers and Public Speaking —See STAGE FRIGHT AND HOW TO DEAL WITH IT

Birthdays

You know you're getting older when you light the candles on your birthday cake—and the air-conditioning switches on.

It was fascinating watching them celebrate his 72nd birthday. It's the first time I ever saw an orthopedic cake.

Sixty is when you come out of the shower, look at yourself in a full-length mirror and realize the awesome power of gravity.

Sixty is when you get socks, underwear and ear-muffs for Christmas—and you're glad.

Blank Piece of Paper / Empty Screen —See WRITER'S BLOCK AND HOW TO GET AROUND IT

Brevity in Delivering a Roast —See *Serving the Roast* at ROASTS

Briefing Books / Material of the Savvy Humorist —See THE HARD WORK OF HUMOR

Business and Show Business —See SPICING UP THOSE DULL SPEECHES

Butterflies —See STAGE FRIGHT AND HOW TO DEAL WITH IT

C

Calling for a Vote —See Vote Call/Voting

"Can Everyone Hear Me?" —See ADVICE—AND HOW TO IGNORE IT

Car with Lights on

Would the owner of a green Pontiac, license plate number 123–074, please report to the parking lot. You left your lights on. I think it's the attendant's tactful way of telling you that your battery may run down before I do.

Celebrations —See (1) Anniversary Celebrations; (2) Birthdays; (3) Retirement Events, Dinners and Roasts

Church

If You're on the Finance Committee: Blessed are they that fall asleep during the sermon but stay awake during the collection.

I like the motto of our church finance committee. It goes: "The Lord loveth a cheerful giver!" We also accept from those too embarrassed to say no.

Class Reunions —See Reunions

Closing —See Ending an Evening/Program

Closing Acknowledgment —See Ending an Evening/ Program

Closing a Disastrous Meeting —See Ending an Evening/Program

Clues to an Audience's Reaction —See LESSONS I LEARNED FROM LOWELL THOMAS

"Collaborative Spontaneity" —See THE HARD WORK OF HUMOR

Comfort Level in Telling Jokes —See SPICING UP THOSE DULL SPEECHES

Command of a Situation Using Humor —See "WHY HUMOR?"

Committees

Committees seem to fall into two categories: Those that achieve results by means of collective cogitation—and those that are more like a group goof.

A committee is eight stalks of chaff trying to be wheat.

Communications and Humor —See "WHY HUMOR?"

Confidence —See *Don't Preface* at DON'TS . . . IF YOU WANT TO GET LAUGHS

Connecting Humor and Substance in a Speech —See USING HUMOR WHEN YOU'RE AFRAID TO USE HUMOR

Continuing a Long Program

Well, as our speakers have so ably demonstrated, the show must go on—and on . . . and on . . . and on. . . .

I've attended many a three-hour meeting and I've come to the conclusion that any committee is only as strong as its weakest kidney.

Control —See (1) CONTROLLING YOUR AUDIENCE; (2) "WHY HUMOR?"

CONTROLLING YOUR AUDIENCE

A speaker has much in common with the captain of a ship. Your listeners are the passengers on this ship. In return for a safe and enjoyable voyage, they voluntarily submit to your expertise, your rules and your leadership. And so, the speaker skipper has to be in control at all times.

Control begins long before the ship even sails. When you accept a speaking engagement, try to get as much information as you can about the sponsoring organization, the composition of the audience and the nature of the program. Learn the names of the high-visibility personalities at the head table and something of the group's background and history. It takes E-mail, phone calls and time—but when you arrive for the event, you will be more of a friend, an associate, than a stranger. This information will also give you the data you'll need to construct "inside" ad-libs. In short, a good captain never sails into uncharted waters.

Secure the printed program or working agenda. Analyze your position in the program and what's expected of you. If you are not slotted to maximum advantage, see if the program can be reordered. There is no plus to going on last in a three-hour program. Sometimes you may have to settle for no-win positioning but

46

quite often, a simple request for a change will do the trick.

A prudent captain gets to the ship well before sailing time. You check out the lectern, lighting, sound system and all the other obvious elements that make for smooth sailing. But don't stop there. Look around the room and see if there are any conditions that may distract an audience.

***

Humor and effective speech communication require a certain intimacy between speaker and audience. The greater the distance between you and your listeners, the less responsive they will be. If you are in a room too large for the size of the audience, try to avoid having the tables and/or chairs evenly spaced throughout. Move them as close to the lectern as possible without crowding. It never hurts to be the captain of a Love Boat.

Further, the closer an audience is to the speaker, the less chance they will have of being aware of possible distractions elsewhere in the room. We're all familiar with the phrase "to upstage." It's a show-business term that refers to one performer doing anything that distracts the audience's attention from another. If one actor is downstage (toward the audience) and is speaking lines—any movement or physical activity by another actor upstage (toward the back of the stage) will immediately attract and divert the eyes and interest of the audience. It is not considered good form in show business to do this—and it makes no sense at all for a speaker to function in an environment that permits inadvertent upstaging.

For example, many meeting rooms have two or more doors and one of the doors may be quite near or beside the head table and lectern. With the inevitability of a Murphy's Law, you can count on someone coming through that door just as you go into the punch line of your biggest joke. What to do? A committee member stationed outside such a door can direct latecomers to the door at the back of the room so that they can make a less intrusive entrance. Spotlights were not meant for sharing.

Occasionally, the potential distraction is a spectacular one. Some meeting rooms are set up with one of the walls as a floor to ceiling picture window. They may look out over rolling green hills with majestic snow-capped mountains in the distance. The lectern is often set right at the center of this window wall so that the speaker is sharing the audience's attention with all the glories of Mother Nature. My suggestion in such setting is: Give Mother the day off. Draw the drapes even if it's ten o'clock in the morning. The Program Committee booked *you*. Let the Rocky Mountains get its own date.

This sort of pre-planning can eliminate many of the embarrassing situations in which speakers have found themselves. But there can never be 100% certainty in a speaking situation. If something loud, highly visible or dramatic happens while you are speaking, you can't ignore it. If you try to ignore it, the impression the audience receives is that you don't know how to handle it, you don't have the answer, you have lost control of the situation—or all of the above. The unexpected can, does and will happen. When it does, another aspect of control comes into play: You must *regain* control—quickly, adroitly and completely.

***

A case history: I was giving a speech in a hotel meeting room when a phone on the wall began to ring. After the third ring a good part of the audience's attention was diverted to seeing who would answer it. I was just about to refer to it when a member of the hotel's catering staff who was still in the room answered it.

I figured this would end the problem so I kept on with my speech. Instead, in a loud voice that carried across the room, the hotel employee began discussing with the caller an event that was being set up in another of the hotel's meeting rooms. He was running down a list of the tables, the menu—fruit cocktail, chicken with string beans and creamed potatoes, etc.

At this point I stopped speaking, held up my hand for the audience's attention, put my forefinger to my lips for quiet, and indicated to the group that we should all listen to what was being said. Now all I was doing by this was running around to the head of the parade to lead it. All attention had gone to the phone conversation anyway.

Suddenly the room became absolutely still except for the voice of the caterer confirming the arrangements for this other event. And just as suddenly, he now realized that our event had stopped and all attention was on him. To the considerable amusement of our audience, he finished with a garble of menu and music details and sheepishly hung up. Whereupon I said, "And if they need a speaker, I'll be finished in twenty minutes." Immediately, all attention returned to home base, the tension of the unexpected interruption had been resolved—and most important, audience and speaker had joined together in good humor to cope with it.

***

It was not a memorable rejoinder. It didn't have to be. But it spoke to the situation in a confident manner and brought a laugh, applause—and the audience back. When an emergency arises, don't try to ignore it. Tackle it head-on and you'll be surprised to find that even the weakest ad-lib packs a wallop.

But—it need not be weak and it need not be an ad-lib. Every speaker is faced with situations that are unexpected but not unanticipated. If you get up in front of enough audiences, you know that at one time or another the sound system will conk out, the microphone will not be adjustable, you will garble a key sentence, a slide won't appear when it should, a person asking a question will do a speech—fill in your own blanks.

In each case, there is a problem or situation of which the audience is aware. The speaker regains control by immediately addressing the problem with humor.

Every professional speaker and performer has scores of these ad-libs ready to surface at the drop of a glitch. They call them "savers"—and it's an apt name. They "save" both the enjoyment of the moment and the reputation of a lifetime. The audience is reassured. The program sails on.

A speaker has much in common with the captain of a ship. Your listeners are the passengers on this ship. It need not be the Titanic.

Conventions —See Meetings/Conventions

Correcting Oneself —See ALWAYS LEAD THEM LAUGHING

Courting Creativity —See WRITER'S BLOCK AND HOW TO GET AROUND IT

Creative Drought —See WRITER'S BLOCK AND HOW TO GET AROUND IT

Criticism (and its value to the public speaker) —See LESSONS I LEARNED FROM LOWELL THOMAS

Cross-Indexing Jokes and Other Speech Material —See SPICING UP THOSE DULL SPEECHES

Crying Baby —See A Baby Is Crying

Current Jokes —See TOPICAL HUMOR: THE CUTTING EDGE

Cursing —See After an Off-Color Joke/Cursing

Cut and Slash Humor —See KINDER, GENTLER COMEDY

Cynicism —See KINDER, GENTLER COMEDY

D

Daily Routine and Writing —See WRITER'S BLOCK AND HOW TO GET AROUND IT

Deadlines —See WRITER'S BLOCK AND HOW TO GET AROUND IT

Dealing with a Drunk

Sir, you may hate yourself in the morning, but the rest of us are doing it tonight.

You'll have to excuse him. He's going through his religious period. For Lent he's giving up his liver.

Sir, would you mind inhaling? You're melting the glue on my hairpiece.

Has it ever occurred to you that you could be a stand-up comic? If you were funny—and if you could stand up.

Dealing with a Faux Pas

When You Commit a Faux Pas

Mouths are like doors. They should only be opened when you know where you're going.

Did you ever get the feeling you've started off on the wrong foot—and it's the one in your mouth?

Is there a dentist in the house? I'd like to have something removed from my mouth. A foot!

I'm sorry. Sometimes I say what I'm thinking before I think what I'm saying.

When Somebody Else Commits a Faux Pas

I think you've just performed the world's first do-it-yourself lobotomy.

—See also (1) MISTAKES; (2) ALWAYS LEAD THEM LAUGHING; (3) *Don't Neglect the Facts* at DON'TS . . . IF YOU WANT TO GET LAUGHS

Dealing with Hecklers and Interrupters

Tell me, do you have a license to carry that tongue?

Sir, I can read your mind and frankly, I don't have to be a speed-reader to do it.

Sir, let's not get into a battle of the wits. You could be arrested for assault with a dead weapon.

Sir, I don't know how to tell you this, but your imagination has just taken flight—while your facts are still on standby.

Sir, I'm sorry to hear that you've made thinking a spectator sport.

Sir, I need you like Blue Cross needs another ski slope.

And now, let's all listen to the man with the walk-in mouth.

Sir, I need you like the Indianapolis 500 needs speed bumps.

Sir, this conversation—it isn't toxic, but it is a waste.

Thank you for that insight. It's a little like putting ketchup on food for thought.

Sir, have you ever considered having a wisdom tooth put *in*?

I wouldn't exactly refer to that as the fast food of reasoning. Let's just call it McThinking.

Sir, I really think the world of what you're saying—but before you go any further, maybe I'd better tell you what I think of the world.

Before winging it, make sure you're an eagle, not a penguin.

Sir, obviously a thought has just entered your head—evidently in search of privacy.

Sir, if you ever get a penny for your thoughts— give change!

To a Garbled Heckler: Isn't that fascinating? Sir, you talk like my doctor writes!

Tell me, have you ever considered freezing yourself until they find a cure?

Sir, is it true that you're the only man Dale Carnegie ever punched out?

Sir, I really appreciate your giving me a piece of your mind—particularly when your inventory is so low.

Sir, in the Great Bridge Game of Life—how does it feel to be the dummy?

Sir, I know your brain is trying to communicate with your tongue—but it's getting a busy signal.

Sir, I'd like to get on the good side of you—but I can't find it.

To an Interrupter: Sir, we have much in common. I'm not accustomed to speaking—and obviously, you're not accustomed to listening.

Sir, what did you have for dinner? Chicken? How much chicken? Half a chicken. I'll tell you why I ask. I just can't understand how a person who's eaten that much chicken could be so full of bull!

To a Talkative Person: Haven't we met before? I never forget a tongue!

Sir, I don't know quite how to put this—but I think your train of thought may be short some rolling stock.

Sir, you're a little confused. I'm the speaker. You are the speakee.

Sir, you have the right to remain silent. Why don't you use it?

Sir, conversation may be a lost art, but this is no time to send out a search party.

Sir, I don't mind having words with you, but when do I get the chance to use mine?

Sir, I know you're being the devil's advocate— and with that sponsor in mind, let me tell you where to go.

Sir, you're getting your harass backwards.

After a Long Interruption: Sir, I don't mind your having the last word—if only you'd get to it.

Sir, I don't know what makes you tick—but you're sure self-winding.

Please, you're trying to confuse me and I think you're too late.

I'd ask you to eat those words but maybe you don't like junk food.

Sir, I'd like to conduct an exit poll—why don't you?

Sir, having heard, analyzed and reflected on your remarks, I've come to this conclusion: That you could blow up a kiddie pool in 32 seconds.

Sir, why don't we make this a TV evening? I'm the audio and you're the video.

When Someone Makes a Bizarre Comment or Observation: Thank you for that thought, but actually, we do things a bit differently here on Earth.

Sir, not only do you have a one-track mind—but it's narrow-gauge.

—See also CONTROLLING YOUR AUDIENCE

Dealing with Interruption —See (1) CONTROLLING YOUR AUDIENCE; (2) Dealing with Hecklers and Interrupters

Dealing with Stage Fright —See STAGE FRIGHT AND HOW TO DEAL WITH IT

Debating Points

Sir, you're suffering from what can only be called logic interruptus.

To Somebody Who Has Just Been Topped in an Exchange: Sir, you've just found out it doesn't help to be in the fast lane if you're driving an Edsel.

We have a surefire method for keeping our debates short. We ask each participant to make a brief opening statement; we put a time limit on rebuttals; we don't allow questions from the floor; and finally, and perhaps most important of all, the milk we put in their coffee is magnesia.

They say that what you don't know won't hurt you and right now I'd like to congratulate my opponent on feeling no pain.

I have my own way of looking at debates. To me, the winner of any debate is the one who shuts up first.

I've played golf courses that didn't have as many holes as that argument.

Sir, I don't know how to tell you this, but I think you're suffering from analytical anorexia.

When Challenged: If I'm wrong, not only will I eat my words, but I'll ask for seconds!

When You Take an Unpopular Position: I feel a little like a guy who's spilled a glass of water on his lap. No matter what he says nobody is going to believe him!

When Your Argument Is Going Badly: Tell me, how can you get cornered at a round table discussion?

After a Disagreeable Exchange: I know this sounds strange, but I always get something out of a meeting like this. Fortunately, aspirin cures it.

Declining an Invitation to Appear in a Roast —See *Preparing the Roast* at ROASTS

Dedication —See HOW TO SUCCEED IN HUMOR BY REALLY TRYING

Deferral —See MISTAKES

Delivering the Roast —See *Delivering the Roast* at ROASTS

Demand-Laugh Jokes and How to Tell Them —See *Demand-Laugh Jokes* at OPENER: THE FIRST TWO MINUTES OF YOUR SPEECH

Destructive Humor —See TOPICAL HUMOR: THE CUTTING EDGE

Disastrous Meeting —See Ending an Evening/Program

Distractions —See CONTROLLING YOUR AUDIENCE

DON'TS . . . IF YOU WANT TO GET LAUGHS

Six Don'ts . . . If You Do Want to Get Laughs:

Don't Preface
Don't Read the Jokes—Tell 'em!
Don't Use Print Language in Verbal Jokes
Don't Let Your Punch Lines Trail Off
Don't Step on Your Laughs
Don't Neglect the Facts

Don't Preface

How many times have you heard a speaker lead into a joke by saying, "Which reminds me of a story"? Or even worse, "Which reminds me of an *old* story"? This effectively tells the audience that the speaker doesn't think enough of them to even come up with a new story.

Laughter is frequently the result of surprise and playfulness. When a speaker says to an audience that he is going to tell them a joke, both of those key elements vanish. In their place is a challenge: "I am going to tell you a joke and I am going to try to make you laugh." It immediately sets up a modest confrontation.

The listeners psychologically fold their arms, square their shoulders and think, "So you're going to be funny. Well, we'll be the judge of that."

When possible, humor should always be positioned and told as truth. The one-liner, joke, story or anecdote should follow and be a natural consequence of the text that precedes it. The ideal speech is one that weaves substance and humor into a single seamless fabric.

Humor should never be dragged in by the heels. Just as the songs in a properly constructed musical further the action of the plot, jokes should complement and provide a fun corollary to the more serious points being made.

Why *do* speakers preface jokes? Fear is the unconscious motivator. They are telling a joke but don't want to be held responsible for the joke if it doesn't go over. Prefacing is often an unrecognized way of saying to an audience, "Please be kind."

But audiences respond to confidence, not timidity—in substance and in humor. So choose the right material, position it for best effect, lead into it with subtlety, tell it with style, and then, with coolness and confidence, dare the audience *not* to laugh.

Don't Read the Jokes—Tell 'em!

The essence of effective humor is spontaneity. A one-liner or anecdote should always sound as if it is being told for the first time.

In the days of vaudeville and burlesque, comedians would make their first entrance by running out, looking around to see if anyone in the wings or backstage might be listening, and then furtively sharing with the audience something that "just happened." It was a more comedic and high-energy version of "A funny thing happened to me on the way to the theater." By this approach, the comedian immediately established a one-to-one relationship with everyone in eye contact. The joke, the story, the happening was for their ears only.

Now I'm not suggesting that a political figure or CEO of a large company begin a speech by hurtling up to the microphone and opening with, "Hey, I gotta tell ya—." But if the lead-in to the joke is properly constructed—and the lead-in and jokes are not read—the sense of immediacy can be the same.

When a speaker reads a joke and it is apparent to his audience that he is reading the joke—it's another facet of prefacing. The surprise factor disappears. Playfulness goes out the window. The speaker is trying to make the audience laugh but in a way that spotlights premeditation.

Read the rest of the speech if you must—but *tell* the jokes!

Don't Use Print Language in Verbal Jokes

Speech humor should be conversational. Many jokes and anecdotes gleaned from newspapers, magazines and books are not. Print stories always have sentences like: "'I'm dancing as fast as I can,' she remonstrated." Or: "'Some people can tell them—some can't,' he replied."

Print jokes always have people replying, remonstrating, interjecting or opining. But if you were to hear the same joke told person to person, chances are the dialogue would be connected to a simple "I said" or "he said" regardless of whether the sentence is a statement, a question, or an answer.

Platform humor should come as close to everyday language and conversation as possible. Jokes are judged by the laughs they generate, not the syllables.

Don't Let Your Punch Lines Trail Off

A fellow comedy writer once paid me a great compliment. He was looking through one of my books and observed that "every joke ended with a rim shot." It was his way of saying they were constructed to get a laugh.

The structure of a joke is extremely important, but the rhythm, placement and make-up of the punch line are critical. Consider the expression "punch line." It says *POWIE.* A punch line is sometimes referred to as the "snapper" or as the "tag." Again, the emphasis is on impact and finality.

The properly constructed laugh line has the key words or word that make the joke funny, positioned at the very end of the punch line. Nothing should follow it but laughter.

This may seem obvious but this type of joke construction has not always been the norm. Humor books a century or two back, would always tack a little moral onto the ending of every joke. If the story ended with someone being put down, the punch line might be followed with: "And he was justly rebuked."

Audiences today will justly rebuke any humorist who allows a punch line to trail off. They do it by not laughing as much, or as long, or at all. So never tack on a "he said," or "she explained," or moral to the end of a punch line. The straight line is the fuse, the punch line is the explosion.

Don't Step on Your Laughs

Sure. Anybody knows that. So why do so many speakers do it? Fear strikes again! The fear that they will tell a joke, nobody will laugh, and they'll be embarrassed. How do they handle this? They tell the joke and almost immediately charge into their next sentence—

thus insuring that the audience won't laugh because there is no open space to laugh in.

Audiences need four things before they can respond to a joke: An effective joke, expectation on the part of the speaker that they will laugh, sufficient time to absorb and understand the joke, and an uncluttered interval in which to laugh. That sounds like a lot, but the last three ingredients happen in a few seconds.

Unfortunately, Einstein's Theory of Relativity has a direct application to humor. The time between the finish of your punch line and the start of the audience's laughter is less than a second. To the speaker, it often feels like an eternity. The instinct is to try to fill this one second gap with more words. The audience doesn't want to miss what's next, so they stop laughing.

So wait for your laughs but never let them die completely before starting your next line. As the reaction comes down to about 25% of its peak, begin your next paragraph. This creates a feeling of flow rather than an episodic joke, laugh, silence, start up again pattern.

A lot of books on public speaking tell you not to laugh at your own jokes. Who says? Red Skelton has always laughed along with his audiences and in so doing he created a party, let's all have fun together, atmosphere. If you and the audience are having a good time, why shouldn't you show it?

Don't Neglect the Facts

So this couple is having a terrific marital spat and finally she says, "Horses! That's all you're interested in. Horses, racetracks, betting! You know what horses ran yesterday. You know what horses are running today. And you know what horses will be running tomorrow. That's all you ever think about—horses! I'll bet you don't even remember the year we got married." He said,

"Sure I do. It was the same year Native Dancer won the Kentucky Derby!"

Now what's wrong with that joke? Native Dancer never won the Kentucky Derby and any dedicated follower of the sport would know it. As soon as they heard the punch line, all their attention would go to thinking, "Wait a minute. Native Dancer won the Preakness and the Belmont Stakes. Never the Kentucky Derby." They would be analyzing instead of laughing.

This may seem like a rare occurrence but it happens more often than you may think. If you are doing an inside joke to an audience of engineers and the set-up line to your joke is illogical or technologically incorrect—they won't even hear the rest. Their minds will try to sort out what is wrong with what you've just said and while this is happening, the joke is lost.

There is such a thing as comedic logic that defies everyday logic and audiences readily accept it. Mistakes, on the other hand, are a distraction. Avoid them if you can.

Drafts of Your Speech —See PREPARING FOR YOUR SPEECH

Dress —See ADVICE—AND HOW TO IGNORE IT

Dress Codes for Speakers —See ADVICE—AND HOW TO IGNORE IT

Drink —See (1) Food and Drink; (2) After You Sip From a Glass

Dropping Something —See Tripping, Dropping Something, or Injuring Yourself on Your Way to the Lectern or at the Lectern

Drugs, Stimulants, Depressants and Public Speaking —See STAGE FRIGHT AND HOW TO DEAL WITH IT

Drunk —See Dealing with a Drunk

Dullness —See SPICING UP THOSE DULL SPEECHES

During a Snowstorm

Our next speaker is one of the great motivators of our time. I am personally convinced that if he wanted to, at this very moment he could go down to the hotel gift store—and get them to stock up on Coppertone.

I want to thank all those who have braved this weather to be here tonight. This morning the snow was so bad, the only one who got to the office was our bookkeeper—Nanook.

(Name of town) is the only place I know that has answered the question: "Where are the snows of yesteryear?" Right under the snows of this year!

Tonight we pay tribute to the gallant members of the Highway Department who have worked night and day through this snow emergency—keeping our highways open and our driveways closed.

—See also Winter and Cold Places

During a Heavy Rain

To People Coming in out of the Rain: Come in and take off those wet things. You look like a yard sale in Venice.

E

Elections

But let's settle this once and for all. *(Name of candidate)* has said he's not interested in the Presidency and there is absolutely no truth to the rumor that he has "YES" embroidered on napkins in case someone asks him while he's eating.

What the convention really needs is another dark horse. But this time, the entire horse.

Electronic / Mechanical Prompters —See ALWAYS LEAD THEM LAUGHING

Ending an Evening / Program

When it comes to trash compactors, nothing beats a program with a time limit.

Regretfully, this wonderful evening is coming to an end. The fat lady hasn't sung yet—but she's getting out her music.

At the End of a Long Program: I'm going to keep this short. *(Look at your watch:)* I see by my watch it's a quarter past August.

Adjournment is what keeps the mumbo from getting too jumbo.

In conclusion—the two words your bladder has been praying for. . . .

In conclusion, let me say that a bird in the hand is worth two in the bush. This offer good only at participating hands and bushes.

When You Recount Something with a Surprise Finish: That's my martini story. It comes with a twist.

When You Recap Your Thesis at the Conclusion of a Speech: And so, as you can see, like airline luggage, I eventually wind up where I'm supposed to.

There comes a time in every speaker's life, when he or she looks out over the audience and sees every face filled with appreciation, expectation, and unalloyed pleasure. It's shortly after the words "so, in conclusion." So, in conclusion . . .

Closing

Live, love and enjoy. None of us have a warranty, but we all have an expiration date.

And so, let me close with a thought that has always brought tears to my eyes: Remember— home is where the payments are.

This has been such a fantastic evening. Tell me, can you O.D. on ecstasy?

And so, in conclusion, let us never forget those immortal words of Marcel Marceau. . . .

And in conclusion, I'd like to say to you one word about applause—PLEASE!

(To adjourn, pause, look at your watch and say:) It's ten o'clock. Do you know where your evening has been shot to?

Right now we're out of time—but we do expect another shipment for the next meeting.

Closing a Disastrous Meeting: Well, it's been a wonderful evening. Kind of a shame we spent it here.

There are two types of speakers I can do without: Those who never stop to think and those who never think to stop. I sincerely hope I haven't been either. Thank you and good night!

In closing, I would like to leave you with this thought: If a 6,000 pound rhinoceros charges you—pay him!

Some of the suggestions I made in this speech may seem a little far out to you, but before you reject them, all I ask is that you sleep on them. And as I look about me, I see that some of you have already begun.

First, let me thank you for allowing me to be a part of an evening that will live forever in my memory. How often do you see 500 people come into a place, sit down and order the same meal?

I have a lot more to say but I always try to observe the first rule of public speaking. Nice guys finish fast!

Closing Acknowledgment

I want to thank who is responsible for the club's entertainment—for hiring me anyway.

Equipment

A lot of speakers are intimidated by the room, the audience and the microphone—but not me. *(Lean over, tap the water pitcher and speak into it:)* Testing! Testing!

If You're Having Trouble with the Microphone: Why don't we use the one that says "Made in America"?

When Lowering the Microphone

First, we have to do a little "downloading." They must have been expecting *(tall personality)*.

How do you like that? I've been waiting so long to talk, I think I've shrunk!

When Raising the Microphone

It's like my pension. It's fixed—but not high enough.

If You're Having Trouble Raising the Microphone: Where are steroids when you really need them?

If you Can't Raise the Microphone: Would somebody please call Roto-Rooter?. . . I think my roto has rooted.

When Raising or Lowering the Microphone

Excuse me while I adjust this for inflation. . . .

When the Microphone Squeals

If you had to listen to as much nonsense as this mike, you'd squeal too!

If the Sound System Begins to Squeal: (Indicate that you have an idea, step back, take out your keys, loose change and watch and put them on the table beside you; explain:) Well, it works at airports.

If You're Getting Feedback from the Sound System: That's all we need. A sound system on steroids.

When the Sound System Fails

You can tell it's Christmas. We've got a sound system and batteries are not included.

First, let me pay tribute to the person who set up this sound system—a person who obviously believes that actions should speak louder than words.

Not to worry. We'll just switch to our non-electronic back-up amplification system. Everyone cup your hands behind your ears.

I'm just glad this outfit doesn't make pacemakers.

There's a name for something like this. And when the electrician arrives, I'm going to call him it.

Pick up two napkins, one in each hand, and start making semaphore signals.

Suddenly it feels like I'm talking to my kids.

When the Lights Go Out

Don't panic. If we all cooperate, we can fix this. Will everybody in the audience please raise both your hands over your head and shake them? *(Ad-lib these instructions until the lights come back on again.)* You know how I learned that? It's from an old proverb: Many Hands Make Light Work!

I think Tom Edison's patent just ran out!

Other Equipment Problems

I want you to know that I'm giving this speech for free. What I'm charging for is using this equipment.

This is about as useful as an ashtray on a motorcycle.

While Something Is Being Repaired: This is one of the nice things about being away from home. It's great to have something go wrong that you're not expected to fix.

If You Have Trouble Pulling a Pen from Your Pocket: I haven't written an order in so long, it took root!

Ethnic Jokes —See ASSESSING YOUR AUDIENCE

Eulogies and Humor —See "WHY HUMOR?"

Excuses for a Bad Presentation —See STAGE FRIGHT AND HOW TO DEAL WITH IT

Expanding Punch Lines —See USING HUMOR WHEN YOU'RE AFRAID TO USE HUMOR

Eye Contact —See (1) REHEARSING YOUR SPEECH; (2) PREPARING FOR YOUR SPEECH; (3) LESSONS LEARNED FROM LOWELL THOMAS

F

Facts —See *Don't Neglect the Facts* at DON'TS . . . IF YOU WANT TO GET LAUGHS

Fair Play and Humor —See THE USES AND LIMITS OF HUMOR

Family Reunions —See Reunions

Faux Pas —See Dealing with a Faux Pas

Fear of Speaking in Public (and how to overcome it) —See STAGE FRIGHT AND HOW TO DEAL WITH IT

Financial Aspects of Speechwriting —See MONEY AND SPEECHWRITING

First Performer at a Roast —See *Delivering the Roast* at ROASTS

First Two Minutes of a Speech —See OPENER: THE FIRST TWO MINUTES OF YOUR SPEECH

A Flattering or Glowing Introduction, Responding to

Wow! That's what I call an introduction on steroids!

What can I say? I don't think anyone should get an introduction like that without first having the courtesy to die.

That's the kind of introduction I like. One where the praise comes with stretch marks.

Well, I wouldn't say all that—but I'm mighty glad that *you* did.

I loved that introduction. I have to be honest—I never worry about cholesterol when I'm being buttered up.

That's what I call a Burger King introduction—one whopper after another!

All I can say is—be careful. I know guys who are running for Congress with less encouragement than that!

I dunno. When you get a send-off like that, somehow it never seems necessary to get a second opinion.

Thank you for that wonderful introduction. By the way, do you do resumés?

—See also Introductions

Food and Drink

What did you think of the red table wine? Wasn't it great? I didn't even know you could make wine from red tables.

Wasn't that a great dinner? I think I just had my spare tire retreaded.

Food prices are so high, it explains why there are so many after-dinner speakers. What they're after is dinner.

In a long-range view of the history of our species, man may be most remembered as a creature who was constantly drinking when he wasn't even thirsty.

I love this wine. Where was it aged—on the truck?

For those of you who are vegetarians, on behalf of the Program Chairman, I'm sorry we served meat tonight. And for those of you who aren't vegetarians, on behalf of the Treasurer, I'm sorry we served meat tonight.

The worst experience I've ever had is speaking to a convention of waiters. You could never get their attention.

Have you checked out what the hotel restaurant gets for a salad? $16.95! I think it's designer greens.

Believe me, it isn't easy eating with a beard like that. _____ is the only one I know with a radar fork.

First, I want to congratulate the chef on this fantastic dinner. I didn't even know that Black & Decker made steaks.

I always get embarrassed at formal dinners because of etiquette. Eating peas, in particular, gives me a problem. I never know which knife to use.

I'm really getting concerned about the preservatives in food. For instance, scientists have just determined why King Tut was able to last for 3,000 years in such good shape. He was embalmed in a gigantic loaf of white bread.

It has been said: We pass this way but once. I don't know who said it. I think it was our waiter.

You know what really gets to me? Paying $9.95 for something called a continental breakfast. It gives you the feeling there is now an eighth continent—Beverly Hills.

And I don't care what hotel you order them in, continental breakfasts are all alike: one and a half cups of coffee, three swallows of orange juice, and a sweet roll that looks like it flunked vending machine.

What I've always admired about this club—it has a fun atmosphere. I mean, where else does an alcohol rub come with vermouth?

In all fairness, banquets have taught me a great deal. For instance, before I started going to banquets, I thought mashed potatoes were supposed to be served hot.

I won't say what the food is like, but I asked the waiter to put a steak on my credit card—and it fit!

Salmon is so expensive, they no longer swim upstream to spawn; they take a cab.

It's amazing what restaurants are charging for bottled water. Water is getting so expensive, one restaurant is listing it as an entree.

This has really been a fantastic, and I may say, unusual dinner. It isn't often you get leg of Spam.

They really have a great bartender in this hotel. He makes a martini that's so strong, it comes with an olive, a twist of lemon, and a warning to denture wearers!

Wasn't that an incredible meal? It's the sort of meal that really cries out for an after-dinner drink—Alka-Seltzer!

Forgetting

I'm sorry. I bought a book that's supposed to improve my memory—but I keep forgetting to read it.

I'm sorry. I have a memory just good enough to remember that I have a very poor memory.

Do you ever get the feeling that someone spilled Wite-Out on your brain?

They say that the new version of *(name of popular software product)* calls for a lot more memory. As you can see, so do I.

Four-Letter Words —See (1) ASSESSING YOUR AUDIENCE; (2) After an Off-Color Joke/Cursing

Frog in Your Throat —See ADVICE—AND HOW TO IGNORE IT

"The Frozen Draft" —See PREPARING FOR YOUR SPEECH

Fundraising

A fund-raising dinner is where you put your money where your mousse is.

I'd also like our club treasurer to stand up and take a bow. He's the one who greets you with open arms—and hands to match.

This is now known as the Pothole Budget. When you don't put enough in the pot, you go into the hole.

There is only one sure way to get people to put their money where their mouth is—gin-flavored twenties.

As you know, our last church dinner was a very successful fund-raiser. The minister shook 94 hands and 82 wallets.

It's amazing how noisy an audience can be when you ask for quiet—and how quiet it can be when you ask for money.

G

Gag Gift or Award —See Acknowledging a Gag Gift or Award

Garble Your Words, If You

As you can see, I've given up lucidity for Lent.

Let me repeat that. I ran off this hard copy of my speech and it's harder than I thought.

By now, those of you familiar with ancient languages have no doubt identified that last sentence as the traditional Latin expression for "my lips are made of vulcanized rubber."

I'll repeat that for those of you who didn't catch it. After all, I was talking at the speed of sound.

And now, let me repeat that for those of you who don't speak flub.

(After you garble a sentence, push up on your upper teeth with your thumbs and comment:) You just can't buy these things at a garage sale.

I'm sorry. My mind wandered and my tongue went out to look for it.

My wife doesn't understand me—and frankly, neither do I.

I'd like to repeat that for those of you who missed it—including myself.

I love that line. I know I love it because you always hurt the one you love.

Giving of Yourself in a Speech —See LESSONS I LEARNED FROM LOWELL THOMAS

Glitches in Your Speech (and how to eliminate them) —See REHEARSING YOUR SPEECH

Glitches That Occur Outside Your Control (and how to deal with them) —See CONTROLLING YOUR AUDIENCE

Glowing or Flattering Introduction —See A Flattering or Glowing Introduction, Responding to

Good Speeches (and what they accomplish) —See LESSONS I LEARNED FROM LOWELL THOMAS

Grabbing an Audience —See OPENER: THE FIRST TWO MINUTES OF YOUR SPEECH

Graduation

A kid gets his first touch of reality at graduation time. There may be 500 students in the senior class—but only one of them is Most Likely To Succeed.

This is the time of year when the people responsible for commencement programs are faced with two big questions: 1. Who tells the graduates the future is theirs? And 2. Who tells the future?

This is a very musical time of the year. It's when they play "The Wedding March" for the brides, "Pomp and Circumstance" for graduates, and "Brother, Can You Spare a Dime" for parents.

There is only one way to cope with the soaring cost of putting your kids through college: When they're very young, you start a special education fund for them and every year you add to it. Then, just when they're ready to enter college, you hold up a bank.

One thing about our educational system disturbs me: Shouldn't you be able to read a diploma to get one?

One school is graduating so many functional illiterates, it's putting their diplomas on cassettes.

One kid was named Grammarian of the Senior Class and it really came as a surprise. He said, "I are?"

I know a school teacher whose goal in life is to be Snow White—because then she'd only have to put up with one Dopey.

Giving an apple to a teacher is a good thing for three people. For the grocer, it's business. For the student, it's goodwill. And for the teacher, it's dinner.

It's fascinating the way modern education stresses positive reinforcement rather than negative correction. Kids today get a beep from a computer. We used to get a bop from a ruler.

Graduation—or, as it could be called, the first day of the rest of your education.

When you leave these halls of learning, very shortly you will be faced with the problems of finding an apartment, finding a job, making a living, paying taxes and paying off your loans. It is precisely this sort of outlook that inspired one of the most comforting quotations of our time: "If you can keep your head when all others around you are losing theirs—you must be going on to graduate school."

Even though you are graduating today, there is still much to be learned in the outside world. For instance, for those of you who spent the last four years eating in the school cafeteria, the first thing you'll learn is that there are other recipes for meat beyond "Burn & Serve."

Now, one of the requirements of every commencement speaker is that they offer at least one bit of sage advice. So get ready. Here it comes. Very shortly you will be leaving the people who think they have all the answers—your instructors, professors and counselors—and going out into the real world. In time you will meet other people who think they have all the answers. These people are called bosses. My advice is: Humor them. A little later you will meet other people who also think they have all the answers. These are called spouses. My advice is: Humor them. And if all goes well, in a few years you will meet still another group of people who think they have all the answers. They are called children. Humor them. Now life will go on, your children will grow up, go to school, and someday they could be taking part in a commencement exercise exactly like this one. And who knows? The speaker responsible for handing out the good advice could very well be you. And it would not be inconceivable that halfway through your speech, the graduate sitting next to your kid will lean over and ask, "Who's the old guy up there who thinks he has all the answers?" Well, thanks to the sound advice you're hearing today and that I hope you'll pass on, he'll be able to say, "That's my father. Humor him." Congratulations on your past achievements. Good luck in the future. And thank you all for humoring me today.

And so, on behalf of your community, the nation, your elected representatives here and in Washington, and everyone associated with the Federal budget—let me just say, "The future is yours. Just keep in touch so we'll know where to send the bills."

I would really like to have my life to live over again. I don't think this one took.

The timing of commencement addresses is all wrong. Don't tell graduates in June that the future is theirs. Tell them in September, when they're no longer all that sure.

This is the month when a few million students will graduate from college and try to sell what they have learned in the real world—which indicates they haven't learned enough.

You can tell the universities are preparing their students for today's world. Not one graduation gown has pockets.

And to parents, graduation day has a special meaning Harry Truman would have loved: The bucks stop here.

I know one graduate who majored in dead languages and it worked out very well. He's an interpreter at Forest Lawn.

When you're a college commencement speaker, you always have to make a basic decision concerning your audience: Whether to lie and have them eager to get into the real world. Or tell the truth and have them eager to get into graduate school.

But not all learning is a good thing. One kid completed four years of college, put on his graduation gown—and learned he liked dresses.

But it's no wonder Graduation Day and Prom Night are remembered so fondly. They represent three of the happiest events in the life of any teenager: Getting out, going out and making out.

The worst thing that can happen to June graduates and their parents is to leave the ceremonies filled with hope, enthusiasm and expectation—and go home in a cab driven by a Ph.D.

The June graduate who has the least to worry about is the Valedictorian who knows Latin, Greek, French and Japanese, has mastered computer programming and financial planning, has a working knowledge of advanced genetics—and isn't averse to heavy lifting.

Commencement day is a tribute to the willing suspension of disbelief. It's when millions of graduates are told "the future is yours"—and they know that not even the caps and gowns are theirs.

A cap and gown and a liberal arts education have a lot in common. Once you graduate, you have no use for either.

There is no question that higher education is a broadening experience. Part of it comes from the knowledge you get in the classroom—and part of it comes from the starch you get in the cafeteria.

There is one big problem with the road to success—no rest areas.

I'm proud to say that during my graduation ceremony I did some volunteer work. I read the program and explained what was going on to five students who were handicapped. Two were blind and three were football players.

The football players were nice guys but not all that swift. One of them graduated magna cum huh?

He still can't understand why his letter didn't come with a stamp.

A commencement address is a speech frequently given by politicians who tell graduates how to cope with all the stresses and strains and tensions and dangers they wouldn't be facing if it weren't for politicians.

Some people say that academic standards are dropping. I never really believed that until I saw the title of the chancellor's speech: "The Future Is Yores."

June is when graduates are thrilled just to get their sheepskin. July is when they realize there's no meat on it.

H

Handling Stage Fright —See STAGE FRIGHT AND HOW TO DEAL WITH IT

HARD WORK OF HUMOR, THE

Comedy is hot.

The top TV and film comedians have incomes that are in the tens of millions of dollars. Some leading syndicated cartoonists are in that same comfortable category.

Just a few years ago pundits were tolling the death knell of TV situation comedy. For one television season, no new sit-coms appeared. Now sit-coms dominate the Top Ten listings.

When vaudeville, presentation houses, and nightclubs dried up, comedians had no place to show their wares and the comedic stockpile withered. Now there are 300 to 400 comedy clubs using a few thousand joke-tellers. The more promising of the club performers are being snapped up for commercials, and TV and film acting roles.

Professional speakers are well aware that a speech without laughs is a speech without takers. No matter what the subject matter: motivational, inspirational, informational—political, corporate, or academic—speakers are expected to deliver a substantial amount of laughter as well.

To repeat—comedy is hot. And there's a good feeling to watching an accomplished comedian or humorist perform. He or she stands there with authority, confidence, experience—secure in the strength of their material and approach. It all looks so easy.

The trap for newcomers is not recognizing, understanding, and engaging in all the hard work that makes it look so easy. Within every great there's a grunt who has spared no effort to perfect his or her performance. When the effort hasn't been made, it can also make for some memorable moments.

***

I remember attending a slide lecture at a local museum given by an authority in his field. The lecturer began by apologizing for being a poor speaker. The man then proceeded to prove his case. His opening remarks were a mumble. A member of the audience called, "Louder." So he mumbled faster. Another member of the audience said, "Use the microphone!" The light of discovery illuminated the speaker's eyes as he recognized this strange device on the lectern. He leaned into it and for the first time could be heard.

Now he began his slide presentation. First, there was the confusion of who would dim the lights and how and where the lights were dimmed. Then he played with the remote control that advanced, backed up, and focused the slides. We had a brief unfocused preview of some of the slides to come as he mastered the mechanism. Finally, he got it back to Slide One and the principal part of his talk began.

The slides required some pinpointing of details and, of course, there was no pointer. So he moved from the lectern to the screen to point with his hand. Divorced from the microphone, once again he couldn't be heard. Once again, "Louder!" Once again, he mumbled faster.

Once again, "Use the microphone!" This bit of audience instruction seemed to confuse him. The microphone was back at the lectern. What to do? The speaker returned to the lectern and, in a flash of technological insight, realized that the microphone was on a cable and could be removed from its holder. Returning to the screen with microphone in hand, all went well until the slides came to an end. He put the microphone on a ledge beneath the screen, returned to the lectern, and began a closing that once again couldn't be heard. "Louder!" Speed mumbling. "Use the microphone!" And, gamely, the speaker leaned forward and did the rest of his presentation talking into the now empty microphone holder.

It was enough to give incompetence a bad name.

**

On another occasion, at a communications conference, I was sitting through a similarly dreadful presentation. A colleague, seated beside me, got up to leave and asked if I wanted to join him. I shook my head. He whispered, "Why would you want to stay for this?" I said, "I learn from mistakes. Better they're someone else's."

When you watch a well-crafted, expertly delivered performance by a pro, it all does look so easy. It's impossible to imagine or uncover the hard work, the trial and error, the frustrations, roadblocks, and challenges that had to be overcome to achieve the final result.

When you watch a bumbler, the pitfalls are all too obvious. The trick is to analyze what is going wrong and how it should be corrected. In the museum speaker's case, most of his troubles were the result of insufficient planning. He knew what he wanted to say. The words had been carefully written and worth listening to. The circumstances of performing them had been left entirely to chance.

The speaker should have asked as many questions as required to get a total and accurate picture of the speech location. He should have learned the size of the room, its lighting, how and who would control the lighting, the stage layout, the equipment available and how to use it. On-the-job training should never take place in front of your audience.

When rehearsing a speech or presentation, it should be done under conditions that closely approximate the actual event. The problems that might arise will then be recognized in rehearsal—and solved. It's hard, painstaking work but it's owed to every audience. Speakers and performers ask audiences to give them one of their most valuable possessions—the precious minutes of their lives. The responsibility of the people onstage is to make those moments enjoyable and worthwhile. They can't all be great—but they can all be professional.

My heart sinks when I hear a speaker apologize for not being prepared or for not being a better speaker. I always feel like saying, "Before you begin, maybe you could help us find someone who is." I am annoyed when I go to a comedy club and see a comedian slouch out to the microphone, look around, and start asking ringsiders where they're from. I didn't come for a geography lesson and painful improvisation. Where's the act?

I grit my teeth at the presenter who goes to the lectern, looks under it, produces a glass of water and takes a long drink from it before beginning. What was wrong with the glass of water on the table in front of him as he was being introduced?

Details? Sure. But they add up on the audience's scorecard. And in each case, the only path to improvement is the hard work of preparation and practice.

Rehearse and review. Then perform and review and redo and rehearse and perform again. It's an endless cycle through the lower courts of theory and conjecture up to the Supreme Court of audience reaction.

***

What are some of the steps that can and should be taken to ensure that audiences are getting your best effort? When Presidents of the United States schedule a press conference, they don't just show up. A few days before, they are provided with briefing books that list every question they are likely to be asked. Suggested answers and background information follow each question.

The President then studies these briefing books and sometime before the press conference, a mock press conference is held in the Oval Office. Aides ask questions—some softball, some zingers. The President answers and then the answers are critiqued. If the response is unconvincing or inappropriate, an on-the-spot rewrite takes place. Then the question is repeated and the new answer given. The whole idea is to have the President at peak performance in this high-visibility event.

Is this just another example of political smoke and mirrors? Not really. A President has to communicate his programs and actions effectively. This exercise enhances his ability to do so.

***

How does this relate to speakers and comedians? Joke-tellers also have briefing books. They are the joke books, comedy files, and humor services they have acquired through the years. In this book you will find ad-

91

libs to cover the most common situations a communicator will face. These comedic resources should be studied, memorized, and absorbed. They are the briefing books of the savvy humorist.

Next, instead of a mock press conference, stage a mock performance. If you're a speaker, do your speech before a few friends or associates. Their function is not to critique your presentation but, from time to time, to interrupt to state a problem that could occur: a guest at the head table leans back and topples off the platform—the lights go out—your written speech or notes are out of sequence. You respond, not in theory, but in actuality—saying and doing what you would say or do in a real-time situation.

If you can audiotape or, better yet, videotape, these sessions—all to the good. You and your surrogate audience can then analyze what was right and what could be improved. Remember that, in this exercise, we're dealing with the unexpected, the emergencies that confront every speaker. The presumption is that the hard work in fashioning and learning your basic speech has already been done.

For comedy performers, the drill is similar. If you do any interactive talk with your audience, your briefing books should contain material that covers likely exchanges. Consider the ubiquitous "Where you from?" gambit. If you have to use it, stockpile effective observations on major cities and areas of the country. A stock of small town, quiet town, suburban town material can also be used in a generic way to cover locations on which you don't have specifics. A matching set of jokes on occupations would be appropriate if you broaden your questioning to "What do you do?"

Once again, stage a pretend performing situation. A few friends can spontaneously respond with cities, occupations, comments—and drawing from your stockpile of prepared and newly created ad-libs, you respond. These are premeditated exercises, but anytime you witness a speaker or performer work and something out of the ordinary occurs, immediately put yourself in his or her place and imagine your own response. It all amounts to comedic aerobics to strengthen your performing skills.

***

Now the concept of "prepared ad-libs" is an obvious contradiction in terms. But Boy Scouts, speakers, and comedians will never hurt from being prepared. Whenever I work with a speaker or performer expecting a question and answer exchange, special material is always prepared to counter the expected queries. The performers memorize it. The speakers have it right on the lectern following the last page of their text.

Collaborative spontaneity isn't all that new. I was on a radio talk show where the other guest was a well-known comedian. Seated beside the comedian was his writer. During the entire interview, the writer kept scribbling notes, jokes, and suggestions on a note pad for the star to "ad-lib." To the listening audience, it came across as a fun-filled, quick-witted performance.

Well, what about television? You can't do that on television. Oh no? Every major talk show host has creative people who research the guests, determine their best anecdotes, write lead-in questions to prompt those anecdotes, and then the writers come up with bright and witty responses to parry, if not top, what the guests say. It's all there on the host's desk for ready referral.

Head Table

It's always an honor to appear on a program with such a distinguished head table. Looks like a group mid-life crisis.

As I look around this head table, I can't recall when so many distinguished and accomplished and outstanding members of our organization— were absent.

Head Table Behavior —See STARTING YOUR SPEECH A WINNER

Heavy Rain —See During a Heavy Rain

Hecklers —See Dealing with Hecklers and Interrupters

Honoraria

Our guest is a person who doesn't know the meaning of the word fear—who doesn't know the meaning of the word defeat—who doesn't know the meaning of the word impossible—and who is with us tonight because he doesn't know the meaning of the word honorarium either.

I'll never forget my first speaking engagement. It was to one of those groups that don't pay much in the way of honorariums, but they make up for it by not listening too closely.

I love that term "an honorarium." An honorarium is where they pay you—but you're not supposed to know about it.

Hotels

And no matter where you go, hotel rooms are out of sight! $200. $250. $300! You know what this country really needs? Day-old hotel rooms!

I love the hotels that have slogans like: Our aim is your satisfaction! I want to tell you something about their aim: A William Tell they're not.

Hot Room

In view of the temperature, we're going to keep the business meeting short, the program lively, and when it's over, as an extra added treat, we're all going to toast marshmallows over the air-conditioning.

They said this room would be air-conditioned and they didn't lie. I've never seen air in such condition.

Boy, the heat in here is really something. I'd take off my jacket only my shirt isn't monogrammed.

If the Air-Conditioning Breaks Down: It's so humid in my room, I had to take a shower just to dry off.

How Not to Tell a Joke —See (1) DON'TS . . . IF YOU WANT TO GET LAUGHS; (2) OPENER: THE FIRST TWO MINUTES OF YOUR SPEECH

How to Spice Up a Dull Speech —See SPICING UP THOSE DULL SPEECHES

HOW TO SUCCEED IN HUMOR BY REALLY TRYING

Some years ago, as a writer on a television show, I went to Chicago to scout an act. The public relations person for a downtown nightclub had mounted a campaign to convince our producer that a new comedy team would be right for the show. The producer asked me to take a look.

It was a weekday night. It was cold. By show time there were nine people in the audience. I had asked the public relations contact not to tell the comedy team that I would be there as this sometimes affects a performance. Maybe that was a mistake.

The performers came out, looked around, and apparently decided there wasn't enough of an audience to waste their act on. There were "Good evening, ladies and chairs" jokes. A lot of pointless banter and ad-lib clowning between the two. A few snippets of their act were thrown in and their set ended.

The PR person gamely tried to put the best spin on the performance and brought me to the bar to meet the comedy team. When they heard my name, the show I was with, they looked at each other and simultaneously realized they had just torn up a possible winning sweepstakes ticket.

When I got back to the TV show office, the producer asked me what I thought of their act. I said I never saw their act and explained what had happened. He shrugged—I shrugged—and we went on to the next item.

***

By way of contrast, a few years ago I saw a play in London called *The Business of Murder*. It had run for five years and was soon to close. Five years of the cast doing the same play, night after night, matinee after matinee—the same lines, the same expressions, the same bits of business.

I saw it on New Year's Eve and the house was only one-third full. There would have been no surprise if it had been less than a peak performance. The star of the play, Richard Todd, is one of Britain's most successful and distinguished actors. I am sure that Todd, like most of his audience, was heading for a New Year's Eve celebration when the curtain came down.

But there was no hint of this during the play. It was New Year's Eve but there was no breaking of "the fourth wall" with ad-libs to the audience. There were no inside jokes or bits of business between the players. It was a performance—as fresh as on opening night.

It's always a mistake for a speaker or a humorist to prejudge an audience. There is no way we can ever accurately assess the importance of any audience or event. The show business cliché is that "you never know who's out there." Every speech, every performance, has to be opening night.

***

Beyond the promise of recognition or personal gain, there's another very good reason for giving 100%— 100% of the time. Every performance, whether to nine people or nine thousand, is a learning experience. You don't learn delivery, comedy timing, and the best way to routine and structure material in a vacuum or in front of a mirror. Each new audience presents its own challenges and these are opportunities that should not be wasted.

It all comes down to dedication. How determined are you to make it? I can count on getting an average of two phone calls a month from budding writers or performers. The preamble, substance, and conclusion of their calls are almost identical. They go something like this:

"I am an amateur but I would like to be a professional. My family and friends think I am gifted, hilarious, talented, a genius *(choose one)*. I know that I can write or perform as well as Neil Simon, Woody Allen, Bill Cosby, Jerry Seinfeld *(choose your favorite)* if only I had the chance. Could you put me in touch with someone who can recognize real talent and open the doors for me?"

The callers never doubt their ability or that stardom is just a break away. They say their friends and neighbors fall down laughing at everything they do. I think to myself, but never say, "Would they fall down laughing if they had to pay a $15 cover and two drink minimum to see it?" They tell me they're the life of the living room and their families say they ought to be on television—at least cable. I think, but never say, "Good. A family's job is to say 'ooh' and 'ah' and be supportive. Objective critics they ain't."

But what all these would-be writers and performers are looking for is a Fairy Godmother Agent or Manager. Someone who can lead them by the hand into the land of fame and fortune. It is a dream and a fantasy cherished by every newcomer. I try to tell them as kindly and gently as possible that it doesn't work that way.

I have always felt that the formula for success in the performing arts is 60% talent, 40% aggressiveness. You've got to be able to have a door slammed in your face and go right back and knock on it again. The writers and performers who make it are not those who just dream of being discovered—but those who discover that dreams are only the spur to achievement. They become their own Fairy Godmother Agent-Manager-Publicist-Door Opener.

No matter how sensitively delivered, this bit of reality is never welcomed by the caller. This is not to imply that dreams and fantasies aren't necessary. They are—but only to motivate action. If dreams crowd out the steps necessary to making them come true, they can become nightmares.

Years ago I was associated with a variety show that was looking for new talent. I asked one of the applicants what her goal was. She said she wanted to be a star. I asked her if she was taking singing lessons. "No." Was she taking dance lessons? "No." Was she enrolled in an acting class? "No. None of those things. I just want to be a star." She may now be 60—still wanting to be.

***

Making it in the performing and creative arts is hard, exacting work—and then success itself calls for equally hard work. The only way you can coast is to go downhill. There is never an end to learning, rehearsal, performance, evaluation—and then more learning, rehearsal, performance, and evaluation. The goal is to be ready when the break occurs and the doors open.

When vaudeville died in the 1930s, it was followed by a decade or so of what was called "presentation houses." Mostly in larger cities, these theaters offered a big band onstage and a featured singer, comedian, and supporting novelty act. As opposed to the two-a-day shows of vaudeville, presentation houses did four shows a day and five on weekends. In between the live shows, a feature film was shown. If you got in before 11:00 a.m., the price could be as low as 24 cents to see some of the top names in show business.

I remember one show that began with a perfunctory up-tempo big band number that was far from memorable. The audience responded with scattered applause. The bandleader, a jazz great, was obviously put out by the lack of enthusiasm. He came up to the microphone and said, "I want to thank you for all that wonderful round of indifference." And followed it up with a few more audience put-down lines. When he finished, a man sitting behind me called out, "You ain't *done* nuthin' yet!"

When and if the big opportunity comes, the ability and the willingness to "do" has to be there and ready to go. Dreams start the creative engine—hard work is the fuel that takes it to its destination. What it all comes down to is motivation. The drive to achieve and excel has to come from within us, but if we're lucky, sometimes it gets a little outside help.

I was to give a speech to a Chamber of Commerce audience in a small city. During the luncheon that preceded the program, the official responsible for booking me was describing the various activities of the group. She told me about the meetings, the training sessions, and the various programs they sponsored. I said, "That sounds like a very ambitious schedule. What's your yearly budget for speakers?" She looked me straight in the eye and said, "You're it!"

If I hadn't brought my own, that would have been all the motivation I needed.

How to Tell a Joke —See (1) DON'TS . . . IF YOU WANT TO GET LAUGHS; (2) OPENER: THE FIRST TWO MINUTES OF YOUR SPEECH

Humor and Its Uses —See (1) "WHY HUMOR?"; (2) THE USES AND LIMITS OF HUMOR

Humor in Business and Political Communications —See "WHY HUMOR?"

Humor That "Plays" —See SPICING UP THOSE DULL SPEECHES

I

If You Ask for a Question and There Are None —See Questions and Answers

Image-Building / Enhancing through Humor —See "WHY HUMOR?"

Improving Your Presentation —See (1) TAPING; (2) THE HARD WORK OF HUMOR

Inattention by Your Audience —See LESSONS I LEARNED FROM LOWELL THOMAS

Incompetence and Public Speaking (a case history) —See THE HARD WORK OF HUMOR

Injuring Yourself as a Speaker —See Tripping, Dropping Something, or Injuring Yourself on Your Way to the Lectern or at the Lectern

Insects

If You're Bothered by an Insect: I don't have enough troubles, now I'm being attacked by a terrorist moth.

Inside Jokes —See *Don't Neglect the Facts* at DON'TS . . . IF YOU WANT TO GET LAUGHS

Interrupters —See (1) CONTROLLING YOUR AUDI-
ENCE; (2) Dealing with Hecklers and Interrupters

Interruptions —See (1) CONTROLLING YOUR AUDI-
ENCE; (2) Dealing with Hecklers and Interrupters

Intimacy —See *Don't Read the Jokes—Tell 'em!* at
DON'TS . . . IF YOU WANT TO GET LAUGHS

Introductions

He is a powerful speaker. A really powerful
speaker. Any more powerful and we'd need a prescription to hear him.

Our speaker tonight has received so many honors, so many awards, so many ovations—he's the
only man I know who has Carpal Tunnel Syndrome from bowing.

A born speaker, when other babies were saying,
"Goo-goo" and "Ga-ga"—he was calling for questions.

Our speaker goes back a long way with our
organization. How long? When he began, a pager
was a tap on the shoulder. . . . The Internet was
the water-cooler.

We're talking about someone who joined this
company so long ago, the only mission statement was, "Yes, Mr. *(name of CEO)!* Right away,
Mr. *(name of CEO)!*"

It isn't often that we have as our speakers *(name
three celebrities)*—and tonight is no exception.

I'd be less than honest if I didn't admit to having mixed feelings about shaving, turning off my favorite TV show, putting on a tuxedo, stepping out of a warm, dry house and driving 22 miles in the rain so that I could be here tonight to introduce a speaker this introduction says needs no introduction.

Whenever I'm given six pages of copy to introduce a speaker, I'm always tempted to begin by saying: "And now, I'd like to present an introduction that needs no speaker."

I was taught that if you can't say something good about a person, don't say anything. Which could explain why so many speakers are introduced as needing no introduction.

Our guest is a graduate of the Bolshoi Ballet School of Management—where he learned to keep everybody hopping and on their toes.

Our next speaker is someone who needs no introduction—which leads me to wonder what I'm doing up here.

Our speaker is a born leader, a creative thinker, an outstanding executive, and a superb communicator. Of course, that's only my opinion—adjusted for inflation.

Tough? When he became sheriff, all robberies in this town stopped. And if that isn't enough, people who stole before brought it back.

Our next guest is a man who really believes in the American Dream. You can tell he believes in the American Dream because every time he gives a speech he puts people to sleep!

Our next speaker certainly needs no introduction. In his field he's probably as well known as Lord Godiva.

Our next speaker comes to us after thirty years of distinguished achievement in the business community. In fact, he was so highly thought of, when he left the car wash, they retired his rag.

Our next speaker is a man who, in his lifetime, could point with justifiable pride to many incredible accomplishments. Unfortunately none of them were his.

This man is so modest, so shy, so unassuming, his birth certificate was made out to Occupant.

Our next speaker is a man who has led this company out of obscurity into anonymity.

We have come here tonight to honor _____, a man whose limitations know no bounds.

Our next speaker is a journalist whose newspaper column has appeared at the bottom of every major bird cage in America.

Tonight we honor a man whose life is an open book—and you know what kind of books they're publishing these days.

It has been said that our guest of honor has the hands of a surgeon and that's true. They're always wrapped around a golf club.

Our next speaker, you'll he interested to know, played a very important role in one of the world's first brain transplants. He was the donor.

One of the great mysteries of public speaking is why the person who needs no introduction still needs an introducer.

When introduced to an audience, I always like to have it mentioned that I once had my name on the cover of *Forbes*. Let them find out it was on a mailing label.

Our guest burst upon the scene as one of the brightest, most talented, most accomplished executives our industry has ever known. Tonight, he will talk about how he got over it.

Through the years our company has experienced a lot of growing pains—and tonight we have one of them with us.

If a little knowledge is a dangerous thing, our next speaker believes in safety first.

Early in his career he had an original idea. It came to him because it wanted to be alone.

HELP FIGHT INSOMNIA. INVITE A POLITICIAN TO SPEAK.

Our next speaker is an individual who has spurred more people to action than anyone else I know—with the possible exception of the person who operates the blue light at K-Mart.

Important? When he says, "Thank God!"—if you listen real good, you hear, "You're welcome!"

Our guest is a man who believes that the aging process is a lot of balderdash—and what's more, he's proven it. Every year he has less dash and he's a lot balder.

What can you really say about our next speaker? He has two legs and two arms just like anyone else—except in his case, they all touch the floor.

Our speaker is a man who knows full well the price of success—ulcers, high blood pressure, hypertension, nervous tics. The people in his department have them all.

In a world full of commas, semicolons and periods—our next guest is an exclamation point!

Our next guest has been called a self-made man. This, of course, was in the days before quality control.

Our next speaker is a man who's very active in the church. He squirms and wiggles and fidgets and. . . .

One of my goals in life has always been to speak at a dinner like this. It's what comes of being an underachiever.

Our next guest can only be described as holding down one of the most important jobs in television. You've all seen *60 Minutes*. You've all seen Mike Wallace on *60 Minutes*. You've all seen Morley Safer on *60 Minutes*. You've all seen that watch on *60 Minutes*. Who do you think winds it up?

Things haven't been easy for our next guest. As you all know, last year his company had to relocate—and he's still trying to find out where.

He is an outstanding athlete and is the proud possessor of a black belt. He also has a brown belt, a white belt and red suspenders.

Our next speaker is a man who is often mistaken for *(current male star)*. He tells girls he's the *(current male star)* type and they tell him he must be mistaken.

If he seems a little nervous tonight, it's with good reason. Just before he drove here, his dog ate his speech—after he read it.

I'll say one thing for our next speaker: He eats, drinks and breathes his life's work. The unfortunate part of it is, his life's work is eating, drinking and breathing.

As you know, our Program Committee is always on the lookout for speakers who can capture your imagination, stimulate your intellect, captivate your fancy, and rivet your attention. And so, while this search continues, tonight we've settled for _____.

"Genius" is an overused word in our business, but our next speaker is a man who, I think, reinforces, reiterates and epitomizes that overuse.

Our speaker is an attorney—someone who is dedicated to life, liberty and the law suit of happiness.

Our guest of honor is a man of warmth, heart and compassion. Every morning he goes into his office and makes two lists. One is a list of things to do. The other is a list of the people he's going to do them to.

Our next speaker is a poor but honest businessman—which could explain why he's poor.

Introducing the Roaster

And here he is, the man with the Black & Decker tongue—_____!

Acknowledging a Humorous Introduction

I really enjoyed listening to that introduction. At a time when so many speakers are giving us so much food for thought, every now and then it's nice to go on a diet.

St. Patrick's Day reminds us that there are those who have kissed the Blarney Stone. And our emcee tonight has reminded us that there are those who have kissed the Blarney Stone as well.

Thank you for that wonderful introduction. That had all the warmth and affection of a Valentine's Day card addressed to Occupant.

Thank you for that overly generous introduction. If there's one thing I've always appreciated, it's creative sincerity.

I'm not one of those people who say I don't really deserve this honor—because that would be a duplication of effort. I have a wife for that.

When Your Guest of Honor Is Wealthy

Most of us spend all of our lives trying to keep up with the Joneses. Tonight, it gives me great pleasure to present Jones.

Our speaker tonight has risen to fame and fortune, and while I have remained in obscurity and poverty, we still have one thing in common—we'd both rather be him.

Our speaker comes from a family of considerable wealth. When he was three months old, his favorite food was Gerber's Strained Rack of Lamb.

After a Long Introduction

That's what I like about _____. When he introduces you, you're never quite sure if you're going to speak after dinner or before breakfast!

After an Introduction That Includes a Long List of Your Credits

That may not mean much to you, but I love hearing it. When I die, I may have myself bronzed.

First, I want to thank you for that great introduction—although it did confuse my wife. Halfway through she nudged me to find out who else
was speaking tonight.

After a Very Short Abrupt Introduction

First, I want to thank you for that send-off. That
has to be one of the finest introductions I never
got.

—See also Opening an Ad-Lib or Informal Talk

Introductions, Needling —See After a Needling Introduction

Introductions, Overcoming Outrageous —See
OPENER: THE FIRST TWO MINUTES OF YOUR
SPEECH

Introduction to a Last-Minute Replacement

Our speaker tonight has brought new meaning
to the word "truth"; he has brought new meaning to the word "insight"; and above all, he has
brought new meaning to the word "available."

Introduction to a Substitute Speaker

Our guest speaker tonight needs no introduction. An explanation, maybe.

When you hear there's going to be a substitute
speaker, it's a little like predicting the weather for
a picnic. You don't really know what to expect—
but you have a feeling it's going to be bad.

It's never an easy experience when you're called in to be a substitute speaker. A substitute speaker is like a wrong number in the phone call of life.

I know that you were expecting to lean back and watch *(scheduled speaker)* tonight—and I was expecting to lean back and watch television tonight. Well, all I can say is: I'm going to try very hard to make sure that neither of us is disappointed.

"Is It Funny?" —See STORIES: WHERE DO THEY COME FROM?

J

"Jitters" —See STAGE FRIGHT AND HOW TO DEAL WITH IT

Joke, How to Tell a —See (1) *Don't Read the Jokes— Tell 'em!* and *Don't Use Print Language in Verbal Jokes* at DON'TS . . . IF YOU WANT TO GET LAUGHS; (2) OPENER: THE FIRST TWO MINUTES OF YOUR SPEECH

Joke Books —See (1) THE HARD WORK OF HUMOR; (2) SPICING UP THOSE DULL SPEECHES

A Joke Dies

You've heard of the line-item veto? That was the line it should have applied to.

(After a joke dies, look down at your speech and say:) It says here: "Pause for laughter."

Either the microphone's dead or I am!

I wonder if they make steroids for jokes?

And now, if you'll excuse me, I'd like to go to church and confess that joke.

There's a name for this. It's called the mid-laugh crisis.

I wonder if that joke had a next of kin?

That's strange. My pollsters told me that joke would be close.

Joke Elements / Types —See (1) ADVICE—AND HOW TO IGNORE IT; (2) *Demand-Laugh Jokes* at OPENER: THE FIRST TWO MINUTES OF YOUR SPEECH

Jokes Constructed to Get a Laugh —See OPENER: THE FIRST TWO MINUTES OF YOUR SPEECH

"Just Say a Few Words" (as an invitation to terror) — See STAGE FRIGHT AND HOW TO DEAL WITH IT

K

KINDER, GENTLER COMEDY

In 1940, Charlie Chaplin made a sound film *The Great Dictator*. It was a biting satire on the fascist dictators, Adolph Hitler and Benito Mussolini, then at the height of their power. Chaplin played a dual role. He was a Jewish barber and he was also a dictator, Adenoid Hynkel.

Throughout the film, Chaplin's barber, a look-alike for Chaplin's dictator, is mistaken for the dictator. In the final scene, taking advantage of this confusion, he gives a long, serious, stirring speech to the dictator's supporters, espousing the values of a free people and democratic government. One line has special relevance today. He said, "More than cleverness, we need kindness and gentleness."

Kindness and gentleness. Kinder and gentler. We hear those thoughts a lot these days—but rarely from comedians. Contemporary humor is often hostile, aggressive, mean-spirited, when not downright savage. It has been for the last twenty years.

Humor is often the most accurate reflection of what is going on in a society and the mood of a people. It can be argued that the cut-and-slash comedy of today is a direct result of the post-Vietnam, post-Watergate disillusionment. We have produced an entire generation of comedians who are angry and cynical—and communicate this anger and cynicism via one-liners and vitriolic commentary.

114

Lenny Bruce would have felt perfectly at home in today's comedy clubs. In the 1950s and 1960s, he was a brilliant comedian tragically out-of-step with his time. The language, subject matter, and defiance that got him arrested then would seem mild and subdued today compared to the fulminations of today's comedy club and cable TV performers.

***

American humor experienced a sea change in attitude and content during the late 1960s. For decades before and after World War II, humor was essentially good-humored. The popular radio shows of the Thirties and Forties (Jack Benny, Fred Allen, Fibber McGee and Molly, Edgar Bergen and Charlie McCarthy) offered nonsense and non-hurtful put-downs.

On film, Laurel and Hardy got twenty minutes of belly laughs trying to move a piano up a steep flight of steps. It was all surprisingly innocent and upbeat considering the turmoil this nation and the world were experiencing.

This same gentle humor carried into the Fifties and Sixties. The popular sit-coms (*I Love Lucy*, *Father Knows Best*, *Leave It to Beaver*) continued to get their quota of laughs in nondestructive ways: Lucy trying to package chocolates with the production line going faster and faster. Thirty years earlier, Charlie Chaplin played a factory worker trying to keep up with an accelerating production line in *Modern Times*. Our tastes in comedy hadn't really changed much during the years in between.

In the late 1960s, the comedic scene began to change. *Laugh-In* and the Smothers Brothers variety show offered a biting, partisan, politically and socially oriented style of comedy that ushered in the attack humor of the 1970s and 1980s. Within a few years, television was knee-deep in situation comedies that put the accent on hostility. Each new series seemed to push back the heretofore accepted guidelines of taste, language, and content. Dialogue became more confrontational; relationships thrived on anger; an era of the negative began.

The motivating factor in comedy today is attack, attack, attack. It can be argued that the humor of Groucho Marx, W. C. Fields, and The Three Stooges was also attack humor. Of course, but it was such a harmless, pretend type of attack. Nobody could ever accept as reality Groucho's jibes at Margaret Dumont, his perennial foil.

With all the mayhem of The Three Stooges—the poking, bopping, slapping and gouging—you always knew it was an act and nobody was being hurt. It was the ultimate slapstick—the two pieces of light wood comedians have used through the centuries in playful combat. Upon impact, the wood slaps together with a resounding thwack but inflicts no pain and the audience knows it inflicts no pain.

There is no such sense of playfulness in today's attack comedy. Movie comedy echoes and apes the violence and destruction found in most action films today. Cars are trashed, houses are demolished, people are killed or wounded—so graphically, the lasting impression is one of reality, rather than comedic make-believe.

***

So what's the problem? It's a new approach to laughter. Time marches on. Well, my biggest concern with attack comedy is the aftertaste. There was an underlying good feeling to pre-1970s humor. Radio and TV sitcoms may not have been the most accurate reflection of real life, but together with the laughter, they reinforced our ideals and the better side of human nature. They were fun, they were upbeat, they were positive about people, family, nation, and relationships. Having experienced them, after the laughter you felt better about the human condition.

The underlying theme of much of today's humor is almost a complete reversal of this earlier innocence and optimism. The mood is negative. The attitude is combative. The subject matter, language, and demeanor are often distasteful, if not offensive. In short, today's comedy rarely contributes to the human spirit—it hacks away at it.

The question then arises: What is the social responsibility of comedians and comedy writers? Does the laugh justify the means—any means? In an era when topical and viewpoint humor is so popular, the viewpoint becomes critical. In the creation of any joke, the writer takes a stand. The subject of the joke is either boosted or bashed. The attitude of the joke has to be determined—playful or poisonous? The language of the joke—G-rated or X-rated? These are all choices comedy writers make consciously or unconsciously before setting word processors to work.

Comedy writers and comedians are the pointers of society. We put a comedic spotlight on the flaws and problems of our world and the people who are dealing with them. We are mostly bystanders with no solutions of our own. Overwhelmingly, our humor follows the path of least resistance. We occupy a front seat on bandwagons, providing easy, simple, crowd-pleasing commentary on complex matters. We run with the pack.

The humorists of 2000 years ago would have sided with Pontius Pilate and the mob. Galileo with his "crazy" ideas would have been an ideal target. Columbus would have been Topic A in Spanish comedy clubs until he sailed off the edge of the earth. The popular way is not always the right way, but it's always the easiest way. As a result, humor adds fuel to fires that are already burning. Sometimes they are fires that should be put out.

Maybe it's time for comedians and comedy writers to go from being part of the problem to providing part of the solution. Humor is a powerful force in today's world. Laughter can be used to create or destroy—build or tear down. Considering all the negatives in modern life, maybe another sea change is called for. Perhaps humorists have an obligation to go a step beyond finger-pointing. I'm not suggesting that comedians offer answers to all of life's problems, but a more balanced, upbeat, ethical approach to laugh-making may be possible. In other words—kinder and gentler comedy—in concept and performance.

***

Is this just pining for "the good old days"—trying to turn back the clock? Not really. If anything, it may be fast-forwarding the clock to the humor of the future. In show business and in every other aspect of modern life, the norm, the accepted, the sought after, changes with astonishing rapidity. What is hot today may be very cold tomorrow.

Comedy has been at the top of the show business pyramid for a number of years now. Laugh-makers will always be in demand but the intensity and nature of the demand may change. The public tires quickly. They will reach a point where they will no longer be amused by comedian after comedian, sitcom after sitcom, working over the same negative subject matter. They will look for something new—perhaps even something that will add a lift to their lives.

There's a reason why *I Love Lucy, The Jack Benny Show, Father Knows Best,* and other such reruns are still so popular and still so funny. There is a staying power to their humor. It reaches out and touches the best in us. They offer fun instead of fury, comedy instead of cynicism, values instead of vitriol.

Some years ago I read in the Writers Guild of America, West newsletter, an item from the *Jewish Daily Forward* translated by Michael Kanin. It went like this:

> "The garbage collectors in New York are paid
> up to $23,000 a year."
> "Really? Then why are the streets so filthy?"
> "Well, you can't expect a man who makes
> $23,000 a year to fool around with garbage."

Most working comedians and comedy writers make a lot more than $23,000 a year. We shouldn't be fooling around with garbage either.

Knowing Your Territory —See ASSESSING YOUR AUDIENCE

L

Language —See (1) ASSESSING YOUR AUDIENCE; (2) *Don't Use Print Language in Verbal Jokes* at DON'TS . . . IF YOU WANT TO GET LAUGHS

Large Hall

Incidentally, can those of you in the very back rows hear me? If you can, don't yell—just wave your binoculars.

Last Speaker on a Long Program —See Long Speeches, Comments and Harangues

Late Starts

And so, as the program indicates, we're beginning this meeting right on the dot of 9:15—*(local railroad)* time.

Our next speaker will be a little late because of something that happened at one of our seminars this afternoon. He was saying that money can't buy happiness—and someone named Gates hit him in the mouth.

Laugh Lines —See *Don't Let Your Punch Lines Trail Off* at DON'TS . . . IF YOU WANT TO GET LAUGHS

Lectern Logistics —See (1) THE HARD WORK OF HUMOR; (2) OPENER: THE FIRST TWO MINUTES OF YOUR SPEECH; (3) PREPARING FOR YOUR SPEECH; (4) REHEARSING YOUR SPEECH

Length of Your Speech —See ASSESSING YOUR AUDIENCE

Lengthy Meeting —See (1) Long Speeches, Comments and Harangues; (2) Meetings/Conventions; (3) Continuing a Long Program

Lengthy Speaker —See Long Speeches, Comments and Harangues

Lessons from the Greats: Lowell Thomas —See LESSONS I LEARNED FROM LOWELL THOMAS

Lessons from the Greats: Red Skelton —See Part III of THE USES AND LIMITS OF HUMOR

Lessons from the Greats: Ronald Reagan —See Part II of "WHY HUMOR?"

Lessons from the Greats: Winston Churchill —See REHEARSING YOUR SPEECH

LESSONS I LEARNED FROM LOWELL THOMAS

I was not a close friend of Lowell Thomas—the legendary broadcaster, author, adventurer, world traveler and chronicler of the great and not-so-great personalities the world has produced in this century. "Acquaintance" would be more accurate.

I first met Lowell Thomas in 1973 at a meeting of the International Platform Association in Washington, D.C. We exchanged some views on humor in speeches and a comfortable relationship began that lasted until his death in 1981.

Most of our talks took place at these annual I.P.A. meetings in Washington but somehow, whenever I hear or read the name Lowell Thomas, my thoughts go back to a chance lunch we shared in 1975. In retrospect, it seems as if each element of our conversation during that luncheon, as well as how it came about and ended, offered some subtle lessons in communication from which I continue to benefit.

Our getting together had not been planned. I was coming out of the Oval Office after a meeting with President Ford, and Lowell was waiting to go in. We exchanged hellos, and since it was near noon, I asked him if he would care to join me for lunch after his visit with the President. He agreed, and half an hour later we sat down together.

There was a minimum of small talk. Lowell Thomas was now in his early eighties, and it was obvious that he invested his time rather carefully when it came to people, places and conversation. But after I had offered some conversational gambits to which he had politely but not enthusiastically responded, I found our talk becalmed—with what little wind in the sails there was coming from me.

I couldn't understand it. We liked each other. I'm sure we both wanted our meeting to be an enjoyable occasion, but it wasn't happening that way.

Then I asked Lowell if he was still involved with Cinerama. Lowell Thomas had been instrumental in bringing this wide-screen film process to audiences shortly after World War II. It used three cameras and produced an ear-to-ear scan that virtually put you into the picture.

The first Cinerama production began with Lowell Thomas introducing the new concept via a normal-size black-and-white film, which then went to color, expanded to an enormous height and width, and the next thing you knew, you were in the front seat of a roller coaster on one of the most thrilling rides a theater audience had ever experienced. Such roller-coaster sequences have since played a part in many wide and giant screen innovations.

***

Lowell was surprised that I knew about Cinerama and his involvement with it. He started to ask me some questions about how I reacted to various aspects of the concept and to the different Cinerama productions. The private man was emerging from the public figure.

I told him that the last twenty minutes of the first Cinerama film—a breathtaking coast-to-coast flight across the United States—was the best pictorial presentation of our country I had ever seen. I said that I had always felt this segment should have been shown around the world because it presented an unparalleled view of the grandeur of America. He told me it had been shown at a few overseas trade fairs but nothing more.

The conversational dips and pauses had vanished. Now we were cooking. I said, "What about theme parks? How about showing it in hard-top theaters in theme parks?" Lowell was not familiar with theme parks. I described them and said I was a theme park buff and went into detail about a recent visit to Six Flags Over Texas. He asked me where it was located. I said, "Between Dallas and Forth Worth." And I can still remember his saying, "Oh, yes. Fort Worth. I just bought a newspaper there." And somehow I had the feeling it wasn't for 25 cents. But now the trickle of conversation had turned into a torrent.

***

So what was the first lesson?

Lowell Thomas had reached an age and level of achievement and maturity that no longer demanded the spotlight. Further, he was not of a mind to do a one-

123

man show of anecdotes and observations to charm one more admirer. He was looking for equity. What had I to contribute to him to make our talk a sharing experience rather than another speech by Lowell Thomas? The instant I put something special on the conversational table, he responded in kind.

I've seen this same reaction in audiences. Many speakers do cookie-cutter speeches. The words and ideas are of interest and concern to the speaker and perhaps to the company or organization the speaker represents. They may not be of interest or relate to the needs of the audience. The result? The audience emotionally tunes out and turns off. And so it's mandatory that the content and concern of your speech reach out and link up to those of your listeners. The loop will then be completed as they respond positively to you.

By the time coffee was served, Lowell Thomas and I had gotten around to the subject of speaking techniques. He dissected the styles of various well-known personalities and mentioned one extremely erudite speaker who had many annoying mannerisms—topped off by the fact that he really didn't speak so much as mumble.

Lowell said that he once listened to this speaker give an informal talk to a small group of people and even though he was just some ten feet away, Lowell couldn't hear or understand what the speaker was saying. When the talk ended, Lowell went up to him, gave some neutral compliment and then said, "Would you be interested in a suggestion concerning your speaking style?" The speaker didn't hesitate a moment. He said, "No."

Which brings me to the second lesson learned during this luncheon. I'm sure that most of us are properly appalled by anyone who would turn down advice offered by such a master communicator as Lowell Thomas. But if you take away the imposing figure of

Lowell Thomas, are we really that much different from the mumbler when presented with criticism?

Criticism hurts. Even in its most gentle form it says we're not doing as good a job as we might. None of us truly wants to hear that. And so, while we may listen to criticism, we tend to rebut it or discard it as quickly as possible.

Through the years, I've found that the criticism and observations that hurt the most and are the most difficult to accept—are often the most valid and the most helpful when heeded.

My suggestion is to write all critiques and observations concerning your performance on a sheet of paper. Put it away. Pull it out again after some personal triumph and then read it over again. In an atmosphere of success and heightened self-confidence, we are often better able to recognize the truth of the comments and then set about turning negatives into positives.

***

Lunch was now over, and I offered to drive Lowell back to his hotel. He said he had walked over but graciously accepted the lift. We drove the few blocks back to his hotel and pulled into the driveway. I got out, hustled around to his side of the car, opened the door, started to lean forward with one hand outstretched— when my eyes met his. Not a word was spoken but the message I got was clear and unmistakable: "Don't you dare try to help me out of this car!"

I backed off; Lowell got out and then gave me a broad grin—his nonverbal way of saying, "No harm done. All is well."

If we but pay attention, our audiences are also communicating with us nonverbally. It's important to read those silent signals. If you introduce a subject that produces a ripple of motion in an audience—people shifting in their seats or exchanging looks with neighbors—you know that for better or worse you've sparked their attention. Sensitivity to what caused that reaction should then be your guide as you proceed with the rest of your speech. Segments may be dropped, embellished or recast, based on your reading of the audience.

If you've told a joke or story that hasn't gone well, the audience may be telling you what they want to hear or what they don't want to hear and this information can and should affect the humor, content and style of what you still have to offer.

The most obvious display of an audience's nonverbal communication is inattention. If you are monitoring your listeners and maintaining good eye contact with the entire audience and not just a few friendly faces, you will be the first to know if you've lost them. Yawns, fidgeting, program studying, are indisputable storm warnings. An immediate change of approach or attitude is called for. No speaker was ever honored for going down with the ship.

Silent clues may also communicate good news. Smiles, elbows nudging seatmates, people leaning forward—all tell you that the track is clear, the signals are green—pour it on!

***

When Lowell Thomas reached his eighties, he frequently said that at his age, everything reminded him of something else. When he gave a speech, he proved it. Lowell would interrupt any narrative to recount a fascinating anecdote or tidbit of recollection drawn from a lifetime of experiences few could match.

His stories and reminiscences brought history alive, and his personal association with the giant personalities of our time made his audiences part of the scene. He gave of himself to his listeners.

How often do speakers do that? How often do speeches present the personal insights and experiences of the speaker?

If you were to analyze most business and political speeches, you would find them to be examples of production-line rhetoric. If the executive couldn't deliver the speech, anyone else in the executive's office could—without a word being changed.

A good speech should instruct, inspire, motivate, inform and/or entertain—but it should also tell us something about the person making the speech. It should offer some insights your bio didn't. Ideally it should reach out and make your audience a confidant.

You came away from a Lowell Thomas speech with the feeling that you had seen and heard the man behind the legend—and the legend grew in the process.

Lowell Thomas shared his experiences, his insights and his knowledge—onstage and off—and somehow I think he would have approved of my sharing the lessons learned at our long ago luncheon with you.

Light Applause —See Applause

Lighting —See (1) THE HARD WORK OF HUMOR; (2) OPENER: THE FIRST TWO MINUTES OF YOUR SPEECH

Lights Go Out, If the

Is there a Seeing Eye electrician in the house?

May I have the next slide, please?

Does anyone have a kite, some string and a key?

Welcome to the tunnel at the end of the light.

As you can see, we have alternating current. Sometimes it works. Sometimes it doesn't.

Limiting the Number of Roasters at a Roast —See *Preparing the Roast* at ROASTS

Limits of Humor —See THE USES AND LIMITS OF HUMOR

Listening to Other Speakers —See STAGE FRIGHT AND HOW TO DEAL WITH IT

Locale

I never said this town is unsophisticated. What I said was—it's the only place I know where "Is it hot enough for you?" is considered a bon mot.

I try to keep an open mind on things. For instance, I'm a great fan of professional football. On the other hand, I like what the *(local team)* play too.

This is a tough town if you're not making it. People either drop your name—or you.

It's a very strict town. For instance, the cemetery—every night there's a bed check.

_____ is really a fascinating place. This is the only town I know where you brush your teeth after drinking a glass of water.

Expensive? This is the only city I know where it costs $50 a day just to fast.

It's a very straight community. When you buy a mattress it comes with a tag saying: OCCU-PANCY BY MORE THAN 2 PERSONS IS DAN-GEROUS AND UNLAWFUL.

It's a wonderful town. I asked a fella playing the game machine at the bus stop how to get to the entertainment district. He said, "Don't move one damn inch!"

This town is so small, the road map is actual size.

Last week was so cold, *(name of city)* cited a flasher for bravery.

I come from a very dull town. The local smorgas-bord featured 31 varieties of liver.

The great thing about holding an event like this at night and downtown is—there's always a place to park. If all the spaces are filled, just wait a minute until the next car is stolen.

Alaska

There are three good reasons why the post office in Alaska can promise next day delivery: It's effi-cient, it's motivated, and the days are six months long.

Atlanta

I love going to the Atlanta airport. It's the first time I ever took a bus and a train, *before* begin-ning my trip.

California

You have to admire the California lifestyle. This is the only state where a cut in the school lunch program means—no wine.

Californians really love the outdoors. Where else can you see a coffin with a sunroof?

Dallas / Fort Worth

As we all know, the three most effective forms of exercise in America today are running, jogging and walking—to the departure gate at the Dallas/Fort Worth airport.

Florida

You can always spot a workaholic on vacation in Florida. He's the one who goes down to the beach, stretches out on the sand, picks up a seashell, holds it to his ear and asks, "Any messages?"

The next time you feel like criticizing the workmanship, quality and durability of products made in America—take a good look at all the 80-year-olds in Florida.

The Florida Weather Bureau really knows how to rub it in. This morning Miami Beach reported 42 inches of sunshine.

Las Vegas

I have the worst luck. Last week I took a bus to Las Vegas—and it got there early.

Las Vegas is really exhausting. By the end of my fourth day, I was so tired, I could hardly keep my wallet open.

Los Angeles

I'm such a fan of Los Angeles, last week I went out and did something very sentimental. I had the air bronzed.

But Los Angeles is finally going to do something about the smog. It's going to put up signs that say: THANK YOU FOR NOT CHOKING.

Personally, I've always wanted to live in Beverly Hills. People in Beverly Hills have so much money, they don't cut their grass—they have it styled.

Minnesota

I'll tell you what Minnesota is like in the winter. I went to a doctor for a check-up. He said, "Take off your clothes." So I took off my clothes. And he put them on.

New England

I've found that the challenge an emcee faces varies according to the geographical area. For instance, in most parts of the country, a master of ceremonies has to warm up the audience. In New England, he has to defrost it.

New York

New York is such a friendly town. The very first day I was there I shook five hands. Three were in my hotel and two were in my pocket.

Seattle

I always get a little confused when I go to Seattle. I can never quite decide if it has one of America's highest rainfalls—or Canada is leaking.

I won't comment on the weather, but Seattle is the only town I know where you can go to a nightclub and see the Dance of the Seven Raincoats.

An optimist is anyone living in Seattle who orders a car with a sunroof.

Texas

They think big in Texas. That's right. In Texas, they think anyone in a *(name a sub-compact)* is a pedestrian.

Washington, D.C.

Let's face it, there is a lot of deception in our nation's capital. Take a look at the Washington Monument. Doesn't look a thing like him.

Have you noticed how many people pronounce it Washington, Diz-zy?

Logjams (and how to break them) —See WRITER'S BLOCK AND HOW TO GET AROUND IT

Long Introduction —See Introductions

Long Meeting —See (1) Long Speeches, Comments and Harangues; (2) Meetings/Conventions; (3) Continuing a Long Program

Long Question / er

Sir, your reasoning escapes me—and it may have gotten away from you as well.

It's always fascinating to hear someone with a machine gun delivery and a slingshot thought.

Sir, I know where you're coming from and all I can say is—I don't think I ever want to go there.

When Responding to a Long, Rapid-Fire Question: Well, in answer to the questioner with the aerobic tongue, let me just say—

When Someone Gives a Long Opinion During the Q.&A.: Sir, your answer—does it come with a question?

If Someone Asks You a Very Long and Convoluted Question: Would you repeat the question? No, let me change that. Can you repeat the question?

Would you mind repeating that? I must have dozed off.

Sir, your question—could you FedEx it?

Sir, in the spirit of the time, could you downsize your question?

First, I want to thank you for adding something to this program—about five minutes.

Long Speeches, Comments and Harangues

I think that was the oral majority—one big mouth after another.

Many a speaker needs no introduction, because his speech is already too long as it is.

To Someone Who Keeps Talking: Sir.—Sir. . . . Sir, would you consider a course in Remedial Listening?

After a Long Speech

The last time I heard a speech that long, my wife reported me to the police as a missing person.

First, I want to thank the previous speaker for those brief remarks. For a while there, I didn't know if I was on next or on Standby.

It's always a pleasure to hear a man who has never known the meaning of the words "I can't"— who has never known the meaning of the words "second best"—and who, as he has so amply demonstrated tonight, has never known the meaning of the words "in conclusion."

After that speech I'm convinced our guest is going to go to Heaven—because, as we all know, hot air always rises.

I'll say one thing for _____. He has never gone back on his words. It'd be too long a trip.

Isn't that something? First time I ever saw a tongue on steroids.

I'll say one thing for _____. When he gives a speech, there are no wasted words. He uses every last one of them!

Let me thank _____ for a speech that had all the ingredients of a fine cup of coffee. It was rich, full-bodied, satisfying—and it kept us up half the night.

That's the trouble with having a speaker who wears support stockings. They never get tired.

Thank you very much. And now, why don't we take a short break so that those of us with eight day clocks can go up to our rooms and wind them.

Thank you. That was just wonderful. Now has anyone else something to say before we adjourn this century?

My friend, I've heard speeches in my time, *(look at your watch)* and I think that's how you delivered that one—in my time.

After a Long Aimless Comment

Sir, your train of thought—does it have a caboose?

In Response to a Long Aimless Harangue: Sir, I think your problem is timed-release confusion.

—See also (1) Meetings/Conventions; (2) Previous Speaker(s)

Losing a Point

Now I know how it feels to be in a microwave oven. I've only been up here three minutes and my goose is cooked.

"Louder!" —See THE HARD WORK OF HUMOR

Loud Singer —See After a Loud Singer

M

Mechanical / Electronic Prompters —See ALWAYS
LEAD THEM LAUGHING

Media Relations —See ALWAYS LEAD THEM LAUGH-
ING

Meetings / Conventions

It was really a very exciting convention. First
time I ever saw martinis served with a twist of
No-Doz.

I like the meatloaf kind of convention. Half the
time you meet—half the time you loaf.

When there's something to be done,
Is there anything more defeating;
Than to think the battle's won—
Just by calling another meeting?

One of mankind's favorite charities is dispens-
ing—with reading the minutes of the previous
meeting.

Have you ever taken a good look at the person
who spent six hours transcribing, reconstruct-
ing, organizing and typing the minutes of the
previous meeting when the motion is made not to

137

read them? If you put sirloin between their teeth, you'd have hamburger!

Church meetings promise a glimpse of eternity. Business meetings deliver on that promise.

Nowadays, the minutes of a meeting are like psychiatrists. You only go to them when you're in trouble.

If you're thinking about mouths, when hasn't there been an open convention?

There was something about the convention that reminded me of a supermarket shopping cart. All those wheels going in different directions.

A convention is where people who are spending $500 a day to attend hear candidates saying, "Talk is cheap."

There's a great object lesson to be learned from the reading of the minutes of the previous meeting. If it only takes three minutes to describe it, why did it take three hours to do it?

I don't know what makes our meetings so dull, but whatever it is, it works!

A meeting like this always reminds me of golf. You go around for three hours and you end up right back where you started.

The third day of any conference is when the audience has reached the audio-visual stage. If they see one more visual, they'll scream!

Hotels love this convention because they never have to run the air conditioning late at night. The breeze from doors opening and closing is enough.

Sometimes I get the feeling that the two biggest problems in America today are making ends meet—and making meetings end.

I took notes on all the important things that have been said at this convention and sent them back to my home office this morning. I sure hope that postcard doesn't get lost in the mail.

Message (delivering through humor) —See "WHY HUMOR?"

Metaphors —See ASSESSING YOUR AUDIENCE

Microphone Problems —See Equipment

Mike Checks ("Can everyone hear me?") —See (1) ADVICE—AND HOW TO IGNORE IT; (2) THE HARD WORK OF HUMOR

Mishaps and Humor —See THE USES AND LIMITS OF HUMOR

Misspeaking —See (1) ALWAYS LEAD THEM LAUGHING; (2) MISTAKES; (3) Mistakes and Misspeaking

MISTAKES

Al Jolson was about as super a star as show business has produced in this century. His film *The Jazz Singer* was an instant sensation and ushered in the "talkies." Onstage Jolson was a spellbinder and could hold audiences enthralled for encore after encore after encore. His "You ain't seen nuthin' yet!" is still a popular phrase. Jolson not only said it but fulfilled its promise.

Not surprisingly, his popularity and unique style led to thousands of performers doing their versions of Jolson. On one occasion, he was in the audience watching one of these Jolson clones. After the show was over, Jolson went up to the impersonator, poked a forefinger into the mimic's chest and said, "Hey, kid, one of us is lousy!"

MORAL: We are all influenced by the style and approach of writers and performers we admire. No one arrives at a stage of artistic maturity without learning from those who have gone before. But the fastest way to succeed in either public speaking or show business is to develop a unique attitude or approach—a concept so different you can't easily be compared to anyone else. You're an original. Clones can make a comfortable living. Originals can reach for the stars.

The problem with marching to the beat of a different drummer is that it involves taking risks. The minute we set off in a different direction, there will be those who question the wisdom of the new path or are frightened by it. The reason so much humor and so many speeches are so bland is the fear of trying something new. The dictate "When in doubt, cut it out" has turned many a promising corporate or political speech into oatmeal.

***

Humor, in particular, calls for a certain amount of audaciousness. But going out onto the comedic highwire is also very intimidating. Humor calls for an immediate audience reaction. The fear that there might not be one has blue-penciled many an inspired but risky joke. The mistake is not having the courage to try.

I think back to the Gridiron Dinner of 1976 in

Washington, D.C. This annual event is one of Washington's most prestigious dinners and is strictly a fun/ roast occasion. Each featured speaker is asked to give an eight-minute funny speech. The audience consists of the movers and shakers of the business, media and political establishments. The speakers are chosen for their prominence in the current political scene. In the spring of 1976, Jimmy Carter was the Democratic speaker.

Carter had started to move out from the pack of Democratic presidential hopefuls, but the contention was still strong. The Gridiron Dinner is a press-sponsored event and a poor performance at it could negatively influence many important communicators. Jimmy Carter came to this dinner carrying some pretty heavy baggage.

At the smaller winter Gridiron Dinner a few months before, he told a story about bathroom tissue and money that offended virtually everybody in the room. When he returned to his seat, he said that his wife had told him not to tell the story and his seatmate said that Rosalynn was right. Realizing the seriousness of his mistake Carter, before the evening was over, had visited with everybody in the room apologizing for the lapse of taste and judgment.

So at the 1976 Gridiron Dinner, Jimmy Carter had a lot on his mind when he selected that always critical first joke for his fun speech. Now in those days the one sure thing with which people identified Carter was teeth. When Jimmy smiled it always looked as if he had 48 teeth in a 32-teeth mouth. Comedians, comedy writers, and cartoonists had a picnic with Jimmy Carter's teeth. In a very savvy but very risky way, so did the future President.

He began with a frequently used opening to his stump speeches. It went something like, "Hi! I'm Jimmy Carter and I'm running for President of the United States." Then he turned to the far left side of the audience and turned on an incredibly exaggerated version of his incandescent smile. The audience stared. Now the bigger-than-life smile and Jimmy's face started to slowly pan the audience from left to right, like a camera sweeping a panoramic view. Most of the audience was still puzzled, but a few laughs could be heard.

Many timid speakers would have panicked at the few laughs and immediately cut their losses by going to the next joke in their speech. Carter didn't. The blinding grin continued to move across the audience slowly and, as it passed the center, the laughter started to build. The audience now realized that Jimmy Carter was doing an enormous spoof of the public Jimmy Carter. By the time the smile reached the far right side of the ballroom, the laughter and applause was thunderous.

What I will always remember about this opening was Jimmy Carter's guts in holding to his course. It's a mistake not to take the risk. The even greater mistake is not to see it through.

Audiences love the unexpected. They delight in being agreeably and inventively surprised. The risk in straying from the tried and true is always there, but the greater the risk, the greater the reward (or punishment). Another marvelous example of this took place at a Gridiron Dinner, also in the mid-1970s.

***

The Gridiron Club, sponsor of the Gridiron Dinner, had been an all-male club for most of its history. After considerable controversy, the club began admitting women into its membership. By the middle seventies, a few women were in attendance at the Gridiron Dinners. This eventually led to the inevitable breakthrough: the first woman speaker at a Gridiron Dinner. The woman was the late Ella Grasso, then Governor of Connecticut.

Governor Grasso was introduced, went to the lectern, and looked out over this 99% male audience, resplendent in white tie and tails. The mood was one of comfortable liberality for having invited someone of the female persuasion to appear on the program. What they expected from Governor Ella Grasso were some words of homage to the Gridiron institution and some heartfelt gratitude for the honor bestowed upon her.

What they got was Governor Grasso fixing them with a long steady gaze and finally saying, "So this is the Gridiron Dinner. *(Pause)* Big deal! *(Pause)* To think that I gave up a Tupperware Party in Hartford for this!"

Ella Grasso had come out of her corner swinging and the audience loved her for it. A good part of her speech was a mock, funny attack on the organization that had invited her. It was risky, it was different, it was playing against what was expected, it was wonderful. I have rarely written a fan letter, but I did so that night.

***

One of the problems of growing older is that you begin to collect regrets as you did baseball cards when you were a child. Many of my regrets center on the mistake of deferment. For most of our lives we have the feeling there will always be tomorrow. We proceed, as we should, with the feeling that anything is possible—indeed, *everything* is possible. But this feeling also encourages and abets deferment. I'll write it tomorrow. I'll read it tomorrow. I'll learn it tomorrow. I'll do it tomorrow. Missed opportunities.

In the 1960s, while I was a writer on the Red Skelton TV show, my wife and I lived in Santa Monica, California. I learned from a newspaper article that Stan Laurel was living in retirement just six blocks away. Stan Laurel of the legendary comedy team, Laurel and Hardy! What an opportunity to talk to one of the show business giants of the 20th century!

On my first available free day, I walked the six

143

blocks, found Stan Laurel's apartment house, and stood uncertainly in front of it. Then, like a kid on his first date, I walked to the corner and back, trying to gather up the courage to knock on his door. What would I say? All I could think of saying would be, "Please! Talk to me. Share with me some of your fabulous life, your experiences, your comedy genius."

I walked up to the corner and back again. I was overwhelmed by the intrusiveness of it all. What right had I to ask Stan Laurel to give his increasingly precious time to a total stranger? I must have spent fifteen minutes walking to the corner and back to the house—and finally I gave up. I said I would do it on another day when I felt more comfortable in doing it.

A few months later Stan Laurel died. I later learned that his last years were lonely ones and he would have loved that knock on the door and the chance to talk shop with someone else in the comedy business.

***

I have thought about this missed opportunity, this missed meeting, many times since. These thoughts inevitably lead me to consider the mistake of another kind of deferment. For many years I have had on my desk these words written by Bob and Patti Carpenter and published in *Road Rider:* "The trip you can enjoy today because of the person you are, may be a frustratingly unhappy one tomorrow because of the person you have become in the meantime. Go, wherever you have always wanted to go. Go as soon as you can, for as far as you can, for as long as you can."

I look at these words quite frequently, as a spur to travel and anything else being deferred. But the underlying message should be taken to heart by anyone in the performing and creative arts. We are substantially different people capable of substantially different things

144

at the various stages of our lives. Our attitudes, philosophies, talents, and enthusiasms go through surprising transformations—and once gone, can rarely be revisited.

So what I am suggesting is this: At every stage of your creative life, drain the cup dry. If you want to be a comedian, get on line at your local comedy club. If you want to be a speaker, join Toastmasters or send out tapes to every organization that could possibly use you. If you want to write a joke, a speech, or a novel, press the start button on your computer or ballpoint pen— and do it.

These are unique moments in your life for turning out pages or performances that you may not feel motivated to produce, or able to produce, five or ten years from now. Bob and Patti Carpenter's words are equally applicable to your quest for creative fulfillment: "Go as soon as you can, for as far as you can, for as long as you can."

Now.

—See also (1) ALWAYS LEAD THEM LAUGHING; (2) *Don't Neglect the Facts* at DON'TS . . . IF YOU WANT TO GET LAUGHS; (3) Dealing with a Faux Pas

Mistakes and Misspeaking—When Things Go Wrong

When You Misspeak: Do you ever get the feeling your lips should have come with instructions?

When You Make a Mistake: It's a shame. I used to be perfect—but I think it wore off.

When Something Goes Wrong: Tell me, why do I suddenly feel like I'm the barbecue in the high tea of life?

Did you ever get the feeling you left your talent in your other suit?

Now you know why I believe in reincarnation. I just couldn't have become this confused in one lifetime.

MONEY AND SPEECHWRITING
Money Makes the Words Go 'Round

Some years ago I received a phone call from the P.R. Director of a large mid-Western corporation. He said, "I understand you write jokes for speakers." I said, "I do." He said, "The C.E.O. of our company is giving a very important speech tomorrow and wants to start off with two big jokes. Could you provide them?" I said, "Yes."

He said, "Great. I'll give you our phone number. Phone the jokes in to my secretary and send us a bill." I said, "Fine—but perhaps we ought to discuss the bill first." He said, "It's really not necessary. Just send the bill and we'll have a check off to you."

I said, "I'd charge $1,000 for the jokes." There was a long silence on the other end—long enough to rule out any expectation of a done deal.

Finally, the P.R. Director said, "You mean to say you charge $1,000 for just two jokes?" I said, "No, I charge $1,000 for the *right* two jokes." Apparently the distinction wasn't recognized because he then said, "I'll call you back." And as of this writing, I'm still waiting for the call.

***

What is a joke worth? What is a speech worth? What is a song worth?

We find it so much easier to establish the value of a car, a boat, a house. There is substance we can see, touch, and handle. There are materials and a known amount of time to bring them together to form the final product. The price tag can be judged on its own merits and then compared to the price tags of similar items.

How do you taste, weigh, sample, and assess a few dozen words or a few thousand words? Even if you widen the margins and triple-space, the finished product weighs but a few ounces. How does a potential purchaser put a value on these few ounces?

Writers face this same question from the keyboard side of the transaction. What do you charge for a joke, a letter, a speech, or an advertisement? How much time will the research take? How long will you have to wait before the muse beckons? How many drafts, self-imposed and requested, will be required? What will it all add up to in minutes, hours, days, and even, weeks? And finally, how much are your time and talent worth?

These are the building-block considerations that lead to the ultimate two questions: What is the writing worth to the writer? What is the writing worth to the client?

***

It has been said that no piece of writing is ever fairly priced. If *Who's on First?* had been written for Abbott & Costello and the writer had charged one million dollars, he would have been underpaid. On the other hand, if a writer had given them a hundred routines for one dollar each—but Abbott & Costello couldn't use any of them—he would have been overpaid.

Nevertheless, prices have to be arrived at for creative writing, and here, the writer is often at a distinct disadvantage. Most writers have a compulsion to write. As Fannie Hurst put it, "I'm not happy when I'm writing, but I'm more unhappy when I'm not."

Writers, quite sensibly, would like to write for big money. But given the emotional drive to put pen to paper or word processor to printer, writers frequently accept far less than big, or even adequate, money. Newcomers will often write for free or on speculation, as a way of showing their wares. Even established writers are sometimes lulled into gratis work with the promise of getting into something "on the ground floor." But as a veteran scribbler once put it, "I don't mind getting in on the ground floor—but I don't want to be the ground."

Irvin S. Cobb may have summed up the problem when he said, "If writers were good businessmen, they'd have too much sense to be writers."

Writing for small pay or no pay is self-defeating from so many viewpoints—foremost among them, the need to make a decent living. But even more harmful is what this attitude does to a client's perception of the writing itself. People value what they pay for. The more they pay, the higher their regard for the purchase—and vice versa.

Money is negotiable applause.

***

There is no doubt in my mind that if a Rolls Royce, one of the finest pieces of automotive machinery in the world, had been put on the market for $4,998, it would not be as highly regarded as it is—solely because it was selling for $4,998. Same car, same superb engineering, same hand-tooled craftsmanship—the only difference, the price.

Similarly, the price that a writer sets on his or her work, often influences the client's regard for that work. I will never forget an overheard conversation during a political campaign some years ago. The candidate was reviewing the work of one of the writers on his staff. His summation was: "Well, what can you expect of a $300-a-week writer?" Creativity, imagination, experience, productivity—all were overshadowed by the price the writer had sold himself for.

So what is a fair price for the written word? Charging by the word, paragraph, page, or pound is impractical, and even establishing the fair value of a total project, speech, or book is a challenge because the writing process is so unpredictable. A writer may size up an assignment, consider it a piece of cake, and quote a price based on a cut-and-dried, type and mail text. However, when sitting down to do the actual writing, an unconsidered aspect of the idea, plot outline, or storyboard may become apparent, and suddenly the time necessary to overcome the complication quadruples and the writer finds himself working at a rate that rivals the minimum wage and hour law.

***

Even when things go according to plan, writing is hard, lonely, demanding work. I never fully accepted the level of concentration that is called for until the time I went into a diner for breakfast and ordered scrambled eggs and coffee. Then I became totally involved in working out in my mind a writing problem I had been stonewalled by for over a day. By the time the counterman brought me the eggs, coffee and cream, my thoughts were so far removed from breakfast, I picked up the creamer and sprinkled it over the scrambled eggs.

I slowly became aware of the counterman watching this with great curiosity. So to preserve what little savoir faire I had left, I picked up the two shakers, peppered and salted my coffee as if it were my everyday routine—and went back to solving my problem. I have always felt such intense concentration deserves intense payment.

While a line-for-line price list for written material isn't practical, the amount quoted and/or charged should meet one criterion: It should be high enough so that the client knows he or she is dealing with a seasoned, successful professional who can be expected to turn out a first-class writing job. With this substantial investment in the outcome, the client has a vested interest in the success of the arrangement and is much more likely to focus on the strengths, instead of looking for flaws in the final product. Putting it another way, the price of the purchase predisposes the purchaser to find value in the purchase.

***

Money also plays a vital part in establishing the image of success. It's the "If he's getting that much money, he must be good" syndrome. Money and success lead clients and audiences to put on rose-colored glasses when viewing the moneyed and successful.

Some forty years ago I remember stopping in to see the show at #1 Fifth Avenue, a small New York nightclub. The featured performer was a young comedian who did a perfectly acceptable comedy act to virtually no audience reaction. He did the routines. The audience stared. The flop sweat poured. It was bombing worthy of World War II.

Ten years later I saw this same comedian perform as the headliner at one of the top Las Vegas showrooms. He did virtually the same act I witnessed ten years earlier in New York, but now the audience reaction was tremendous. The laughs came in salvos! What made the difference? In the interim, he became the star of a TV situation comedy that was in the Top Ten. He was an indisputable success—a proven commodity. The audience no longer questioned his ability to be funny. In show business terminology, they were laughing on their way in.

In short: Money equates with success—success equates with money—and they both equate with acceptance. If you value your work, others are more likely to value it as well.

Besides, what's wrong with getting paid? Writers should never lose sight of the immortal words of Dorothy Parker who said, "The two most beautiful words in the English language are: CHECK ENCLOSED."

Motivation and Public Speaking —See HOW TO SUCCEED IN HUMOR BY REALLY TRYING

Mumbling —See THE HARD WORK OF HUMOR

N

National Speakers Association —See STAGE FRIGHT AND HOW TO DEAL WITH IT

Need for Humor in Speeches —See ADVICE—AND HOW TO IGNORE IT

Needling Introduction —See After a Needling Introduction

Negative Humor —See KINDER, GENTLER COMEDY

Noisy Audience

Before we begin, I have a message for that table in the rear: The airport called and asked if you could hold it down a bit.

Could everybody please quiet down? From up here this looks like a group anxiety attack.

Could we have a little quiet in the back, please? There are people up here trying to sleep.

I just got a disturbing note from the people next door asking us to be more quiet. What makes it so disturbing, it's a bowling alley.

Non-Verbal Communication from Your Audience —See LESSONS I LEARNED FROM LOWELL THOMAS

Novice Speakers —See (1) STAGE FRIGHT AND HOW TO DEAL WITH IT; (2) USING HUMOR WHEN YOU'RE AFRAID TO USE HUMOR

Number of Speeches at a Successful Roast —See *Preparing the Roast* at ROASTS

O

Objectives —See OPENER: THE FIRST TWO MINUTES OF YOUR SPEECH

Obligatory Openings —See SPEECHWRITERS

Off-Color Joke —See After an Off-Color Joke/Cursing

One-Liners vs. Stories —See STORIES: WHERE DO THEY COME FROM?

OPENER: THE FIRST TWO MINUTES OF YOUR SPEECH

BAM! ZAP! POWIE!

I don't believe in starting slow and picking up speed as you go along. If you're not a celebrity or a proven winner to the audience you're facing, you'd better grab them in your first two minutes—or you may not grab them at all. If you're opening with a joke, go with a big one. If it's a serious beginning, start with a fact, a statement or an illustration that will make them put down their coffee cups and lean forward to give you their undivided attention.

Studies validate this quick-start approach. An audience's first impression tends to be its last. We remember more of what is said earlier in a program than later. And, so, you can't go wrong if you think of the first two minutes of your speech as an audition. It's a 120 second sample that has to convince your listeners that the remaining twenty minutes are worth their time and attention.

How do you do this? First, you have to clear the deck of all encumbrances that might get in the way of BAM! ZAP! POWIE! One of the biggest encumbrances is being introduced in an interminable or inept way. Every speaker has suffered the slings and arrows of outrageous introductions. If you're a humorist, inevitably you will be introduced by toastmasters trying to prove that they are the superior humorists. If you are a pundit giving a 20-minute talk on world affairs, you will sometimes be introduced via a 30-minute talk by the resident pundit. If your name isn't exactly a household word, that's when you can count on being welcomed in ten seconds as someone "who needs no introduction,"— while the audience is thinking, "Who?"

You can count on all of the above happening at least once in your public-speaking career. But then there is the introduction that comes at you so unexpectedly and is so devastating in its impact that you wonder if you shouldn't open with your closing. Such an introduction was reported in *Variety*. Freddie Sadler, a British performer, had been booked to do a stand-up comedy act for an audience of former British servicemen. The secretary of the group brought Sadler on with the following introduction: "We're going to have the entertainment now. We couldn't get the comedian we wanted so we've got Freddie Sadler. I've never heard of him. But before he tries to make us laugh, I want you to stand for a minute's silence for our two members who died since our last meeting." . . . Take it, Freddie!

How do you avoid this kind of scintillating send-off? You do it by writing your own introduction and sending a copy of it to the emcee or toastmaster of the event at which you are speaking. The introduction should be short—tell who you are, what you've done, and what you're going to talk about. It should whet your audience's appetite—not sate it.

***

What other encumbrances might there be to a successful speech opening? Well, there are all those little problems and annoyances that you solve by coming in an hour before the audience arrives. You check out the microphone to make sure you can be heard in all parts of the house. Test the lectern and see that your notes or speech fit comfortably on it. Do you need a lectern light, and is there one, and do you know how to turn it on?

Take a look at the lighting. Can the audience see you? Can you see the audience? Is the level of the house lights satisfactory and, if so, will the lights remain at that level during the program? Do you hear music playing over the hotel's sound system? "What's that? It will be turned off when my speech begins? Wonderful, but to save the committee that extra chore, why don't we just turn it off now?"

Every speaker should run down a personalized "laundry list" of checkpoints before the first member of the audience arrives. You might say that many of these concerns are not your job. The Program Chairman or Committee should take care of them. True. But when you begin your presentation, in the eyes and ears of your listeners you assume full responsibility for your presentation. If you look bad because the microphone isn't working or you're standing in shadow, you can't call the committee up to share the death scene. So when you approach the lectern, make certain that everything has been done and everything is in place to give you a running start.

***

Your first words—do you go right into BAM! ZAP! POWIE? Not quite. I'm a firm believer in moving to the lectern with authority and speaking up without hesitation. I'm appalled by the speakers who amble up to the microphone, put their notes down, rearrange and adjust them, then take a lengthy drink of water while silence envelopes the room and the audience wonders when the curtain will go up.

By all means, get your first words out just as soon as you face the microphone. But the first ten seconds or so of your remarks should be "fill"—or what I call "yammer." An audience always goes through a brief period of readjustment immediately after they applaud the upcoming speaker. They push back the coffee cups, rearrange their chairs, and just get comfortable for the upcoming remarks. If you begin with substance immediately, part of it will be swallowed by this temporary inattention. So give them ten seconds of amiable "thank you and nice to be here," and then go for your attention-grabber.

Should it be a joke? Why not? Audiences are conditioned to expect humor at the start of a speech and as long as it doesn't assume the aspect of ritual, properly constructed and performed humor usually works. But your first joke should be a very special kind of joke. Obviously, it should get a laugh, but it should also be designed to bring you and your audience closer together.

157

How do you do that? By a relevant demand-laugh joke. And what's a relevant demand-laugh joke? The biggest mistake made by speakers who are afraid of humor is that they try to tell a joke in such a way that if it doesn't get a laugh, they can pretend they didn't tell a joke and just continue on. This is a sure-fire, guaranteed path to comedic failure. It's the equivalent of a baseball player who tries for a bunt each time he steps up to the plate, instead of a home run. If you ever saw movies of Babe Ruth in action, you'll remember that when he took a cut at the ball, he put everything he had into it. And if he missed, sometimes he would spin completely around and even fall to the ground—which was embarrassing. Sure! But when he connected, it sailed right out of the park. When you're doing opening humor, it's the far fence you want to be going for.

A good salesman asks for the order—a good joke asks for the laugh.

***

So much for theory. Now let's demonstrate a relevant demand-laugh joke.

Demand-Laugh Jokes. My earliest professional speeches were before women's clubs and to lecture series audiences. I began by saying, "Thank you for that very kind introduction and thank you for allowing me to share this evening with you." (The coffee cups have now been pushed back and the chairs repositioned. I begin the build to the joke.)

"Even though I've been in show business all of my life, as a comedy writer I've spent very little time in front of audiences—and I guess it shows. Just before the program began, I was standing in a little room down the hall when Mary Jones, your very capable Program

Director, came up to me and said, 'Do you do much public speaking?' I said, 'No, I really don't.' She said, 'Are you nervous?' I said, 'Of course not!' She said, 'Then what are you doing in the Ladies Room?'

It never missed because it had the four basic elements of a relevant demand-laugh joke: Surprise, Relevance, Rhythm, and it was Constructed to Get a Laugh.

The first and perhaps most important element is Surprise. The audience was led along a path of pleasant chitchat that also sketched in a little plot and character development along the way. Here was the big-shot guest speaker implicitly crowing about how cool, calm and collected he was—only to have the embarrassing truth revealed and the topper delivered by a member of the home team.

***

The second element—Relevance. Until the punch line, this was simple, everyday conversation that was germane to the situation, and the audience had no doubt that a true incident was being related. There was nothing implausible in what I said about myself, and I was talking to their Mary Jones, their Program Director, in an exchange of small talk they must have witnessed many times.

Rhythm. A good joke has rhythm. It flows and moves and builds with a calculated momentum until the laugh is realized. Note the short sentences of the dialogue—the undercurrent of challenge in Mary Jones' questions, and the hint of unjustified bravado in my answers. A rhythm of tension and confrontation was being established.

The final element and triggerpoint of a relevant demand-laugh joke is the fact that it's Constructed to

Get a Laugh. It has a clear-cut, unmistakable punch line and—if the assessment of the audience is correct, the concept of the joke viable, and the performance adequate—it demands the laugh.

There is another component to demand-laugh opening humor that isn't mandatory, but often helps. As a speaker, you can rarely go wrong by putting yourself down in a funny way. Self-deprecating humor has become a staple in today's speeches because it eliminates an emotional gulf between speaker and audience. The listeners can relate to the speaker more as an ordinary person than as a Senator or Chairman of the Board.

Also, opening humor need not be a story-type of joke. A one-liner or series of one-liners can be used providing you preface them with just enough "yammer" to make sure you have the audience's attention.

I occasionally open with a series of self-deprecating one-liners when my introduction or my printed credits refer to me as an "expert on humor." With some amount of false modesty, I point out the correctness of that statement: "I *am* an expert on humor. But before anyone gets too carried away with that, maybe I'd better tell you the last thing I was an expert on—*How to prevent baldness*." (For many years I have sported a very short crewcut from which most of the crew has bailed out.)

Immediately the bubble of self-importance bursts, but I try to make a comeback: "Frankly, I never realized that I was bald until two weeks ago, when a fly landed on top of my head—and slid off."

Now for the final payoff and reverse spin: "But I'm not really worried about it because I know there's a Biblical explanation for baldness. That's right—a Biblical explanation for baldness. It is written that the good Lord has created millions and millions and millions of heads—and those He's ashamed of, He covers with hair!"

And so the balance is restored and all the baldies in the audience who have been getting nudged by their friends, can nudge back. You've made your case as a friendly, humorous, down-to-earth human being—and you're ready to go on to the substance of your talk.

***

How many jokes should you do in the upfront part of your speech? If the first is a blockbuster, quit while you're ahead. For most business and political speakers, two should be the maximum. The whole point of this opening humor is to bring the audience over to your side. Business speakers should never lose sight of the fact that humor is a tool—not an end unto itself. What you are doing is staging a comedic commando raid on your audience. You roar in, reach your objective, secure it, and then move on.

Does it work? Whenever I reach the punch line of the relevant, demand-laugh joke I am using to open a speech, I look over at the Program Director (or whoever booked me for the event) during the laugh. Just as I am settling down in the knowledge that, yes, it's going to be all right—he or she is doing the same. You can almost hear the sigh of relief.

When your two opening minutes are right, you prove to the committee members and to your audience that you are in control of the situation and that they have every reason to look forward to what follows.

BAM! ZAP! POWIE! You're playing their song.

Openers —See USING HUMOR WHEN YOU'RE AFRAID TO USE HUMOR

Opening an Ad-Lib or Informal Talk

My name is . . . *(Hesitate, concentrate, then look down at your name tag and read it out loud.)*

Ladies and gentlemen—and those of you who couldn't wait to get started on the fruit salad.

Before I begin, I would like to apologize for a small speech impediment—my heart is in my mouth!

After Opening Remarks: I'll hold the other announcements for a little later on in the dinner. To put it poetically:

There you sit all broken-hearted,
You came to eat but then I started.
So let me end my little ballad,
This ham will follow your soup and salad!

It's a great thrill to be here tonight. You know, everybody says that, and maybe it's about time for a speaker to be completely honest: It's okay to be here tonight. . . . I'll be even more honest. It was either this or fill out my income tax return!

Before I begin, I'd like to take a moment to recognize some very important people in the audience. *(Shade your eyes, look around slowly and every so often your face lights up as you wave to someone.)*

I've practiced this speech all week and I feel pretty good about it. So, if you could just manage to look a little more like a bathroom mirror, we'll begin.

Tonight, we have gathered here together to try to find the answers to the two greatest questions facing America today: Who listens to a bartender's troubles? . . . And even more important: Who does an umpire boo?

Openings

Tonight, I am going to speak softly *(hold up your speech)* and carry a big script!

Before we begin, I want to make sure that you finish all of your Baked Alaska. Remember, there are dieters in Beverly Hills going to sleep hungry.

Before we begin, I have one message to read: Would the owner of the blue sedan with license plate 602-334 and the headlights on—please report to the parking lot. Services for your battery begin in fifteen minutes.

Following that rather lengthy reception, you'll be pleased to know that this speech will be close-captioned for the martini-impaired.

It's always a pleasure to be here in one of my favorite cities—*(pause, pull out a card and read from it the name of the city)*. . . . And it's an even greater pleasure to be standing here before one of my all-time favorite organizations—*(pause again, pull out the card and read from it the name of the group)*. . . . For those of you who just came in, I'm your speaker for the evening and my name is—*(pause again, pull out the card and read from it your name)*. . . .

Before we begin, headquarters has asked me to make this announcement: Until further notice, please do not put anything more into the Suggestion Box. The handle is broken and it won't flush.

Good evening, ladies and gentlemen. As you can see, I have a prepared text here. But I know I'm among friends. I know exactly what I want to say. I know precisely how I want to say it—and I certainly don't need the words of any anonymous speechwriter to get my message across. There-fore—*(with an extravagant flourish, throw the speech pages aside or onto the floor)*. And so, once again, good evening, jedies and ladlemen. *(Hesitate a moment and then deliberately retrieve the pages.)*

Optimum Conditions for Speech / Roast —See *Serving the Roast* at ROASTS

Other Speakers as Instructors —See (1) STAGE FRIGHT AND HOW TO DEAL WITH IT; (2) THE HARD WORK OF HUMOR

Outrageous Introductions (and how to overcome them) —See OPENER: THE FIRST TWO MINUTES OF YOUR SPEECH

Overcoming Stage Fright —See STAGE FRIGHT AND HOW TO DEAL WITH IT

Overlooking Something —See Forgetting

P

Package and Present a Speech —See PREPARING
FOR YOUR SPEECH

Paper and Binders for Your Speech —See PREPARING
FOR YOUR SPEECH

Path of Least Resistance —See KINDER, GENTLER
COMEDY

Patterns of Speech, Dress, and Behavior —See
(1) ADVICE—AND HOW TO IGNORE IT; (2) START-
ING YOUR SPEECH A WINNER

Payment for Speechwriting —See MONEY AND
SPEECHWRITING

Performability and True Stories —See STORIES:
WHERE DO THEY COME FROM?

Performability of Written Humor —See SPICING UP
THOSE DULL SPEECHES

Physical Aspects of a Speech (layout, paper, binder)
—See PREPARING FOR YOUR SPEECH

Pitfalls of Public Speaking —See THE HARD WORK
OF HUMOR

Placement on a Program —See *Serving the Roast* at ROASTS

Points of Reference —See ASSESSING YOUR AUDIENCE

Political Correctness —See ASSESSING YOUR AUDIENCE

Political Occasions

Ignorance is bliss—which could explain why you see all those posters of my opponent smiling.

He's smiled so much during this campaign, he has the only teeth in town with a tan.

You might say my opponent has a winning smile and a losing platform.

If it's true that we learn from our mistakes, someday my opponent is going to be a very smart man.

I'll say one thing for my opponent. He always manages to have the last word—and it's usually "Ooops!"

My opponent has a very point-blank approach to the issues. Every time I point to an issue, he looks blank.

He's one of those politicians who believes in talking straight from the shoulder. Unfortunately the brain is somewhat higher.

My opponent's advertising proves one thing: Crass will tell!

If you vote for my opponent, it's a case of forgive and forget. You'll forgive his record and he'll forget his promises.

I'll say one thing for my opponent. When he gives a speech there's never a dull moment. Hours, yes!

I loved that speech. Now I know what they mean by pulling the bull over your eyes.

Positioning Yourself for Delivering a Roast —See *Serving the Roast* at ROASTS

Positive Aspects of Humor —See TOPICAL HUMOR: THE CUTTING EDGE

Practice Audiences —See STAGE FRIGHT AND HOW TO DEAL WITH IT

Practicing Your Speech —See REHEARSING YOUR SPEECH

Prayer

I've never quite understood why we always have the prayer before dinner, when it's the program that needs the help.

Prejudging Audiences —See HOW TO SUCCEED IN HUMOR BY REALLY TRYING

"Prepared" Ad-Libs —See (1) THE HARD WORK OF HUMOR; (2) PREPARING FOR YOUR SPEECH

Preparing for a Roast —See *Preparing the Roast* at
ROASTS

Professional Writers —See MONEY AND SPEECH-
WRITING

PREPARING FOR YOUR SPEECH

Content, style, relevance, delivery, impact—these
are all vital elements that go into the creation of a successful speech. They also tend to be the aspects of a
speech that get most of the attention in the "how-to"
books. When we get a birthday or Christmas present,
we do focus on the gift itself, but the wrapping, pack-
aging and presentation play a considerable role in our
enjoyment of the moment.

How do you wrap, package and present a speech for
maximum effect?

It all starts with the initial draft. I'm a firm believer
in the positive benefits of speech drafts that *look* appealing.

As a speechwriter, I've found that the acceptance
ratio soars when speech drafts are submitted to speakers in a form that invites the eye. Use the K.I.S.S. formula—Keep it Simple, Speechwriter! Lay out your copy
using wide margins, double- or triple-spacing, one- and
two-sentence paragraphs, and short sentences in a sea
of white space.

Avoid solid blocks of text that convey a subliminal
message of dullness. Eschew obfuscation and jettison
jargon. Aim for a draft that looks up at you and yells,
"Read me! Read me! Read me!"

***

Let's face it, most of us are perfectly willing to climb
the highest mountain, swim the deepest river, cross the
widest desert to reach our objectives—but only if the
all-expenses-paid-tour has already left. With few excep-

tions, we're all patsies for the easy way. If your copy is cosmetically appealing, it will not only be read first, but it will be perceived as more interesting, apt and usable than similar copy submitted in textbook form.

The concept also applies to speech drafts you write yourself. Call it self-hype. I tend to write a draft and if time permits, put it away for a few days. When I pull it out again for review, a polish and a rewrite, I find that my emotional reaction is always influenced by the look of the copy on the pages. Obviously the words have to be the right words, but quite often our perception of what is right is substantially influenced by the visual appeal or lack thereof of the speech draft.

Too simple? So is the paper clip—but it works.

I would also recommend that each draft of a speech be spoken out loud by the writer—to eliminate the inevitable combinations of words or syllables that human tongues were not meant to utter.

Reading a speech out loud also provides a fairly accurate idea of how many minutes it will run in performance. The resulting realistic time assessment has altered many a speech.

Perhaps the best reason writers or speakers should read the early drafts out loud is to experience their own gut reactions to the words. If it sounds dull, vapid and uninspiring to the writer and/or speaker, there's no reason to assume an audience won't have the same reaction.

***

With the exception of the Ten Commandments, most speech drafts are rethought, rewritten, restructured and, occasionally, improved. Each draft is numbered, dated and, sometimes, even "houred." The tendency then is to retype or print out these subsequent drafts creating a new configuration of copy, paragraphs and pages beginning with Page One.

This is great for saving paper and gets an "A" for neatness. Unfortunately, every new draft puts the speaker back at Square One in her or his conscious or subconscious attempts to commit part of the text to memory.

I suggest that the physical layout of individual pages or different drafts be changed as little as possible. If you eliminate a paragraph, don't move up the next paragraph to fill the space, thereby changing the structure of each subsequent page.

This may leave some blank spaces—or, if you're adding copy, some slightly crowded sections. But it will also allow the speaker to become acquainted and comfortable with the speech copy. When he or she hits the top of page 14, the speaker knows it's the chunk concerned with "whatever." By speech time the speaker knows the gist of it and can paraphrase the copy while maintaining eye contact with the audience.

If the physical layout of the speech is changed with every draft, the speaker is less able to develop this familiarity with the words. The speech becomes a reading rather than a performance.

I'm also a firm believer in "humor to come." How many times have we all seen the first page of a speech draft left blank with those three little words in the center—"HUMOR TO COME." Well, I don't think that's a bad way to go.

***

The problem with dropping even the best of jokes into an early draft is that familiarity does breed contempt—or, at least, insecurity. The first time you hear or read a joke, you may burst into spontaneous laughter and think it's priceless. The second time you hear or read that same joke, you may smile and think it's pretty good. The tenth time you hear or read it, you wonder how your speechwriter had the gall to give you this old joke.

So, whether humor is provided by someone else or you develop it on your own, leave this aspect of your talk for last. The closer to speech time, the greater will be your own enthusiasm for the humor and your own perception of its freshness.

If you do begin to doubt the effectiveness of a joke or an opening that's been in your speech since the first draft, do this: Think back to the very first time you heard it or saw it. Did you laugh? If you did, remember that your audience will be reacting to it for the very first time as well—and should also reward it with laughter.

***

We have now arrived at Draft 4 or maybe even Draft 14 of your speech. It's finally been frozen and it's ready to be made up into a performing manuscript. Ideally, this freezing of the words should be done a few days in advance of the event so that the speaker has the opportunity to become familiar and comfortable with the words.

If there is one common complaint made by all speechwriters, it's about rewrites. I have found that a few drafts usually produce the most effective vehicle for the speaker. When the number of drafts go far beyond a few, it becomes an exercise in creative wheel-spinning.

Changes are made but they are just that—changes. The copy doesn't get better. It doesn't get worse. It's just different.

A dozen drafts also do a marvelous job of demoralizing the speaker. "Which is better? The closing in Draft 3 or the one in Draft 10?" "Do we still have Draft 3?" "Maybe we can bend that closing into the finish we tried in Draft 8." "What do you mean we don't have draft 8?"

By this point, the speaker's best hope is that the Baskin-Robbins Flavor-of-the-Month is Valium.

This will be the most unheeded advice since "Have a nice day!"—but I still feel impelled to give it: Limit the number of your drafts, freeze the copy early and allow much more time for rehearsing than speeches ever seem to get.

***

The final, frozen draft of your speech should then be transferred to a good 24-point, rag-content bond paper. I've found that this weight and texture doesn't stick together and is most easily handled. The type should be large and dark enough to be easily read under the dimmest of lectern lights.

This performing copy of your speech should then be put into a sturdy folder that opens and stays flat on the lectern. This folder provides a neat concealment of the pages of your speech as you proceed to the lectern.

There's a very good reason for this concealment. It's the same reason for never starting a speech with a premise that offers eight ways to lick inflation or ten rules for better health. Most members of an audience can count pretty good. If the first way or rule runs nine minutes—they multiply that nine minutes by eight or by ten and quickly begin to wonder if they'll be home by Easter.

Abraham Lincoln's Gettysburg Address may not have been written on the back of an envelope, but if it had been, the audience would have taken heart at the sight of it in Abe's hand. So don't telegraph the length of your speech by going to the lectern with an exposed sheaf of speech copy. Conceal it in a businesslike folder.

Don't put your speech into a loose-leaf binder. This often seems like a good idea because it keeps the pages secure and in sequence. The big minus is that it forces you to turn each page completely over. As a result, every time you turn a page the attention of the audience is momentarily directed to this movement. Further, each time a page is turned, they're reminded that you are reading to them and not speaking to them.

It is far better to keep your speech as a deck of loose pages. Place the deck on the lectern and immediately slide the top page to the left or right of the deck (your preference). This gives you a scan of two pages at all times. As you finish reading each page, you just slide the top page of the deck across and onto the top of the completed page. The front of the average lectern is high enough to completely conceal this sliding action.

***

Setting up your speech as loose pages has other advantages. If previous speakers or events in the program dictate last minute-changes in your speech, it's a lot easier to shuffle pages than to click them into and out of binders.

If you feel you may have to make cuts in your speech as you're delivering it, put a slightly larger-than-page-size piece of cardboard above the page in your deck to which you might want to cut. The cutboard is easily grasped. Slide it across to the top of your completed pages and it will carry with it all of the pages you won't be using. The very next page is your new continuing point.

You can also manage on-the-spot deleting by putting tabs on the side of speech pages indicating specific sections of your talk.

Bottom line: If you have to read a speech, make certain that your reading copy helps instead of hinders your performance. It's the mark of a pro. It's another element in achieving a feeling of total self-confidence—

a feeling that may have been best expressed by basketball's Elvin Hayes when he said, "I'd pay to see me play."

—See also (1) THE HARD WORK OF HUMOR; (2) REHEARSING YOUR SPEECH

Presidential Speeches —See SPEECHWRITERS

Pretending the Audience Does Not Exist —See STAGE FRIGHT AND HOW TO DEAL WITH IT

Previous Speaker(s)

I won't comment on the previous speaker. Let's just say that some speakers put audiences to sleep. With him, they coma.

I'll say one thing for our previous speaker: He really knows when to quit. It's about 32 minutes before he does.

I'll say one thing: With that speech, _____ finally got it all together—which is what you have to do when they pick up the garbage.

First, let me say how much all of the previous comments are depreciated.

What can I really say about the previous speaker? I mean—he tried.

First, on behalf of the previous speakers, I want to thank you for the enthusiastic and warm reception you gave to their speeches. It's always nice to have an audience that doesn't get out much.

174

I'd like to congratulate the previous speakers on what can only be called a Niagara of words and a Sahara of thought.

First, I want to thank you all for those hamburger speeches. I call them hamburger speeches because they contain a lot less meat than we were expecting.

I won't comment on the previous speakers. Let's just say I mourn for the 200 chickens and 4000 string beans that have given their lives to make this dinner possible.

Aren't they a great looking group? Look like a polyester farm.

It's hard to describe what they just did. In medicine it would be called a placebo.

What can I tell you? That was a speech to be remembered. Not repeated. Just remembered.

In all fairness to the previous speaker, he is recovering from major surgery. Had a talent bypass.

That's what makes me so proud to be living in America. Where else but in this free and democratic and accepting nation of ours, could a speaker like that find work?

I'd like to thank the previous speaker for saying what is in his heart. I know he said what is in his heart. If he said what is in his head, it would have only taken a minute and a half.

This has really been a drip-dry sort of evening. The speeches have all been dry and the speakers have all been—different.

Let me congratulate the previous speakers on achieving what can only be called an oratorical first—humor gridlock.

I don't want to put down the previous speakers, but there has to be a reason why the Happy Hour is the name given to that period of time immediately *preceding* the program.

Do you ever get the feeling that _____'s speeches come from Frederick's of Hollywood? You can see right through them.

I won't say anything about one of the previous speakers because he's known for playing hard-ball. The minute you say something hard, he bawls.

That was really a wonderful speech when you consider the handicap he's working under—Terminal Talent.

Wasn't that great? What a remarkable speech for a man who still thinks Taco Bell is the Mexican phone company.

About a Young Person: Isn't she wonderful? I was 24 once. *(Pause, frown and shake your head.)* Then twice.

I love the way _____ delivers a speech—so placid, so tranquil, so uninvolved. It's almost as if he's having a calm breakdown.

Sir, I have to admit you're a very forthright speaker. About every fourth word is right.

First, I'd like to acknowledge the previous speakers. There's an old expression: Always leave them laughing, which could explain why they're still here.

I want to congratulate the previous speakers on that interesting display of what can only be called—humor anorexia.

Printed vs. Verbal Jokes —See *Don't Use Print Language in Verbal Jokes* at DON'TS . . . IF YOU WANT TO GET LAUGHS

Procrastination (as the booking agent for stage fright) —See STAGE FRIGHT AND HOW TO DEAL WITH IT

"Production-Line Rhetoric" —See LESSONS I LEARNED FROM LOWELL THOMAS

Professional Speechwriters —See SPEECHWRITERS

The Program / Program Committee / Program Chairman

Hasn't this been just a wonderful evening? The setting, the music, the program—and the dinner was served just the way I like it—free.

Tonight, I'm proud to say your committee has put together a perfect evening. A four-star hotel, a three-course dinner, a two-drink reception, and a one-speaker program.

Why have I volunteered to be Program Chairman? Let's just say I'm into pain.

As members of the audience, we'd like you to know what we've planned for this evening. First we'll have the food—followed by a few speeches—and then we'll have some music. It's called the Three D's—dinner, dozing and dancing.

It isn't easy being a Program Chairman. Let's face it, speakers are a lot like mushrooms. You never know if you're getting a bad one until it's too late.

Since this is a rather lengthy presentation, in order to preserve a certain sense of discipline, dignity and decorum, I would ask that anyone wishing to be excused during the program, please raise your hand. One finger if you want to go; two fingers if you want to go badly; and three fingers if you want a mop.

Prom

It's always a pleasure to see so many people putting on the ritz. And just a reminder to all you fellas in the audience: The ritz has to be returned by 10 a.m. or they charge you for another day.

Punch Lines —See *Don't Let Your Punch Lines Trail Off* at DON'TS . . . IF YOU WANT TO GET LAUGHS

Punch Lines (and the need for them) —See STORIES: WHERE DO THEY COME FROM?

Q

Questions and Answers

And now we come to the final part of this program—the Question and, please Lord, let me have an Answer period.

We have time for just one more question on this rather controversial topic. How about the gentlemen in the back with his wife's hand over his mouth?

I love that expression: "And now, I'll take some questions from the floor." You always have to wonder why the ceiling, walls and door are being ignored.

Sir, like history, you're repeating yourself. Could you get to your closing?

If You Don't Immediately See Someone Who Has Their Hand Raised: I'm sorry. I used to be a waiter.

Sir, that's what I call a pothole question—deep, dangerous and I'd rather not get into it.

When Responding with Just One Word: No! And if you'd like a second opinion: *(turn halfway around to face the rear wall and hold out your hand as if calling on someone. Then complete the turn and when you face the audience again, repeat:)* No!

Are there any questions? . . . *(If none:)* Are there any answers? . . . Are there any survivors?

Replying to a Trick Question: That's what I call a loaded question. It's like your wife asking, "How do you feel today?" Which indicates either an interest in how you feel today—or she wants the oak tree transplanted.

When You Can't Remember Part of a Multiple Part Question: I'm sorry. Would you mind repeating the last part of that question? My mind wandered and it didn't have the exact fare.

When Somebody Disrupts the Q.&A. Period: May I just point out that Q.&A. stands for Question and Answer—not Quibble and Argue?

When Someone Makes a Statement Instead of Asking a Question: Thank you very much. And now for the question to your answer.

Response to a Far Out Question: That's the problem with Q.&A. You ask for questions from the floor and what you get are off the wall.

—See also Long Question/er

Quick-Start Approach —See OPENER: THE FIRST TWO MINUTES OF YOUR SPEECH

Quiet as Preparation for a Speech —See STAGE FRIGHT AND HOW TO DEAL WITH IT

Quotas for Roasters —See *Preparing the Roast* at ROASTS

Quotes in Speeches —See USING HUMOR WHEN YOU'RE AFRAID TO USE HUMOR

R

Rain —See During a Heavy Rain

Reading Jokes or Speeches —See (1) *Don't Read the Jokes—Tell 'em!* at DON'TS . . . IF YOU WANT TO GET LAUGHS; (2) PREPARING FOR YOUR SPEECH; (3) REHEARSING YOUR SPEECH

Real Life as a Source of Humorous Material —See STORIES: WHERE DO THEY COME FROM?

Rebuttals

Sir, what you have just said can only be described as a speed bump on the highway of logic.

Sir, I'm very sympathetic to your problem. It's evident that you've acquired so much misinformation, that you want to share the surplus with others.

Well, once again you're jumping to confusions.

All I can say is, if you took what you just said, added mustard and put it between two slices of bread, you'd have the biggest baloney sandwich in history.

Have you ever noticed how the slowest thinkers have the quickest answers?

After a Long Rebuttal: Have you noticed how some people are like enamel paint? It takes them a long time to dry up.

Sir, have you finished? Because your thought did a few minutes ago.

Could you put that another way? For starters, how about accurately?

Sir, has it ever occurred to you that you might be ten minutes ahead in your talking and an hour behind in your listening?

Astrologically speaking, I've never heard so much Taurus in all my life.

Rebutting Humor (the futility of) —See "WHY HU-MOR?"

Recovering from a Mistake with the Aid of Humor —See "WHY HUMOR?"

Recovering from an Outrageous or Weak Introduction —See OPENER: THE FIRST TWO MINUTES OF YOUR SPEECH

Regrets —See MISTAKES

REHEARSING YOUR SPEECH
"I don't have time."
"I know my subject. I'll just wing it."
"Not to worry. I'll review it on the plane."
They've all been used by speakers to postpone or eliminate the rehearsing that can transform a collection of words into a performance.
Rehearsing is the sieve that separates the accom-

plished speaker from the yawn producer. It's not a luxury or a frill that can be discarded without consequence. Rehearsing is a vital and mandatory part of the speechmaking process.

"Too busy" is the most frequently used excuse for avoiding practice. Whenever I hear it, I cite the example set by one of the greatest communicators of our century—Winston Churchill.

Churchill rehearsed. Words, attitude and gestures—he rehearsed them all. He found the time—he took the time, even during the life-and-death months of the Battle of Britain—to make sure that his speeches would be listened to and remembered.

On one occasion, Churchill was taking a bath and his valet thought he heard him saying something through the bathroom door. His valet tapped on the door and said, "Excuse me, sir, but were you speaking to me?" "No," Churchill replied, "I was addressing the House of Commons."

If argument is necessary for adequate speech preparation and rehearsal, consider this: If your speech runs 20 minutes and you're giving it to 300 people—that's 100 hours of human existence being placed in your care. It's a considerable responsibility. Even people who have time to kill don't want to see it done in with a blunt weapon.

The final and perhaps best motivation for making the performance of your speech as good as it can be: Vanity. We all strive for excellence and the psychic and material rewards that it brings. But excellence is not a one-night stand. Unlike baseball players who are considered exceptional if they stand at the plate and connect three times out of ten, speakers have to make a connection every time. As theatrical agent Bill Liebling put it: "You're only as good as the night they catch you."

So let's talk about rehearsing. When, where and how?

Ideally, the writing of your speech should be completed in sufficient time to allow you to rehearse it once on each of three separate occasions. There is a value to allowing time for reflection between rehearsals. It allows you to look at the copy with a fresh eye and gives you some time to absorb the lessons learned from the previous run-through.

If you plan to read your speech, the text or notes used in rehearsal should be the text or notes you will use in performance. The text should be set up in such a way that you are comfortable and familiar with it. I would also suggest that the copy be typed on only the top half of each page. If the text runs all the way down to the bottom of the page, for half the speech you will have your chin in your chest trying to read it. The audience will see a lot more of your haircut than of you.

If the lectern at the event is large and angled, placing your text on the lower lip of it will sometimes create the same reading problem. Ask if the lectern has a bar that can be positioned mid-way so that the speech text resting on it is not at belly-button level.

***

Should the speech be read or memorized?

Humor should *not* be read. The essence of good humor is spontaneity. It should always sound as if it's happening for the first time and if you read a joke, this sense of "now" is lost.

As for the rest of the speech, practicality has to be considered. Obviously, a speaker who can maintain total eye contact with an audience and foster the perception of a one-on-one relationship is way ahead of someone scanning a text. But here the time factor intrudes. It just isn't realistic for executives or political figures to memorize speeches, particularly when the speech load is a heavy one. There are also many speeches requiring precise wording or providing detailed information, that dictate a carefully followed text.

Three rehearsals serve to return some of the eye contact opportunities that are lost in reading from a text. Paragraphs and even entire pages become familiar to the speaker. They can then be paraphrased or restated without doing injury to the content. The speech becomes more personal and little nuggets of vitality are added to the performance.

The "where" of rehearsing is also quite important. I'm always amused when speakers rehearse a speech by reading it to themselves while sitting in their favorite easy chair at home. You don't give the speech sitting in an easy chair. Why then, rehearse in one?

***

Rehearsals should approximate the real event as closely as possible. Primarily, this means delivering the speech out loud, while standing up and at a lectern. If you don't have access to a lectern, buy one of those lightweight plastic study aids for reading in bed. When placed on a desk or table, it is an ideal surrogate lectern.

While rehearsing, keep in mind your audience and speech location. Speechwriters often provide their clients with a fact sheet to go along with the speech. This fact sheet will list the date, location and sponsor of the event. It will also provide background information on the interests and composition of the audience, who will be at the head table (with a brief bio of each) and even such details as nicknames and whether or not the client has met or previously appeared with them. The physical layout of the room is described and any other information that may prepare the speaker for the event is appended.

In the absence of such a fact sheet, make up your own. Then, when you approach your desk-top lectern, visualize the room in which you will be speaking. As you perform your speech, in your imagination make eye contact with the members of an audience you know something about. When you finish, rehearse even the closing of your speech folder and acknowledging your applause.

Rehearse so that when you actually do the event, it feels as if you've been there before.

As you deliver the speech in rehearsal, pay particular attention to any glitches that occur. If you hesitate because the physical layout of a sentence or phrase is confusing—or you have difficulty in pronouncing a word, name or combination of syllables—see what happens the next time you rehearse.

If the problem recurs, correct it by adding slashes, underscores and/or phonetics to the text—or, if necessary, rewriting or restructuring the text. Don't say to yourself, "I'll get that right when I do it for real." If you repeatedly misspeak in rehearsal, under the pressure of the event itself, chances are you'll do it again. Don't put any more of a burden on yourself than you have to. Solve the problem in rehearsal.

For the second rehearsal, you might want to tape your delivery of the speech. A playback will give you the opportunity to consider the speech from the audience's viewpoint and may help you to fine-tune it. Listening to the tape while driving to work, jogging or eating lunch is a painless way of committing some of the words to memory.

Rehearsals are also the ideal time to plan ahead. It never hurts to anticipate and solve problems before the crisis occurs. If you have a 60-minute presentation and the audience is tired, hostile, overheated, restive or all of the above—pre-selected cuts can tailor your speech without damaging the fabric.

On the other hand, if you've completely won over the audience and they're hanging on your every word— a few prepared-in-advance embellishments might be called into action.

It all takes a considerable amount of time, thought and effort. True. But it may save you from being in the position of the governor who was speaking at the largest university in his state. Naturally, a compliment to the school was called for. He was supposed to refer to "this venerable institution." Adequate rehearsal may have kept him from saying what he did say—namely: "This venereal institution . . ."

—See also THE HARD WORK OF HUMOR

Relevance as an Element in Demand-Laugh Jokes —See *Demand-Laugh Jokes* at OPENER: THE FIRST TWO MINUTES OF YOUR SPEECH

Repetition, Fear of —See TAPING

Repetitive Words or Phrases (like, you know) —See TAPING

Researching for a Roast —See *Delivering the Roast* at ROASTS

Responding to a Far Out Question —See Questions and Answers

Responding to a Gag Gift or Award —See Acknowledging a Gag Gift or Award

Responding to a Glowing or Flattering Introduction —See A Flattering or Glowing Introduction, Responding to

Responding to a Needling Introduction —See After a Needling Introduction

Responding to Interruption —See (1) CONTROLLING YOUR AUDIENCE; (2) Dealing with Hecklers and Interrupters

Retirement Events, Dinners and Roasts

Retirement is when the only surprises you ever get come from prune juice.

Anybody who wants to retire has rockers in his head!

Retirement is a fascinating time of life. It's when you experience an effluence of affluence.

Retirement is when your azalea isn't the only thing that's bushed.

Retirement is when you finally have enough time to do all the things you no longer want to do.

The problem with being retired is that you never know what day it is—what time it is—where you're supposed to be or what you're supposed to be doing. It's a lot like working for the city.

The problem with retiring at fifty-five is that people keep telling you how good you look for sixty-five.

Work is the elevator that carries you up to the heights of influence, prestige and self-fulfillment. And retirement is the shaft.

I retired four years ago. My biggest problem is keeping the boss from finding out.

I'll never forget the first company I ever worked for. This company was so small, when I was promoted from office boy to Executive Vice President—my duties didn't change.

I won't say that thirty years on the job haven't taken their toll. When I first started here I put in all the overtime I could get because I wanted the bread. Now I'm glad if I can just get my buns home.

Retirement is a more or less situation. You have a lot more of less and a lot less of more.

You know you're approaching retirement when you can't quite tell if junior executives are fresh out of the Management Training Program or the Day Care Center.

As you know, our company has a unique retirement program. You work until you die.

There are two ways to look at retirement. Some people hit sixty-five. Others embrace it.

In retirement, it's important to maintain your health, well-being and a positive frame of mind. That's why I have a prescription martini glass—with the label "FILL TWICE DAILY."

Retirement is eating the carrot while thumbing your nose at the stick.

What I've always liked about retirement communities is the complete air of practicality. You go into the drugstore and you find Ben-Gay with the perfumes.

You can always tell former military in a retirement community. They're the ones who every night do KP, take out the garbage—and march the dog.

Think of it this way: Most of your life you're in the army of taxpayers. Retirement is when you join the reserves.

Retirement—it's the first day of the *rest* of your life.

During his many years with the company, _____ could always be counted on to put in a good day's work. Our problem is, we had him on the night shift.

For all of his thirty years with our company, he has always held firm to one basic philosophy. He has always believed that time flies—but work can be a rest stop.

He has seen many changes in his thirty years with our company. When he began in the Accounting Department, software was a number two pencil.

As I stand up here tonight, I can't help but tell you it is a little unnerving to know that 300 people would come out on a night like this—just to see you quit.

Tonight we've come together to honor _____ as he begins the new adventure of retirement—which goes to show that old bankers never die, they just yield to maturity.

_____ has put in a memorable thirty years with this company—twenty-two years if you subtract coffee breaks.

Retirement is that ideal stage of life when the only thing you have to take a stand on is the bathroom scale.

After all that's been said tonight, there's no doubt that _____ has been able to cut the mustard. Now let's see if he can cut the cake.

When a Sales Manager Retires: It won't be easy to break the conditioning and work patterns of a lifetime. Something tells me, the _____ family may be the first one in their neighborhood ever to have a Marketing Plan, Advertising Program and Quota for a garage sale.

Wrinkles are the service stripes of life.

I'll tell you how I feel about retirement. I don't mind so much that the parade has passed me by. What does bother me is when they hand you a broom and tell you to follow it.

I have no problem with retirement. I'd much rather be put out to pasture than under it.

It helps if you don't think of yourself as a worker, but as a trainee for retirement.

The best time to pack it in is when you fully realize what you have put into your savings account, what the company has put into your retirement plan, and what the cafeteria has put into your chicken salad.

Retirement is when the only hostile takeover bid you have to worry about is crabgrass.

Retirement is such a comfortable period. It's when the only creative juices you really need are prunes.

You can always tell the retirees at the company picnic. When the CEO tells a joke, they're the ones who say they've heard it before.

Just because people are retired doesn't mean they've lost their zest for life. You'd be surprised how many homes you can go into in Sun City and find two La-Z-Boy loungers side-by-side—with a mirror on the ceiling.

Tonight we honor a member of our organization who began with this company so far back, the executive washroom didn't have a key—it had a Sears Roebuck catalog.

As _____ put it, he's worked here for thirty years and he's been married for thirty years, so as he begins staying at home full-time, he doesn't really think of it as retirement. It's more like just changing bosses.

The Social Security years are when time hangs heavy and your wallet doesn't.

I'm going to keep my speech short and I'll tell you why I'm going to keep my speech short. I've been sitting up here for two hours. When I was young, my heart ruled my head. When I was middle-aged, my head ruled my heart. Now I'm 65 and my kidneys rule both.

Thirty years ago, I came into this company with nothing—and through the years, the Payroll Department has seen no reason to change that.

Actually, you've given me everything I could ever want in retirement—an old-fashioned gold watch and a digital check.

I'd be all in favor of making Social Security voluntary—but only if we could do the same for old age.

God isn't dead. Maybe He just retired on a fixed income.

Retirement really doesn't change our lives that much. The biggest difference is that all those things you never had the time to do—now become all those things you don't have the money to do.

Retirement is an educational experience. The first thing you learn is how very wrong Ben Franklin was when he said that "time is money."

I told my wife, when I retire we're converting our twin beds into one king-sized bed. I'm never going to commute again.

My ship never did come in—but thanks to our pension plan a rowboat makes monthly calls.

Two women were sitting on a park bench discussing retirement and the conversation went something like this:

"Ever since my husband George retired, he's set up a strict schedule for everything we do—shopping, cleaning, gardening."
"Just like my husband Sam, may he rest in peace."
"You know, I'm really enjoying this cigarette. When George retired he gave up smoking and won't allow it in the house."
"Just like Sam, may he rest in peace."
"Well, I'd better get going. George throws a fit if lunch isn't ready on time."
"Just like Sam, may he rest in peace."
"Tell me, when did you lose Sam?"
"He starts tomorrow."

And so, _____ and his cat are going into retirement. Both, in their own way, fixed for life.

When I first came to work here thirty years ago, _____ said we get sick pay. Then, a week later he handed me my first paycheck and proved it.

All I want are three things in a retirement community: a warm climate, a nearby golf course and a cocktails-on-wheels program.

Personally, I will never get used to being retired. There's something about drinking coffee on your own time.

195

When a great football player goes into retirement, they honor him by retiring his jersey. So now that _____ is leaving us, we'd like to retire the one item that is most closely associated with his 30 years in our company. *(Hold up—ashtray if retiree is a constant smoker—or a coffee cup— or a similar identifying object.)*

This is a very special evening for our guest of honor. After thirty-three years of retirement, this week he finally made it official.

In a way, retirement is like a vasectomy. You retain all of your faculties only now they're just for fun.

As you probably know, he's already bought a beach-front condo in a swinging retirement village. It's the only place in the state that permits nude wading.

The nice part about retirement is it gives you both the time and the necessity to experiment with exotic gourmet dishes—like Peking Spam.

My wife is firmly convinced that when it comes to household pests—nothing is worse than a retired husband.

The best retirement is when you have the whole day to do nothing in—and it isn't enough.

The nicest part about retiring is to be able to sit at your desk for that one last time—to review all the company problems yet to be solved, all the corporate hassles in search of resolution, and the rocky economic road still to be trod—and softly say to yourself, "Th-th-th-th-th-that's all, folks!"

As we all recognize, retirement is something we have to prepare for. And I have. Two years ago I started doing home repairs a lot. A year ago I started shopping at the supermarket a lot. Six months ago I started going over our financial affairs a lot. And six weeks ago I started crying a lot.

Retirement is that awesome period of adjustment when you go from three martini lunches and expense account dinners—to Gruel Helper.

If you're thinking of retirement,
May I please have your attention.
With prices going up and up,
What rhymes with pension? Tension!

I've always wanted to settle down in California because people out there really know how to spend their retirement years. I mean, where else can you find hot tubs filled with Postum?

In his thirty years with the company, he has always been a team player. In the winter, the team is the *(football loser)* and in the summer, the team is the *(baseball loser)*.

Ever since he retired, his wife has asked him to make her life easier by doing little things around the house. Like stay out of it.

And so, as he begins this well-deserved retirement, he has only two wishes for the future: That his bowling score be as high as his hopes—and his golf score as low as his pension.

It was a little embarrassing planning for this event. When _____ announced he was going to retire, it came as a complete surprise—because most of us thought he already had.

I'll tell you how far back he goes with us. When he joined _____, the company car was a Schwinn.

I haven't quite decided how I'm going to spend my retirement—but for starters, I'm going to drive down to Florida—by golf cart.

You know you're ready for retirement when you take off your shoes, put on your slippers—and even *they* hurt.

I never realized how many people have gone to Hawaii to retire until I saw surfboards with arch supports.

After all these years of living in big cities with the traffic, the noise, the people and the congestion—all I want in retirement is a house so far out in the woods—that dialing the operator will be a long-distance call.

Retirement is when the only time there is something you have to do—is when you get up in the middle of the night.

Retirement is when the living is easy but the payments are hard.

Tonight, we're not losing an employee. We're gaining a space at the coffee machine.

Retirement is when you like to watch the sunset—whenever you stay up that late.

Retirement is a wonderful time of your life. It's like being on strike only you don't have to picket.

Sixty-five is when you realize that just because you've been put out to pasture, doesn't mean you're in clover!

The happiest part of retiring isn't the farewell dinner, the gold watch or even the pension. It's when you mulch your commuter's ticket.

A successful retiree is one who moves to Florida with five gift books on how to cope with retirement—and five years later, he's still too busy to read them.

Anyone who works past his retirement age is off his rocker.

Personally, I look forward to retirement. I will always think of 65 as not a working number.

A lot of retired people take up new hobbies. They collect stamps, coins, butterflies, art. All I want to collect is dust.

If you stopped working twenty years ago and you really want to get depressed—compare your retirement pay to your grandson's allowance.

I won't say how much work I aim to do in the next few years, but if you're planning to give me a gold watch, it better be self-winding!

The biggest shock that comes when you retire after a lifetime of office work—is learning that some people actually *buy* pencils, pens and paper.

For those of you who are concerned, _____
just told me he's fixed for life. I don't know if that
means he got a pension or a vasectomy.

In preparation for this dinner, the head office put
out a thumbnail sketch of all of his accomplishments since joining this company. It's called a
thumbnail sketch because that's what it fits on.

A lot of people going into retirement find that
the biggest challenge is adjusting to just sitting
around doing nothing. With _____ this won't
be a problem. With our company alone, he's had
over thirty years of practice.

Unlike some other members of our staff, he has
never spent his time in daydreams—mostly because they'd interfere with his naps.

In his long career with our company, our bookkeeper has been honored many, many times—
which is good news and bad news. The good
news, he once won an award for originality and
creative imagination. The bad news—it was from
the I.R.S.

And since his retirement, he's begun a second
career in the take-out business. That's right.
Every day his wife tells him, "Take out the garbage. Take out the dog. Take out the weeds."

Don't think of yourself as retired. Think of yourself as a leisure consumer.

The first big shock of retirement is when you
realize there are no days off.

Retirement is when you can't decide if you're getting deaf or the rest of the world has laryngitis.

Sixty is when you begin to wonder if going through puberty is a round-trip.

Retirement is that special time of life when you get too much gray and not enough green.

Retirement is when you finally reach your station in life—and it feels like you got there by Amtrak.

For a really comfortable retirement, you need a good investment plan. So twenty years ago I started one and it's really worked. My broker has comfortably retired. My accountant has comfortably retired. My lawyer has comfortably retired.

Laugh and the world laughs with you. Cry and you were counting on Social Security.

As I look back, there is only one thing I wish I could have saved for my old age—the years between twenty and thirty.

Retirement is when millions of Americans finally have the opportunity to adopt an alternate lifestyle—poverty.

Obviously, our guest of honor has prospered in his years with (company). When he first came here he weighed 138 pounds. I won't say what he weighs now, but you know how some people have pants that say LEVI? And others have pants that say CALVIN KLEIN? His say WIDE LOAD.

201

Acknowledging a Retirement Gift: First, I want to thank you for this handsome watch. *(Shake it and hold it up to your ear.)* How do you like that? I think it quit before I did?

Looking back, there are so many memories. Who can ever forget that fateful day thirty years ago, when out of the 5,000 employees in our company, the Chairman of the Board took _____ aside—and left him there.

I've been punching a time clock for thirty years and some habits are hard to break. And so, after I retire, I'm still going to punch a clock. If it ever goes off at six in the morning, I'm going to punch it clear across the room.

Retirement is when you finally find out what your spouse has been doing all day long—and you're sorry you asked.

I don't mind sharing the housework but there is such a thing as overdoing it. I mean, who waxes ceilings?

The nice part about retirement is that you're past the point of intimidation. Yesterday a mugger tried to rob me in a supermarket parking lot. I said, "Sorry. I just gave."

The whole trick in retiring is planning ahead. *(Pick up a roll from the bread tray, hold it up, look it over and put it in your pocket.)*

The best way to handle retirement is to take all the money you've saved for a rainy day—and move to the desert.

Food prices are so high, retirement is when you go from Safeway to No Way.

It has often been said that when _____ retires, it will leave a huge, gaping hole to be filled. And you know why it will leave a huge, gaping hole? Because when he finds out what his pension is going to be, he'll go right through the roof!

Retirement is that marvelous time of life when the sun rises and you don't.

The problem in a lot of companies is workers who settle for early retirement—two years before they quit.

And now, let us all join together and sing the Retirement Anthem. The one that goes: "If retirement is the prime of my life—why am I eating hamburger?"

Getting old is no crime, but the government is beginning to look on it as mighty inconsiderate.

Relax. Retirement may be when you're over the hill—but at least you're over the Hell as well.

A number of people have retired from our office in the last few years and they always look so cheerful and relaxed and rested when they come in to chat and borrow lunch money.

Many people retire and then vegetate. Who can afford meat?

As a token of our appreciation, we have created this special gold watch to serve as a constant reminder of your many years with our company. It needs a lot of winding up—is always a little late—and every day, at a quarter to five, it stops working.

Reunions

Class reunions are where you hug, kiss, laugh, cry, and reminisce with total strangers.

Class reunions can be an unnerving experience. I wanted to ask the geeky-looking kid with the thick glasses who was always fooling around with a computer, a modem, and a mouse, what he's doing now—only he couldn't hear me through the window of his Rolls.

At a class reunion, the most embarrassing thing you can ask anybody is "What are you doing now?" Because you get answers like, "Oh, I'm still C.E.O. of General Motors." After something like that, you just don't feel much like talking about your VCR repair shop.

Twenty-five year class reunions, in particular, can be very confusing. You see the girl you took to the senior prom—and you can't decide if there's still some love-light in her eyes—or whether it's just the glint of trifocals.

Ten-year class reunions aren't so bad. Twenty-five-year class reunions can be a little daunting. But the real problem is fifty-year class reunions. Even the name tags have wrinkles.

The best class reunion of all is where everyone looks older, fatter, softer, slower, balder, dumber and poorer than you do.

Family reunions are where you travel thousands of miles to visit people you left home to get away from.

A reunion is where a few hundred people get together—to see who's coming apart.

Rhythm as an Element in Demand-Laugh Jokes
—See *Demand-Laugh Jokes* at OPENER: THE FIRST TWO MINUTES OF YOUR SPEECH

Rim Shots —See *Don't Let Your Punch Lines Trail Off* at DON'TS . . . IF YOU WANT TO GET LAUGHS

Risk / Risk Taking —See (1) USING HUMOR WHEN YOU'RE AFRAID TO USE HUMOR; (2) MISTAKES

ROASTS
The material for this subject is divided into five sections:

(1) Preparing the Roast
(2) Delivering the Roast
(3) Serving the Roast
(4) Jokes for the Roast
(5) Responding to the Roast

Preparing the Roast

Roasts are "in."

The lunch, dinner or get-together that honors people by demolishing them is the current fad. Long popular with show business organizations, roasts have now caught the laughter and imagination of general audiences. Suddenly testimonial dinners became testimonial roasts; retirement luncheons became retirement roasts; political fund-raisers assumed the form of political roasts.

And why not? The long evenings of praise, plaques and platitudes have produced 60% of the world's proven reserve of yawns. There are only so many ways you can verbalize the great job being done by good old Joe or Joan before it gets to be watch-checking time.

The roast, when properly prepared, seasoned and served, solves the problem. The guest of honor is praised a little and punctured a lot. Paradoxically, these gentle jabs usually have a bonding effect. They bring the audience emotionally closer to the strengths, weaknesses and personality of the person roasted. And since laughter is the language of equals, the good feeling tends to have a considerable shelf life.

***

So much for the good news. The bad news is that roasts frequently present problems that warrant the label: THIS EVENT MAY BE HAZARDOUS TO YOUR IMAGE.

Sometimes the problems are built into the event. The organizers, in their enthusiasm to involve as many names as possible, may overload the program. I'm always appalled when program committees tell me there will be ten people roasting the guest of honor. When I suggest that ten roasters may be a bit much, they say, "We thought of that and so we're limiting each speaker to three minutes." Three minutes! Some speakers take more time than that just clearing their throats.

Whenever I am told about one of these planned mob scenes, I make a prediction that has never been wrong. I predict that a couple of the speakers will hold to their three minutes—usually by being serious instead of humorous—nice instead of needling.

The remaining speakers will complain about the difficulties of telling jokes for three whole minutes—and then do ten minutes, with occasional gusts up to twenty.

I can still remember one nightmarish roast in which

one of the roasters, with a three minute quota, did twenty-four unrelentingly dull minutes—including one six-minute story with no discernible punch line. He was finally gently led away from the microphone by the emcee who was by now in an advanced state of shock. Later on the roaster complained that he never got to do his best material.

But even if the ten roasters are capable, the parade of speakers with a single topic creates mind-numbing repetition. There are only a few high-visibility aspects of each guest of honor that can be addressed. The first person doing a joke about the honoree's passion for chocolate will get a laugh. The second speaker doing a chocolate joke will get a smile. The third roaster to approach the subject will get a stare. The eighth chocolate reference could very well produce groans or some other put-down of the speaker.

***

Duplication of subject matter isn't the only problem caused by the overstuffed roast. Ten speakers who each have to be introduced, get up, do three-plus hilarious minutes, and sit down again—act out a scenario that can only be endorsed by sleep therapists.

Once the first few speakers do their Jack-in-the-Box routine, the audience gets the idea. Worse, if the first few speakers strike out, programs are surreptitiously consulted. "Seven more roasters to go." Hypochondriacs start worrying if there's such a thing as terminal boredom.

Now the argument could be made that show business roasts always feature a dais that's wall to wall with participants. True. But the participants are professionals. They're accomplished in the selection of material, skilled in delivery, and aware of the need for pace and change of pace. And even with all this, many a show-business roast goes downhill after the second hour and tenth personality.

Program committees that limit roast events to from one to four roasters, each doing a reasonable amount of time, automatically become eligible for membership in the S.P.C.A.—the Society for the Prevention of Cruelty to Audiences.

***

Roasts often present another problem that may not be recognized in the planning stage.

The organization wants to honor Person X. Someone on the program committee jumps up—and with all the enthusiasm of Mickey Rooney and Judy Garland coming up with the idea of putting on a show in the old barn—says, "I know what! Let's make it a roast!" And a roast it is.

But roasts aren't appropriate for all menus or all appetites. Ideally, the guest of honor at a roast should be reasonably well-known to the audience; have some high-visibility job, history, hobby and traits that can be humorously addressed; have the ability to zing back in the rebuttal; and, perhaps most important of all, have a personality that can be comfortably kidded.

Bill Clinton and Bill Gates are perfect guests of honor for a roast. The Pope would present problems.

And so, if your organization is going to do right by a roast and the roasters, choose your roastee with care. If your honoree is a quiet, unassuming, hard worker who has lived an exemplary life and shunned the spotlight—put the roast back in the freezer and polish up the plaque.

To only a slightly lesser extent, the same care and criteria should be applied to the selection of roasters. Roast humor may be the most difficult humor of all. It is pure attack. Attack tempered with affection and make-believe, but attack nevertheless. It's not easy to do and not everyone can do it.

Some speakers who are otherwise quite skillful in the delivery of humor, become uncomfortable with roasts. They can score with self-deprecating humor but don't feel at ease poking fun at others. And such discomfort is quickly felt by an audience.

Roasts call for a special kind of recipe—a delivery that combines just the right amounts of mock seriousness and comedic attack. You don't mean what you're saying and the audience knows you don't mean what you're saying—but for the moment, it's accepted as fun reality.

Good roasters are people who can kid, josh and gently needle those around them without raising hackles. This characteristic is so much a part of their personalities that it's comfortably accepted, even by their targets. But there is a social contract involved. They observe the STOP signs. Good roasts know just how far to go before the laughter turns to hurt.

And so, for the well-done roast, committees should not choose their roasters indiscriminately. On the other hand, it takes two to complete an invitation—the inviter and the invited.

***

Through the years I've received hundreds of phone calls from speakers who, spurred by a variety of motivations, have agreed to participate in a roast. In many cases, the honor of being asked, a sense of obligation to the honoree, or the prominence of the event has obscured all the potential minefields that come with the territory.

Then as the date of the event draws near, they suddenly say, "Good Lord, what have I done?"

Quite often the speaker has never done a roast

before, doesn't like attack humor, doesn't want to offend the guest of honor, has nothing prepared and no time for preparation, the event is the day after next—and the question to me is "What should I do?"

There are no pluses to being an amateur-night loser in front of prestigious audiences. Richard Nixon would have been far better off if he had skipped the Nixon-Kennedy TV debates and spent the time buying pancake make-up and attending Personality 101.

In humor, as in politics, you enter the races you think you can win.

If you are wrong for the roast—or the roast is wrong for you—let someone else do it. The Titanic is always overbooked.

Delivering the Roast

So you've been asked to do a roast as one of the roasters. You've accepted. Now what?

A good performance should appear effortless, but to achieve this, a great amount of effort is required.

For a roast, the effort goes into research and preparation. Not the day of the roast. Not the week of the roast. Your research, writing and gathering of material should begin the day you accept the invitation and continue until you stand up to speak.

Procrastination is the thief of time and of good speeches. So put away the unconscious thought that the event will never take place or that the date will never come.

Then set out to get all of the biographical information available on the guest of honor—the roastee. The formal bio is important because it gives you a framework of dates, places and events upon which to hang your barbs. But personal references and idiosyncrasies are much more important in creating roast material. Try to round up biographical articles and personality profiles that highlight the flesh-and-blood person behind the public persona.

Contact family, friends and business associates of the roastee. In addition to further biographical tidbits, see if you can glean from them any appropriate retellable anecdotes or incidents. Quite often, these recollections can only be used by someone other than the target of the evening.

Now it's list time. Using the information gained from all sources, make up three lists.

The first list will be a skeletal bio that lists the high points in the guest of honor's life with emphasis on the gaffes, failures and flaws.

The second list should catalog the more colorful and high-visibility aspects of your subject's personality, appearance, dress style and way of life.

The third list is a catch-all list of everyone and everything associated with the event that might be grist for your comedic mill. Included would be the roasters who precede you on the program, the toastmaster, the sponsoring organization, the decor of the room, the order of the program, the dinner menu—any aspect of the event that would be instantaneously recognized by the audience.

There might even be a fourth list of events in the news and in your community that might have some bearing on the roastee.

***

When these lists are reasonably complete, read through them a number of times so that you become totally familiar with the subject matter they contain. If you have a knack for humor writing, now is the time to put that ability to work. Place the lists side by side and using the time-honored devices of exaggeration, understatement, misdirection, word play, misunderstanding, etc., construct your roast material with the information on these lists as your foundation and building blocks.

If you are not a humorist, prepare to be an ex-humerist. Dig out the folder, loose-leaf book or shoe box with all the scraps of jokes and stories you've collected and used through the years. Add to this the joke books you may have in your library.

Now carefully go through this storehouse of humor with the specific interests, jobs, hobbies and personality traits of the roastee in mind. When you see a joke, one-liner or story that speaks to one of these topics, put it aside for possible inclusion.

At this point, don't try to make a judgment as to the worth or performability of the material. If the subject matter is right, add it to your collection. Quite often, a weak line coupled with another thought or application can trigger you into a blockbuster.

In addition to the jokes that have a specific application to the life or career of the guest of honor, be on the lookout for more generic roast humor. Put-down lines in general can easily be adapted to roast situations.

Finally, make sure you include the true funny stories and incidents you have researched from family and friends.

***

Now it's time to "routine" them. First, consider your position in the program.

If you are the first roaster, a more or less biographical approach to the guest of honor's life is called for. But also take full advantage of your lead-off spot. Go for every easy, high-recognition peg you've found—the roastee's passion for lichee nuts, the time he played football in college and threw the game-losing interception, the time she turned Michael Jackson down for the neighborhood glee club.

If you are not the lead-off roaster but appear soon after, a more judicious selection of the easy subjects is called for. Use fewer of them and be prepared to cut if the previous speakers preempt either your joke or your thought.

Should you be slotted toward the end of the parade of roasters, forget the high-recognition points entirely. Explore the minutia of the guest's life. Invent comic incidents. Throw some jibes at the other speakers, the head table, the host organization, the hotel, the air-conditioning—anything that would add a new element of subject matter to the event.

This latter approach is particularly important when you have a guest of honor who is not well-known or who is such a quiet, well-mannered, low-profile type of person that he never should have been chosen to be the roastee in the first place. If such is the case, your material can be almost entirely divorced from reality.

Make up a fanciful life history. If the guest comes from a small town, do small town jokes. (So small the Baskin-Robbins has only one flavor.) If there was military service, do army or navy jokes. (In World War II, he fought and fought and fought—but they drafted him anyway.) Time spent in college can be explored. (He didn't exactly graduate summa cum laude. He didn't exactly graduate magna cum laude. Well, let's be honest about it. What he majored in was "Huh?")

A largely bogus life history can be the best way to go with guests of honor who don't fit comfortably into the roast pattern. And it's wise to keep another thing in mind: A bolt of lightning will not strike you down if you stray from the topic.

If you have a sure-fire chunk of material or never-miss anecdote that would be new to the audience, use it. You can always find a comedically acceptable way to link the extraneous material to the subject of the event. It adds an element of known strength to the untried portions of your presentation and if you're the nervous type, starting off with this material isn't a bad idea.

The tone of roast material is all-important. Perhaps the most overworked line in roasts today is: "A man who is a legend in his own mind." But it serves as a useful example of what a good roast joke should be. It has bite without being bitter. It jabs but it doesn't jolt.

In choosing a role model for your roast performance, the good-natured approach of Mark Russell is much more in keeping with the tone of non-show business roasts than the attack style of Don Rickles.

And this sensitivity to feelings should not be restricted to your material alone. Your speaking style and attitude should indicate that no matter what is being said, it's all in fun. Even though the put-down lines are being delivered with mock seriousness, every now and then, break up a little or look over to the guest of honor with a grin. "Smile when you say that, podnuh" is the best way to keep feathers unruffled.

Finally, hold to your allotted time—and if your allotted time is too long, do less. At a roast, brevity is the soul of twit.

Serving the Roast

A roast is sort of a testy-monial—and in one form or another, it has been with us through the centuries.

Poking fun at our peers and our leaders seems to be a part of human nature. It is instant egalitarianism. For the moment, the poker and the pokee become equals, and all listeners join in at the same level. And, providing the pokes are based on mirth instead of malice, no harm is done.

Throughout history, many societies have provided times, places and events to let off this comedic steam. The court jesters of old needled Numero Uno as roasters do today. Many of Gilbert and Sullivan's operettas were thinly disguised spoofs of contemporary British leaders and royalty. Political cabarets in Germany during the twenties and early thirties provided laughter and dissenting viewpoints until Hitler came to power and all debate ended.

An often quoted line by a character in Shakespeare's *King Henry VI* is, "The first thing we do, let's kill all the lawyers." But in practice, one of the first actions repressive regimes seem to take is to eliminate all the humorists. Tyrants have always found it easier to deal with being talked at than being laughed at.

***

Freedom, therefore, can find no better measurement than the scope and frequency of anti-establishment humor. Which establishment? Any establishment. The Democrats. The Republicans. The Board of Directors. The electric and gas company. The boss. You name it.

Fortunately, we're living at a time and under a political system that imposes no arms limitations on comedic shafting. As a result, the roast has never been more popular, and chances are, before long, you will be asked to participate in one. If the conditions, advantages and risks are acceptable and you choose to do the roast, here are some suggestions that may keep you from getting burnt:

First, positioning. Obviously, if you are the roastee, the guest of honor, you go on last.

If you are one of the roasters, you automatically become part of a group of speakers who will be sharing a limited amount of subject material. Your position in the program becomes a key element in your success.

Now it might be felt that the order and structure of an event is the prerogative and responsibility of the program committee. On the other hand, it usually isn't all that easy to get speakers—particularly speakers for a roast. I have also found that since most participants accept the performing slot they are given—those who negotiate get what they ask for.

I have never been shy about nudging, pushing, wheeling and dealing my speaker clients into that position on a program where they will be seen and heard to best advantage.

***

An audience rarely analyzes why a speaker goes well or badly. They don't consider the effectiveness of the sound system, the ventilation in the room, the lighting, the length of the program, the order of the program and all of the other major and minor conditions that affect their judgment and appreciation of the entire event and each element in it.

Consequently, speakers performing under optimum conditions will meet with considerably more laughter, applause and good will than if they made the very same presentation under minimum or adverse conditions. Need selling? Take your best two jokes or stories and do one of them early in a three-hour program. Do the other late in the three-hour program. The audience will be your instructor.

So what sort of positioning do you negotiate for in a roast? I used to ask for the second spot among the roasters. I did this on the theory that it would be best to let the first speaker cope with getting the audience's attention and interest. The emcee or toastmaster *should* break the ice and focus the group on the program, but all too often it falls to the first speaker to overcome the remnants of restlessness, conversation, and dessert and coffee consumption.

These factors still concern me, but I no longer ask for second slot on a roast program. I try to get first. I feel that the disadvantages are far outweighed by the one big advantage: You get first crack at all the fat, juicy recognition points associated with the roastee's personality, job and career.

***

In a roast situation, when you get there first, you don't even have to have the most. The audience is hearing the high-recognition subject matter for the first time at this event. The initial impact of the irreverence and the freshness of it all can turn even weak lines into winners.

But with each succeeding use of the identical subject peg, the audience's resistance stiffens. If they hear the word "golf" and you're the fifth speaker to address the guest of honor's golf game, the audience is already thinking, "All right, how bad is he?" and your joke answer had better be a blockbuster.

To avoid this problem, try to snare first place in the roast line-up and let those next in line deal with repetition as best they can.

What if you can't lead the parade? Sometimes the best laid plans of mice and Machiavellis "gang aft agley." What do you do if first spot is taken but you still have a choice?

I would then go over the list of your fellow roasters and ask for a spot as early in the program as possible but immediately following the speaker who figures to be the bomb of the evening. The whole idea is to follow someone who doesn't stop the show—but who does slow it up.

***

While roasts aren't an Olympic event, there is always a competitive factor involved. You don't want to follow a professional comedian or an experienced banquet speaker. Even if you do well, if they do substantially better, your efforts will suffer in comparison. So pick your spot and try to spot the easy pickings.

Now what about the roast situation where you don't have a choice and you're positioned at the end of a long line of roasters? If you decide against suddenly remembering a previous engagement, then keep your presentation short, lively and different.

Short—because, to the audience, five minutes of jokes early in the program will seem like three. Five minutes of jokes late in the program will seem like twenty-three.

Lively—because a tiring audience requires more to hold its attention. Become a little more expansive. Step up your pace a bit. Address or involve other members of the head table or audience. It's the home stretch; psychologically and literally you're at the back of the pack, so your oratorical stretch drive has to be a strong one.

Most important of all, your presentation should be different. Don't even consider addressing any of the easy, high-visibility aspects of the guest of honor. By the fourth roaster, it will be old news. Concentrate on peripheral or invented bio material, and book passage on any additional flights of fancy you may have. These could include gag awards, plaques, gifts, visuals, props—anything to add a new comedic note to the proceedings.

***

Roasts do tend to excite the competitive spirit. After such events, you frequently hear postmortems that decide who did best, who didn't. Who won, who lost. But in preparing for a roast, it might be useful to consider Grantland Rice's thought: "It's not who won or lost, it's how you played the game."

Except for show business roasts where the competition is traditional and intense, the average business or charity roast need not result in winners and losers. All can be winners if a little cooperation is employed.

On occasion I have written for a speaker who has frequently shared events with a top comedian. The two are good friends, and so the goal is not for one to top the other, but for both to look good and be well received.

To achieve this, I am in touch with the comedian's head writer, and between us, we divvy up the subject matter. He tells me what subjects his client will cover, and I tell him what areas my client will address. We keep in touch right up until the event so that we are not blindsided by a new approach on either side. We may also exchange jokes or premises that more appropriately belong in the other client's speech.

The result of this comedic detente is a balanced performance, the elimination of potential tensions between the two performers, a better total product for audience, and dual winners. If there are only a few roasters, this humane approach should be considered.

Now it may appear to some that this obsession with placement on a program is overdone. So you do your thing first, fifth or tenth—does it really matter that much?

***

I can only tell you about an incident that happened over thirty years ago, but it has been a useful reminder to me ever since. I was friends with a young comedian who sometimes volunteered to be on shows that were given at civic organizations or hospitals. (In the days before comedy clubs, these shows provided a good place to try our new material.)

During the week before Christmas, I went with the comedian to a veterans hospital where he was to be the featured performer on their show. There were a few hundred servicemen and women in the audience. Most were seated in chairs, but a few rows of wheel-chair and wheeled stretcher patients were up front. The hall had an overlay of Christmas and New Year decorations in a brave attempt to add a festive seasonal note to the event.

Well, the first part of the show was acceptable but unexceptional. A dance act and a juggler got on and off without mishap. But then, as my comedian friend was getting ready to go on, the producer of the show came up to him leading a rather forlorn looking young man in a faded hospital bathrobe. He explained that the young man was a patient and would the comedian mind if he just went out and sang a song or two before the comedian closed the show? After a quick and un-impressed survey of the newcomer's appearance, my friend, with a magnanimous sweep of his hand, said, "Be my guest."

The comedian and I stood in the wings as this waif-like veteran padded out to center stage, tightened the belt on his bathrobe, nodded to the piano player, and then proceeded to sing "I'm Dreaming of a White Christmas" in a soft tenor voice that had to be fashioned by angels. My friend started to groan quietly.

The second number was "Danny Boy," and before it was half over, the audience was experiencing a group lump in its throat. Beside me, the groan had turned into a whimper.

And finally, to these few hundred sick and lonely patients, miles and miles away from family, friends and loved ones, our bathrobe Caruso closed with "Going Home." The collective tears, before and behind the curtain, would have threatened Hoover Dam.

The bathrobe left, the emcee returned, and my comedian friend was then introduced as that "funny, funny man who'll have you rolling in the aisles"—and out he went. What can I tell you? For the next ten minutes, if that auditorium had been a public library, no one would ever have had to point to the SILENCE IS REQUESTED sign.

So if you are ever tempted to doubt the importance or the wisdom of positioning, think again—or you may also be "Going Home"—in silence.

Jokes for the Roast

Note that most of the put-downs in this section are aimed at men. At this time, very few women participate on roast panels, and it is even more unusual to see a woman being roasted. Should this pattern change in the future, you will find that most of the jokes in this section (and every other category in this handbook) are not gender-specific. The lines can easily be targeted at the opposite sex. However, as with all put-down jokes, caution is advised. Current social mores and personal sensitivities should always be taken into consideration.

First, let's talk about how long he's been with us. When he first joined this company James Earl Jones was a soprano.

In his many years with our company, he has always taken advantage of fringe benefits. With his fringe—the benefit is—he has never had to buy a comb.

When it comes to romance, he has now reached that age, when if his wife has a headache—he hides the aspirin.

A determined man, you always know where he stands. It's usually right in front of a refrigerator.

We're talking about a man so rich, he actually uses the mini-bar in his hotel room.

A sensitive man. A vulnerable man. Last year he went to Ireland—and to this day wonders why the Blarney Stone didn't kiss back.

A self-made man, you can tell that from the car he drives. First time I've ever seen a Ferrari pickup.

A man who was once given the key to the city—and asked to lock it as he left

Is this man a salesman? He could sell microwave ovens to sushi restaurants.

We're talking about a man who, even before the age of computers, had a laptop. It was his stomach.

Throughout his many years with our company he has developed a well-deserved reputation as a go-getter. And we all know what he goes to get—coffee and a jelly doughnut.

In the race for excellence he has always lead by example. And you know how fast moving lead is.

Our guest has given new meaning to the phrase "self-esteem." Self-esteem is the joining of two words: Self—an awareness of one's being, one's position, one's status. And steem, which as we all know—is hot air.

There are many who have described our speaker by simply saying, "This is a leader!" There are even more who have said, "This—is a leader?"

They don't call _____ mega-mouth for nothing.

I think I can say without fear of contradiction that we are here tonight to honor a man who wouldn't be here tonight if we weren't here tonight to honor him.

He has spoken to audiences in all fifty states and in twelve foreign countries—a tribute to his subject, his eloquence, his style and his wash-and-wear tuxedo.

I'm sure you all remember that last year he was kidnapped and the kidnappers asked his wife for $10,000 to bring him back. And I'm sure you also remember his wife's answer: "I only give to worthy causes."

A convention like this is such a learning experience. For one thing, you learn that time is money. Just last night _____ learned that time is money when someone asked him, "Wanna have a good time?"—and it cost him $100 and his watch.

The person we honor tonight is a man of Olympian modesty—the only one I know who ever got a gold medal in humble.

A religious man, he has been known to spend four hours a day with his head bowed down. One hour at prayer, asking for divine forgiveness—and three hours at golf, asking for divine forgiveness.

I won't say how much he's in the rough, but he does have the only golf cart with four-wheel drive.

He hasn't had an easy life. We're talking about the only person who ever got a letter in the mail telling him he may already be a loser.

He had all the usual childhood afflictions—measles, mumps, chicken pox, parents.

He always wanted to be his own best friend but his mother wouldn't let him hang around with that kind of person.

A proud man, he has never considered himself bald. He prefers to think of it as having a full head of skin.

In his long career as a public speaker, he has often been referred to as bombastic. Some have called him a bom—and the rest have called him a bastic.

What can I tell you? This man is a spellbinder. And you all know what a spell is. It's something that puts you to sleep.

You wouldn't call him the most exciting speaker in the world. When he gives a talk, anything after "Good evening, ladies and gentlemen" is a comeback.

If the Roastee Is Short: He is a man we have all put on a pedestal—the better to honor him, the better to revere him, and the better to see him.

As you know, he is something of a casual dresser. I won't say what he usually looks like, but we're talking about a man who has to stay indoors on trash pick-up day.

Fast? You're looking at the only jogger who suffers from jet lag.

Clumsy? Who trips over rain?

Tonight we honor a man who has proven beyond the shadow of a doubt that you don't have to have dyslexia to get things backwards.

. . . a man who is ready for anything—he's the only one I know who carries a Swiss Army beeper.

. . . a man who, early in his career, was told there is no such thing as free lunch—and ever since, he's been stuffing rolls in his pocket at breakfast.

Clever? He once got a $65,000 government grant to study whether there were more important things than money.

You might say the boss is our leading indicator. He indicates what he wants done and then he leads you to it.

Our office was a pioneer in the use of flextime. 9 to 5 when the boss is in—10 to 3 when he's not.

The nice part about working for *(boss)* is, you can rest secure in the knowledge that a robot will never take your job. Where are they going to find a machine that grovels?

Rich? Who else do you know keeps in shape by folding money?

Rich? The I.R.S. uses him as a credit reference.

Confused? This man has a callus on his head just from scratching.

We originally put him in charge of refreshments but it didn't work out. He flunked Kool-Aid. Couldn't figure out how to get a quart of water into that little envelope.

I won't say how old our guest of honor is, but there's a reason why his college diploma is written in Latin. That's what people were speaking then.

He has always followed one guiding principle: "Lead me not into temptation—I can get there quicker by myself!"

A man who, when it comes to romance, can only be described as Lincolnesque. His last four scores were seven years ago.

Isn't he great? There's a man of a thousand stories—if you count the 500 times he's told all two of them.

A religious man, his one goal in life was to become a priest—but he didn't want to work on Sundays.

As for the work he has done for our company, it goes without saying—mostly because, every afternoon there's a ball game, he goes without saying.

She's at that stage of life where she needs only three things to keep her happy—the scent of magnolia, the Oil of Olay, and the Milk of Magnesia.

She's very proud of the fact that she and her daughter are often mistaken for sisters. Oldest looking kid you've ever seen!

I asked _____ how they were going to celebrate their Golden Wedding anniversary and he said they were going to eat, drink, sing, dance and then go home for some bonsai sex. I said, "What's bonsai sex?" He said, "When you keep it to a minimum."

It's fascinating the way he changes his position. He has the only set of convictions with a rollbar.

They say you can't take it with you. Right? Wrong! Our guest tonight has the world's only set of asbestos luggage.

He comes from a poor but honest family. How poor? They were so poor that living in poverty was beyond their means.

Conservative? Our guest is the only man I know who wears a button-down T-shirt.

A cautious man, he has always been known for planning ahead. In fact, he got his very first job at the age of nine when he became a paper boy for the _(local newspaper)_—after being assured they had a retirement plan.

It's all right to be neat, but who combs sauerkraut?

Dull? This man is boring even when he's listening!

Even as a kid, those far-away places with strange-sounding names were calling him— Pocatello, Kankakee, Ashtabula.

He's a little upset tonight. We went out to the bar for a drink and he remembered to bring money.

Cheap? Let's just say he saves for tomorrow like there was no today.

As we all know, he is a relaxed, laid-back sort of person who never lets things get to him. These things have included hard work, long hours and punctuality.

Careless? How do you misplace a tattoo?

Old? He can remember when fast food was running over a chicken.

Our guest began life in poor and humble circumstances in Miami Beach. Born in a log cabana . . .

I like that outfit. I didn't know L.L. Bean made tuxedos.

Do you ever get the feeling that life is a test—and you've lost your crib notes?

Now we come to the question: What kind of a job has our guest of honor done for our company over all these years? And for this I'm going to ask all of you to join me in the answer. Everybody—

hold one hand out in front of you, palm down. Good. Now spread your fingers ever so slightly. Very good. Now the last part calls for a little bit of coordination. Shrug and then rock your hand from side to side. *(Lead the audience through each step.)*

It's one thing to take a little work home from the office—but tonight we're talking about someone whose briefcase comes with four wheels and a turn signal.

There is such a thing as being too conscientious. I mean, who wears a beeper to a nude beach?

Today he stands alone in his field—which speaks to either the success of his accomplishments or the failure of his deodorants.

Rich? We're talking about a man whose wallet has its own zip code.

Influential? Dial-A-Prayer calls *him.*

Persuasive? His favorite drink is a martini with a twist of arm.

To his credit, when he first came into this business, he didn't want to make it on his father's reputation. Which was a good thing because his father couldn't make it on it either.

Oh, he may try to put on airs, but a sophisticate he isn't. Give him twelve paper bags and he uses them for a wine rack.

As you know, his favorite sport is golf. I won't say how much time he spends in the rough, but his favorite club is a combination putter and machete.

He's feeling particularly good this evening because last night he bowled 60 points above his I.Q. Bowled a hundred and six!

They say you can't take it with you. Maybe so, but if that includes strawberry shortcake (*or guest's favorite food or drink*), he ain't going.

We're talking about a fella who really enjoys his food. I mean, who else carries around a picture of a refrigerator in his wallet?

In spite of all evidence to the contrary, we are talking about a man who looks on his body as a place of worship—even though he personally may have gone to one too many cake sales.

You can always tell when he's on a serious diet. He leaves the anchovies off his pizza.

His wife, in particular, has been looking forward to this evening. She says life hasn't been much fun for her since that barbecue last summer—when the tenderizer fell into his lap.

He hasn't had an easy time of it. Early in life he heard that women went wild over a guy in uniform—so he became a priest.

He is a man who knows how to survive in the wilderness. And if you ever played golf with him, you know why.

Sneaky? He's the type who'd gift-wrap zucchini.

He came from a very poor family. How poor was it? We're talking about a man who's still holding IOUs from the Tooth Fairy.

In his youth, he was a very serious scholar. Very serious. At college, he used to love football week-ends—because there would always be empty chairs in the library.

He is a man who has always had his eye on politics. Even as a child he collected bubble gum cards of lobbyists.

As a child he was always getting mixed signals from his parents about his height. His mother kept reassuring him that, for his age, he wasn't too short—while his father used him for a foot-stool.

I won't say he's out of fashion, but who else has a necktie with lapels?

You might say it was inevitable that he became a doctor. Even as a kid, his favorite color was pale.

We honor a man whose sex life is directly linked to the Gettysburg Address: "Four score—seven years ago."

He was once married to a computer expert but it was evident from the honeymoon that it wouldn't work out. He could never get used to someone who moaned in Windows 97.

He has always been a man who takes a different view of life from the rest of us. I once looked in his little black book and beside *(female star)*'s name he had written: "Good posture. Likes to bowl."

Unpopular? We're talking about a guy who, last week, tried to join a movie rental club—but the membership voted him down.

And when it comes to golf, we're talking about the only man who yells "Fore!" while putting.

Eat? This is the only man I know who suffers from a very rare ailment—forklift elbow.

A man who has carved a brilliant career for himself by being forthright. Whatever the boss says, he comes forth with "Right!"

A fiercely self-sufficient and independent man— you can tell it by the determined stride he takes while being walked to work by his mother.

During the war, he served his country in the Pentagon. What he served his country was breakfast, lunch and dinner.

When it comes to hobbies, I'm sure we're all aware of his interest in the horse-and-buggy days. If he can't bet on the horses, it drives him buggy.

Some people call him a born loser. This is untrue. He is not a born loser. He had to work at it.

His first job was selling anchovy paste—which wasn't easy. How many anchovies need mending?

He's at that age where he's substituted golf for sex. For three reasons: He scores more; he misses less; and he's always sure of a starting time.

Let's not kid ourselves, when it comes to class, he does have a problem. Who else do you know who goes to the ballet and tries to cut in?

He's a little upset over something that happened today. A moth flew out of his clothes closet and died of a very unusual ailment—Terminal Polyester.

He is a man of all seasons—salt, pepper, paprika, oregano—just so long as it's over food.

Eat? They don't call him the fastest gums in the West for nothing.

I'll tell you what kind of an eater this man is. When he drives home from work and pulls into his driveway, he presses a little button on the dashboard of his car—and his refrigerator door automatically opens.

He's just begun a new exercise program. He takes three quick steps forward, stops—and then his stomach jogs for ten minutes.

As you know, he's been married ____ times. I think he's trying to build up an immunity.

An old-fashioned, conservative kind of guy—he didn't even kiss his wife until after their third date—and fourth child.

A roast is when all is said and fun.

If you want to know what the pecking order around here is, yesterday I phoned DIAL-A-PRAYER—and *(name of boss)* said, "Can you hold?"

The first month as President and Chief Executive Officer of a corporation is always a very painful experience. You get chapped lips from kissing cold mirrors.

It has been said that many executives have within them the seeds of greatness—and with that thought in mind, it gives me great pleasure to introduce one of the seediest our industry has produced.

Self-confident? This man is without a doubt—without a doubt.

A very humble man. A very unobtrusive man. A very democratic man. He doesn't want anyone calling him sir. Kneeling is enough.

A man who, in his thirty years with this company, has made competence a spectator sport.

He is a friendly man, a gregarious man, a communicative man—and through the years I've heard from him on many an occasion—mostly because they always let him make one phone call.

Cheap? Tonight we're honoring a man who will never die—until he can go tourist.

Rich? When he buys a suit, the only thing he has to let out are the pockets.

Rich? You could retire on just what's fallen into his couch.

As you all know, he played basketball in college and who can ever forget that once-in-a-lifetime moment when his teammates hoisted him onto their shoulders and carried him off the court? And told him not to come back until the season was over.

A trusting man, he once sent away for a cologne they said was guaranteed to make him smell taller.

And he's very health conscious. You can tell that from the dinner order they sent in to the chef tonight—186 steaks and a trail-mix.

I won't comment on his physique. Let's just say that if you tried to bury him in the sand, you could run out of beach.

It's not that he hasn't tried. It's just that when it comes to dieting, he takes the cake.

Life hasn't been easy for our guest of honor. One time things got so bad, he wanted to take 100 sleeping pills and end it all. But after the first two, he fell asleep.

His love of travel began at an early age. He was the only kid in the first grade with a pencil box and a passport.

As you all know, he's a hands-on executive. For instance, what he had his hands on today is pretzels, beer and golf-clubs.

In any crisis, he has given new meaning to the phrase "one-minute manager." For one minute, he manages. Then he panics.

Through the years he's acquired a considerable reputation in our company as a troubleshooter. Whenever there's trouble, he's been the first to shoot right out the door.

He is a man who could never be called anti-union. On the other hand, if you added up all of the hours he's spent away from his desk, he is definitely against organized labor.

A man whose work pattern has inspired the Payroll Department to come up with a brand new classification: On-The-Job Retirement.

He is a businessman with an impressive track record. Monday he was at the track. Tuesday he was at the track. Wednesday he was . . .

Our guest tonight is a man who has proven by his own example that where there is smoke—there is a cheap cigar.

Tough? When he was three months old, he was wearing denim diapers.

A confident man. You can tell that from his resume. It's the first time I ever saw Omnipotence listed under Job Skills.

The offspring of very sophisticated parents, he may have been the first baby ever to have been raised on Gerber's Quiche.

He grew up in Beverly Hills and that's tougher than you might think. Bullies used to go up to him and say, "My butler can whip your butler!"

He has known hardship. All of his life he has suffered from poor driving skills—as anyone who has ever played golf with him already knows.

I won't comment on his golf game. Suffice it to say he loses an average of eight golf balls a game—and when he does find one, it's usually lying next to an unconscious person.

He would have excelled in sports if it weren't for one small problem—coordination. We're talking about a man who created one of basketball's most unusual moves—the slam-miss.

He has always been a man of few words—and not too good at spelling those.

As you know, he is a veterinarian. In fact, he graduated from a very prestigious and practical school of veterinary medicine. The first thing they taught him was how to ask a sheep if it has Blue Cross.

A man thousands of people have called "friend"— mostly because they can never remember his name.

I won't say he holds on tight to every penny, but he's the only man I know with Velcro money.

During World War II he was part of the Resistance—but they drafted him anyway.

I won't say how old he is. Let's just say he's at that age when he can no longer put on his socks while standing.

Throughout his many years he has always had a way with women. It's called celibacy.

Our guest is a man of charity who has been widely acclaimed for his work with the Terminally Left-Handed.

This man is so likable—dogs come up and pet *him*.

You can tell so much about a person just by observing the way they dress. For instance, just looking at that outfit he's wearing tonight tells you four things about our guest of honor: He's neat, tidy, affluent and color blind.

He will never be known as a fashion plate. I realize that lots of people wear clip-on ties. He's the only one I know who wears clip-on socks.

And let's face it, he isn't exactly the best-looking person you've ever seen. I mean, let's be honest—he has the only I.D. photo that comes with a warning.

He hasn't been well these past few years. Suffers from a very rare ailment—sclerosis of the charisma.

You might say his destiny was determined when his mother didn't quite make it to the hospital, so he was born in the family car—an Edsel.

Our guest tonight is a man of ambition who once confided to me that his ultimate dream was to have his picture on a postage stamp. It isn't there yet but at least it's in the post office.

Our guest is solid, stable, cautious and conservative in everything he does. Even as a child, his dream was to run away with a traveling law firm.

Oh, there have been times when his astuteness wasn't all that it should have been. For instance, early on when he bought the Brooklyn Bridge. Well, a lot of people have bought the Brooklyn Bridge. On the other hand, he's the only one who ever bought a ticket to San Francisco to see it.

You might have noticed that our guest has been on a diet. I won't say how much weight he's lost but he's now wearing the only shorts in town with a safety catch.

Willpower? He could lose weight on a cruise!

_____ and _____ are both middle-of-the road. Then again, so are potholes.

Doesn't he look great? I've always had the feeling that _____ was vaccinated against middle-age.

A sensitive, compassionate, caring man—he is best known as the creator of our company's motto: IF AT FIRST YOU DON'T SUCCEED—OUT!

Crass? Who opens a six-pack to watch Master-piece Theatre?

Concluding a Roast: And now, we come to the part of the program where we honor our guest posthumorously.

An astute and brilliant leader, in his previous association there was good news and bad news. The good news is that through his efforts, and his efforts alone, an entire new chapter was added to that company's history. The bad news is, it was Chapter Eleven.

He is a man who is known far and wide for his ability to approach every target—far and wide.

A man who can size up a difficult situation in an instant, there is no truth to the base canard that his desk trays are labeled IN, OUT and HUH?

He has always been known as a man who takes his work home with him. Then again, so was Willie Sutton.

Aggressive? He's the only one I know who ever had Executive Burn Out in kindergarten.

Conscientious? He's been on the road so much, his kids think the telephone is Daddy.

For thirty years he's put his nose to the grind-stone—which means it must have been a beaut when he started.

Through the years he has consistently risen to new heights. I know. I've seen his expense account.

He is a man who believes in old-fashioned values—which goes a long way to explaining the quarter tips he leaves in restaurants.

He has a well-deserved reputation for keeping his ear to the ground. That's right. He'll sleep anywhere.

He is a man who has achieved a well-deserved reputation for consistently standing behind his work—watching it pile up and up.

He comes from a very old and a very wealthy family. For 2,000 years after the Garden of Eden, they held the patent rights to sex.

Rich? When he flies, his wallet is considered carry-on luggage.

I couldn't help but notice him out at the buffet where he was eating like a bird—jumping from one plate to another.

Eat? Halfway through Thanksgiving dinner, he sent out for pizza.

He is a quiet man, a humble man, a modest man—except for that brief moment at the end of each week when he locks the door of his office, looks in the mirror and says, "T.G.I.F. Thank God I'm Famous!"

If You Have To Go On Late at a Roast: I know the hour is late and it's been a long evening, but I don't intend to leave this microphone until I've told you every good thing I know about our guest of honor. *(Pause.)* Thank you very much. *(And sit down.)*

241

Do you realize, if it weren't for this lectern, he could have been arrested for loitering?

I want you to know that what you have just heard is nothing but a collection of half-truths—and by now, I don't even know which half.

I listened to the previous speaker with great interest. They say we are what we eat—and I couldn't help but notice that baloney sandwich on his plate.

Everything about our guest projects an image of goodwill. His shirt, his tie, his suit, his shoes—all of them came from Goodwill.

If _____'s mouth were any bigger, it could go condominium.

In all these years, I have never heard anyone say one bad word about him. It usually took several paragraphs.

Always a gentleman, as a youth he helped little old ladies across the street. Which wasn't easy. He lived in Venice.

It has been said that the human body is the epitome of fine art. His is more like a cave painting.

He's a very excitable person. He's the only person I know who has ever yelled, "You lie!" at a fortune cookie!

I won't say how conscientious he is, but last week he was on vacation—and from force of habit he called in sick.

I won't comment on his work habits. Let's just say he's a restaholic.

When Roasting Your Boss: Oh, I could go on—but frankly, I don't want to ruin what up till now has been a very promising career—namely mine.

I won't say how _____ spent most of his time with this company—but rumor has it that the only way he could find his way back to his desk—was to start at the coffee machine.

I'll say one thing for _____, he isn't vain. When the weather turns cold, he has the only toupee with ear flaps.

_____ has one big problem. It takes him an hour and a half to get to work—after he gets there.

Lazy? He once got an Incomplete on a urine test.

A public meeting in _____ said it all. Halfway through, the moderator stopped, looked out over the audience and said, "I heard that! Who called our leader a clown?" And a voice from the back answered, "Who called that clown a leader?"

Old? He remembers when a home computer was an egg timer.

He really looks great. It's as if he's worn out his wrinkles.

He still has a full, thick, luxuriant head of hair but he isn't taking any chances. He's the only one I know who asks the barber for a doggy bag.

In our company, tonight's guest of honor occupies the office where the buck ultimately stops. Mostly because he runs the football pool.

As I look out over this audience, in an age of workaholics, never before have I seen so many people on the wagon.

He started in our business at a very early age. How early? You ever see pin-striped Pampers?

In his many years with the company, he has proven himself an expert in the area of crisis management. Whenever we needed a crisis, he managed it.

Our guest of honor has also known failure. In fact, he left his very first position because of job burnout. The boss took one look at the job he was doing, burned and said, "Out!"

When he left home, they said there would always be a light burning in the window for him. And there is. It says "NO VACANCY."

I'm always suspicious of anyone who fills out an application form and where it says "Interests," puts down "Prurient."

_____ is a man of a few words. Of course, they're recycled a lot.

Fat? If there's anything to reincarnation, he's going to come back as Gary, Indiana.

Her idea of a fast crowd is the express line at the supermarket.

Old? He can remember when if people were "spaced out," they were having trouble with their typewriter.

It's not fair to say he doesn't get any exercise. This man happens to be a very brisk eater.

He's quite modest about it but when it comes to dieting, he's really on a roll—not to mention a doughnut, a Danish, a Twinkie and a Belgium Waffle.

Heavy? Two of his shorts fill the washing machine!

Have you ever seen him in a bathing suit? Looks like a cellulite farm.

I happen to know that deep down this man is very self-centered. Very self-centered. If he had been at the Last Supper, he would have worried about which fork to use.

And lately he's had the feeling that his wife doesn't trust him when he goes away on business trips. She sews name tapes into his clothes—hers.

Loaded? His wallet is a member of the F.D.I.C.

He's also very thrifty. Very thrifty. The only man I know who's listed in the Yellow Pages under CHEAP.

Cheap? On Valentine's Day, who else do you know gives generic perfume?

He is a man with his shoulder to the wheel, his nose to the grindstone and his ear to the ground. Worst posture you ever saw!

You may be interested to know that _____ wrote his speech on recycled paper—which could explain some of the jokes.

You could say that our guest is talented, witty, urbane and intellectually gifted. You could say that—but not if you're under oath.

His idea of a diet is waiting for the microwave oven to finish cooking.

Even as a child he displayed a unique aptitude for business. He was the only kid on his block who had a lemonade stand—with a two-drink minimum.

Our next guest is a man who was always known for being ahead of his time. Then, one day he got his watch fixed and (shrug) . . .

He is also a man of religious convictions. He once did six months for impersonating a priest.

I'd like to give you a penny for your thoughts, but it would be taxation without representation.

Lazy? Last night he called up a Singles Bar and asked if they deliver.

Today we honor a man who doesn't know the meaning of the word dissemble, who doesn't know the meaning of the word fear, who doesn't know the meaning of the word quit. And so, we've all chipped in to get him this dictionary.

What can you really say about a man who has a sign over his desk: THE BEST THINGS IN LIFE ARE ME.

I have never said that _____ is a company man. On the other hand, he's the only one I know with a bumper sticker that says "I BRAKE FOR *(name of boss or CEO)*."

Among his many accomplishments, he has a green thumb. It's from fishing olives out of martinis.

Let's not say he drinks. Let's just say he's forty-six years old and still believes in the Vermouth Fairy.

As you know, he's a little on the short side. A little! He'd have to use elevator shoes to play Toulouse Lautrec.

There are those who say he isn't as sharp as he could be, but there is no truth to the rumor that his mantra is "Huh?"

It's one thing to be neat, but who has a crease in their socks?

Eat? It's the first time I ever saw a mouth with stretch marks.

Unlucky? You know how some people get in *Who's Who?* He gets in *Why Me?*

_____ is rich. How rich is he? How many people do you know have a three-room wallet?

When you're _____, money doesn't mean anything to you anymore. He's so rich, he still bets on the Cubs.

I never said he was cheap. I just said that when it comes to spending, he has a love-hate relationship. He loves money and hates to let it go.

Mean? Who else do you know, would rearrange the chocolates in a Whitman Sampler?

I won't say how much time he's spent in sand traps, but you know how some people go around in a golf cart? With him it's a dune buggy.

Is this man a golfer? He even prays with an interlocking grip.

I'll say one thing for _____: He has always given this company an honest day's work. Sometimes it took him a week to do it.

Our next speaker is a man of science. The inventor of the Rolaid umbrella for acid rain.

Who can ever forget that day, many years ago, when _____ had greatness thrust upon him—with instructions to deliver it to Winston Churchill.

Old? His copy of *Playboy* comes with a snooze alarm.

Creative? He couldn't ad-lib "Shhhh!" in a public library.

Through the years he has managed his department as competently, as effectively and as unobtrusively as any organization I know—with the possible exception of the EPA.

Furthermore, he has given new insights into the age-old work ethic. For instance, some people might say that he consistently arrives late for work. He looks on it as arriving early for the coffee break.

As you know, our guest of honor is a humanitarian. Who can ever forget his impassioned support of mercy flushing for terminal roaches.

Tonight we honor a humble man. A man who has only wanted two things from this world: 1. For his body to be sent to Johns Hopkins when he passes on. And 2. For it to be sent to *(current femme fatale)* while he's still here.

When the Roastee Is Fat: And I love to see _____'s gorgeous bride standing beside him—the "10" and the ton.

He is a man of strict moral and fiscal standards. Never in his life has he ever grabbed for a drink, a blonde or a check.

He isn't cheap. He just has an impediment in his reach.

I won't comment on his lack of class. Suffice it to say, he still can't understand why they don't sell Chivas Regal in cans.

Lately he's been on a half-hearted diet. You can tell it's half-hearted. Who orders grapefruit with gravy?

Rich? When his daughter got married, they had a money tree at the reception. It was a sequoia.

Rich? Last year he took a cab when he went to the hospital for an operation—and told the driver to wait.

If the Roastee Is a Lawyer: I won't comment on his practice but when it comes to serving his clients, he believes in leaving no stone unturned. Which is fortunate, because that's where he finds a lot of his clients.

During World War II, he worked in the underground. He was a clerk in Macy's basement.

Old? The only thing 38-24-36 reminds him of is his Captain Midnight Decoder Ring.

If there were a Tooth Fairy for hair, can you imagine what *(bald roastee)* would be worth today?

Let's not say he's lazy. Let's just say that when it comes to burning ambition, he could be classified as flame retardant.

Our guest of honor was in *(profession or field)* for five years before he told anybody. He likes to keep his troubles to himself.

Our guest tonight has often been compared to the Vice President of the United States. No one's been able to figure out what he does either.

Early in his career he stood apart as a person who believes in just three words—GO FOR IT! And he did—coffee, cigarettes, Danish, you name it.

Even as a child, our guest of honor had his eye on the big-time. Other kids had imaginary playmates. He had an imaginary board of directors.

He's also the author of a book that has been so helpful to those in academe. It's called *How to Get Out of Teaching and into Money.*

He's also very much into health. Before every meal he orders a double martini with a twist of lemon—for medicinal purposes. The double martini to avoid stress, anxiety and tension—and the twist of lemon to avoid scurvy.

He comes from a very poor family. Very poor. You know how kids today borrow the family car on Saturday nights? He used to borrow the family shoes.

He has what can only be described as a dream job. Every fifteen minutes they have to wake him up.

And before we go any further, I want you to know there is no truth to the rumor that _____'s speeches cause boredom in laboratory rats.

One of his outstanding features is a glorious head of hair. No one has ever questioned the magnificence of what can only be described as his exceptional head of hair. In all fairness, there are those who contend that it's nature's way of compensating for what's underneath.

He isn't exactly the sharpest person I've ever met. I came to that conclusion the day I saw him trying to buy a motorcycle with a four wheel drive.

I won't say how long he took to graduate, but for a while there they weren't sure which he'd reach first—Senior Prom or Senior Citizen.

You might say he's reached the age where they only put four or five candles on the birthday cake—one for each tooth.

Tonight we honor a man whose career and figure have grown by leaps and pounds.

A man whose face is his fortune—because he spends most of his money feeding it.

I happen to know that he is a little concerned about his weight. To _____, designer jeans is a toga.

Fat? Who else has a driver's license with the words: PHOTO CONTINUED ON THE OTHER SIDE.

I once tried to meet _____ through a mutual friend—only he didn't have one.

You have to admit one thing: _____ does not make the same mistake twice. But he does have a way of finding new ones.

Our guest is well-known for his support of so many noble causes. He has always been willing to give of his time—to give of his energy—to give of his creative thinking. Money—*(shake your head and waggle your outstretched hand)*.

The boss just complimented me on running a very safe department. I think that's what he meant. He said that none of my people seem to be straining themselves.

We have a boss who eats, drinks, sleeps and breathes business. When you go to his home, he shows you office movies.

He is a generous boss. Who can ever forget that time he went on a profit-sharing kick? If you mentioned profit-sharing, that's what you'd get.

Our company finally gave up its very fair, very liberal, very progressive "promote from within" policy. The boss ran out of sons.

The boss is really into exercise. If you ask for a raise, he tells you to take a walk.

Our boss is something of a conservative. He still thinks an obscene gesture is reaching for your paycheck.

He's a very sensitive boss. You can tell that by the way he fires people. He takes them to lunch and orders theirs to go.

What can you really say about _____? He's like a whoopee cushion on the seat of power.

He is a boss with a sense of humor. Many's the time he has told us about the funny thing that happened to him on his way to the office. And if you don't laugh, a funny thing happens to you on your way out of the office.

For a young man to succeed in his job these days, it never hurts to be an S.O.B. A Son Of the Boss.

There is only one substitute for being right—being boss.

I don't think the boss is going to be happy until he has a yes-computer.

Tonight we honor a man who, throughout his thirty years with this company, was never too busy to see anyone. Mostly because he was never too busy.

Cheap? He once said to Albert Einstein, "A penny for your thoughts."

Uncouth? If he had a box at the opera, it would be popcorn.

I understand he's a great practitioner of TM—Total Mediocrity.

We've got a boss who's all heart. He said he wouldn't give us an extra week for our summer vacations but he'd do the next best thing—put a sunlamp bulb in the Xerox machine.

What can we really say about our guest of honor tonight? He's the only man I know who signs his name with an X—and then misspells it.

Old? At his last birthday party, they lit the candles on his cake, put a grill over it and cooked nine steaks and a rib roast.

Conceited? His nose is so high in the air, yesterday he inhaled a sparrow.

Important? When he calls DIAL-A-PRAYER—he doesn't get a recording.

Insecure? He goes to confession with a lawyer.

Cheap? Yesterday he found a box of aspirin. Now he's trying to get a headache.

Responding to the Roast

All I can say after a speech like that is "May you be a light sleeper—and may the person living upstairs take a correspondence course in polka."

I want to thank the committee for limiting the previous speakers to five minutes each. It reminded me of something I have in our kitchen—a trash compactor.

I know the previous speakers are sitting there pleased with themselves—but I have to remind them that in the washroom there is also a device that dispenses hot air—but never enough to get the job done.

Thank you and good evening. And for those on the panel with a short attention span—thank YOU and good evening.

I read that men's brains grow smaller as they get older—but somehow I didn't expect a demonstration of it tonight.

If the Roaster Is Short: Hearing those remarks is like digging into a grapefruit. It's amazing what a little squirt can do.

This may be hard to believe, but I've really enjoyed their program. I had never heard drive-by speakers before.

You may have noticed me taking notes during their remarks. Some of you may have thought I was writing down rebuttals. Not so, I was writing down names to take out of the will.

It's always a pleasure to follow speakers whose excellence in communication has never been questioned. Mostly because it's never been mentioned.

I'd like to say what a wonderful job they all did— but I'm under oath.

First, I want to congratulate them for doing the best they could considering their medical condition—osteoporosis of the funny bone.

I want to thank the previous speakers for what can only be described as verbal terrorism.

As I listened to the previous speakers, I realized that the latest findings are correct—airbags can be dangerous.

I want to thank the previous speakers for the way they almost rose to the occasion. It isn't easy being among the humor impaired.

First, I want to thank the previous speakers for their dedication to keeping this a humor-free zone.

Acknowledging a Female Roaster: And what can you say about _____? She's like Mother Teresa with an attitude.

Tonight has brought back so many memories. In particular, it brought back the memory of the time I spent a night in the Kansas City hotel immediately beside the stockyards. And this evening, like that evening, I can truthfully say I have never heard so much bull in all my life.

First, let me say how much I've enjoyed this evening. The reason I can say that is, I'm not under oath.

As you know, in all these years with the company, I have only asked for three things from my staff: honesty, integrity and idolatry.

First, I want to thank the previous speaker—a man of many talents. As you can see, humor isn't one of them.

All I can say after an evening like this "Never mind guns. Register tongues!"

They told me this was going to be a bang-up evening. What they didn't tell me is who was going to get banged up.

They really happen to be a very spiritual, pious and devout group of people. As we all witnessed, they have even given up laughs for Lent.

I was told that in recruiting the speakers for tonight's program, the committee left no stone unturned. I think I should have warned the committee what you find under stones.

First, I want to say how much I've enjoyed the program up till now. And I owe it all to two things *(then pull from each of your ears a wad of cotton) . . .*

Roasts, Taking Risks —See (1) MISTAKES; (2) KINDER, GENTLER COMEDY

Rural Audiences

Our speaker is a man who has been outstanding in his field—praying for rain (or "higher prices").

S

"Savers" —See CONTROLLING YOUR AUDIENCE

School Functions

Before we begin, I have one message to read: Would the owner of the 1998 Cadillac with the telephone, bar, TV set and *(name of school)* faculty parking sticker, please report to the head table? There's nothing wrong. We just want to know how you do it.

Seating

Would all those who are standing please take your seats? I can't see the people in back. *(Wait for them to do so.)* Thank you. *(Then look beyond them and comment:)* Would you mind standing up again?

Self-Deprecating Humor —See THE USES AND LIMITS OF HUMOR

Seminars

Seminars tend to be expensive. In a democracy, speech is free but listening costs.

Sensitive Subjects and Humor —See THE USES AND LIMITS OF HUMOR

Set-Up Line —See *Don't Neglect the Facts* at DON'TS
. . . IF YOU WANT TO GET LAUGHS

Sexism —See (1) ADVICE—AND HOW TO IGNORE IT;
(2) ASSESSING YOUR AUDIENCE

Sexist Jokes —See ASSESSING YOUR AUDIENCE

Shorter Rather Than Longer —See ASSESSING YOUR
AUDIENCE

Singer, Loud —See After a Loud Singer

Singling Out One Audience Member —See USING
HUMOR WHEN YOU'RE AFRAID TO USE HUMOR

Sipping a Drink —See After You Sip From a Glass

Slang —See ASSESSING YOUR AUDIENCE

Slide Presentations (how not to give) —See THE
HARD WORK OF HUMOR

Slides / Visuals

When a Slide Is Upside-Down: Now, as those
of you who are standing on your head already
know, this slide shows the *(and describe the content).*

When a Slide Is Totally Out of Focus: Now for
those of you who don't dig Picasso, let me adjust
this.

Slow to the Lectern

When Someone Is Slow in Coming Up to the Microphone: Isn't that wonderful? I think he has two speeds—SLOW and STOP.

Sneezing, When You

Excuse me. *(Pull a bill from your wallet, handle it as you would a handkerchief, sneeze and then throw the bill away and say:)* If there's one thing I hate it's ostentation.

Excuse me. *(Start your speech again, then stop and "ad-lib:")* I don't know why I did that. This subject is nothing to be sneezed at.

Snowstorm —See (1) During a Snowstorm; (2) Winter and Cold Places

Social Responsibility and Humor —See KINDER, GENTLER COMEDY

Sound System Problems —See Equipment

Speakers Themselves

As a speaker, I've only had two complaints from audiences. One, that I talk so loud they can't fall asleep. And two, that I talk so long they can't stay awake.

As a speaker, he has often been compared to Abraham Lincoln delivering the Gettysburg Address. When he finishes his speech, there is also sorrow, tears and mourning—especially by the program committee.

Poise is when you finish your speech and the toastmaster thanks you for taking time out of your busy schedule to be a part of their program—and you nod and smile graciously knowing full well that the only thing on your calendar is a little coffee from breakfast.

I used to get nervous when giving a speech but then I read that it helps to think of the entire audience as being naked. And so, at this very moment, I'm standing up here imagining everyone in this audience as being naked. And it really works. I no longer suffer from nervousness. Eyestrain, yes.

The First Law of Public Speaking: Whenever anyone is introduced as someone who needs no introduction, at least 60% of the audience will say, "Who?"

Personally, I have never been conceited—and I can't tell you how much I admire myself for that.

Let me put this into plain English. I'll translate it for the lawyers later.

There's an old saying that goes, "Flattery will get you nowhere." That's not true. Flattery is what got me up here on this platform tonight.

If you've already heard this story, please don't stop me because it's the only one I know.

A lot of people dread getting up in front of an audience. As one of them put it, "To me, public speaking is anathema. Every time I do it, I make anathema self!"

We had a real good session this morning. The coffee showed up and the speaker didn't.

Making a speech is like watering a lawn. You're satisfied if just a quarter of it sinks in.

First, let me start off by saying I have some good news and some bad news. The good news is, this is what I had prepared for tonight *(hold up your speech)* and I had planned to read every word of it. The bad news is, I still do.

At the very start, let me just say that we both have something in common. You don't know what I'm going to say—and neither do I.

Before I begin, I want you to know that the following speech has been edited for television. I cut 20 minutes out of it so we could all get home in time for the game on Channel 2.

As some of you may know, I'm appearing here tonight for two very good reasons. The first reason is your Program Committee was trying to find a speaker who's intelligent, entertaining, sophisticated and has a compelling message— and they did. The second reason is, he got sick so they called me.

Some people suffer from stage fright. I don't. The stage doesn't bother me at all. It's the audience that scares the hell out of me!

At one time or another, I think each of us has wished we could turn back the clock. I know if I could turn back the clock just 45 minutes, I'd be the happiest person in this room. 'Cause that's when I left my speech on the kitchen table.

I don't want to brag, but the last time I did this it brought the audience to its feet. And they never sat down again until they reached their cars.

As they say at the Dairy Convention: "Mooing right a long . . ."

If I'm a little hesitant, you'll have to excuse me. This is the first after-dinner speech I've ever made—except for yelling at my kids in McDonald's.

I want you to sit back, relax and enjoy. There won't be anything heavy tonight. You know how some speakers come up with brainstorms? With me, it's more like a light drizzle.

Somebody told me that the way to overcome stage fright is to picture everyone sitting in the audience in the nude. *(Look around the audience with a happy smile; then pick up a few blank pages from the speakers stand, throw them into the air and say:)* To hell with the speech!

I have nothing against an audience that waits with bated breath to hear what I have to say— providing what they bait it with isn't bourbon.

For those of you who have never seen a professional speaker, picture a tongue with a meter.

Too often a speech is when your body rises to the occasion—but your mind remains seated.

On every speaker's wall,
This warning should be hung:
If your problem is holding an audience—
Then why not just hold your tongue?

If you don't mind, I'll be referring to a few speech points I've put on these cards. It's called "Help me fake it through the night."

Beware the speaker who comes with Fortune 500 credentials and a fortune cookie speech.

Unnecessary words are the bane of good speeches. Let me repeat that—

The trouble with many speeches is long sentences—created by people who can't tell the difference between a comma and a coma.

I'm going to make this brief because _____ warned me that this group has a marvelous way of making a long story short. You leave.

You do get a little insecure when your secretary refers to the office machine that collates your speech pages as the pooper scooper.

You could tell the conference wasn't taking any chances when _____ opened the first meeting with "Good morning!"—and it was tabled.

As you know, this is a research facility and we've grown rather accustomed to putting in twelve hour days. Eight hours trying to find a cure for the common cold and four hours trying to find a parking space for the common car.

I worked a room in Vegas that was so big, by the time I got to the microphone, I had jet lag.

After dinner speeches should be like after dinner mints: They should be refreshing, compact and serve a purpose.

Motivational speakers are people who stand up and say there is no such thing as a free lunch—immediately after finishing one.

If You're Obviously Nervous: I'm sorry. The same thing always happens when I have to give a speech—my heartbeat switches from automatic to manual. *(Thump your heart area with the side of your fist.)*

(Pick up a glass of water and start to drink from it. Then pause, hold up your hand for patience, reach under the lectern, bring out a cocktail glass, pour some of the water into it, toast the audience and drink. Explain:) It's still water—but I'm more used to the grip.

I'm always suspicious of any speaker who starts off by saying, "It gives me great pleasure"—and isn't referring to liquor, cigars or sex.

I don't want to be critical, but I can't help but notice that one of the big problems some speakers have is a complete lack of sophistication, savoir faire *(pick up a glass of water, drink a little, throw your head back and gargle; then put the glass down and add:)* and couth.

I'm not used to speaking to such a large audience. The one thing that gives me courage is that I'm speaking on my favorite subject—me.

266

My score for a speaker goes up a few notches,
When he speaks with a watch that he fre-
  quently watches.
But it's lowered again, when before he gets
  through,
He's got us all watching our own watches too!

When you consider how many people have been
bored to death, maybe we ought to register
speeches.

As your brochure sees you, you're a talented, experienced, acclaimed and accomplished speaker
worth every penny of the fee you charge. As the
Program Committee sees you, you're a tongue
with a meter.

The biggest problem speakers have is convincing
program committees it may be gab, but it's not
going to be a gift.

We're living in confused times. Last night I heard
a speaker say, "We've got to keep prayer out of
the public schools." And a voice at the back of
the hall yelled, "Amen!"

People always ask me why I wear a big red ten
gallon hat *(or some other very noticeable article of
clothing)* and I tell them. It has to do with taking
a positive but practical view of life. For instance,
I know that no matter what happens, the good
Lord is watching over us. Then again, there are
now six billion of us, so I want to make darn sure
He can pick *me* out of the crowd.

*If You're Standing Beside Someone Who's Very
Big, Powerful and Muscular:* Now I know how Fay
Wray felt.

267

I realize I may have gone a little over my time—but that's what happens when you have a captive audience and a free speaker.

With your permission, I'm going to read this paper. I'm going to read it for three reasons: One, I have a very poor memory—and the other two I can't remember.

Speaker Who Is Bald —See Bald Speaker

"Speaker Who Needs No Introduction" —See (1) OPENER: THE FIRST TWO MINUTES OF YOUR SPEECH; (2) Introductions

Speaking Techniques —See LESSONS I LEARNED FROM LOWELL THOMAS

Speeches Without Laughs —See THE HARD WORK OF HUMOR

SPEECHWRITERS: The Care and Heeding of Speechwriters

The classic story about speechwriters concerns a corporate wordsmith who considered himself to be overworked, underpaid, unloved, unsung and unappreciated. One day it all became too much for him and he decided to quit—but not with the usual letter of resignation. He decided to do one last speech for his boss, a speech that would wipe the slate clean of all the injustices, real and fancied, he had ever suffered. He began work on the chief executive's speech to the stockholders for the firm's annual meeting.

The date of the event arrived. The chief executive mounted the podium with a smile on his face and the unread speech in his hands. He looked out over the audience, ad-libbed a few pleasantries, put on his reading glasses and began: "My friends, you have read a lot of annual reports and you have heard a lot of optimistic forecasts of future prospects. But what you are about to hear now will make them all pale into insignificance. In the next five minutes I will tell you how, in the coming fiscal year, we will double our gross, triple our net, quadruple the price of our stock and describe a new product that is so profoundly different in its concept that it will be the dominant influence in the world for the next one thousand years!"

The chief executive acknowledged the thunderous applause. He then turned to page two, a page that was blank except for these words in the speechwriter's hand: "Okay, you S.O.B. You're on your own!"

I don't know of an equivalent story that dramatizes the woes that chief executives have suffered at the hands of writers. Late drafts, leaden prose, sloppy research, ten thousand words instead of one verbal picture—speakers have been done in by them all. Nevertheless, the marriage between executive and speechwriter is a necessary one. It may often be past the honeymoon stage but with a little tender loving care on both sides, it need never call for a ticket to Reno.

***

I began my career as a comedy writer for show business. I wrote books of professional humor—46 to date. I went into television and spent almost a decade writing for Jack Paar and Red Skelton. I also began a topical humor service called Orben's Current Comedy.

Initially, subscribers to *Orben's Current Comedy* were performers—comedians, deejays and variety acts looking for new one-liners to add to their material. Then a new type of subscriber became a factor—corporate executives, political figures and community leaders. These speakers had discovered that because of television, audiences were judging all speakers by the professional standards set by their favorite performers.

Executives could no longer tell a time-worn story and then bumble through 45 minutes of deadly drivel and expect to get away with it. Like it or not, corporate and political speakers had entered the world of show business. And so they turned, and continue to turn, to help offered by professionals in the performing arts. So let's take a look at some of the things show business has known for centuries that can also benefit the worlds of business and politics.

In Hollywood or on Broadway, any writer who doesn't show up to see the talk-through, rehearsals and opening night of his or her creation would be considered disinterested, disloyal, foolish—or all of the above. In politics and business, it is usually considered a great honor for the speechwriter to be invited to the final event. It's a reward rather than a condition necessary to his job. I have known speechwriters for major executives who turn out scores of speeches each year and have no idea how the final product went. Was it performed well? Badly? What did the audience respond to? What turned them off? The writer will never know unless he's there and, if he isn't, will go on repeating mistakes and having his creativity frozen in place.

***

Speakers do not perform in a vacuum and writers do not write in one. Each speech, each performance is a learning experience and one that should be shared by both members of the creative team. Curiously, the speaker is less able to assess the impact and effectiveness of a speech than a writer hearing it as part of the audience. The speaker is too caught up with the needs of the moment: Reading, remembering, gesturing, working to all sections of the room, selling and winning over his listeners. The writer, removed from all of these tensions, can make a much more realistic study of what is happening and what can be done to improve both the writing and the speaking next time out.

Beyond the performing considerations, there are other very practical reasons for having the writer accompany the speaker to the event. Quite often, something in the day's news or some special problem that is only discovered when the executive arrives on the scene has to be addressed. The speechwriter, background research in hand, is able to immediately confer with his principal, receive direction, write or rewrite and keep his client on top of the situation.

During my two and a half years at the White House as speechwriter and then Director of the Speechwriting Department for President Ford, a writer always accompanied the President on speaking occasions. Sometimes the last minute fine-tuning of the words was minimal. Sometimes a dramatic improvement was inspired by the excitement of the event itself. There's nothing like a fast-approaching deadline to clear the thinking processes. It's like intellectual caffeine.

Perhaps the most telling justification for the presence of the speechwriter occurred when it was learned at the last minute that we had been misinformed as to the nature and interests of a specific audience. The speech that had been prepared did not really speak to the concerns of the group. Fortunately, the speechwriter (with heroic help and research from home base in Washington) was able to create a brand new speech in the three and a half hours it took for Air Force One to fly to the event.

***

Sometimes the emergency is trivial, but minor crises can also be turned around to good effect. In October 1975, President Ford flew to Knoxville, Tennessee, to speak at a White House Conference on Domestic and

Economic Affairs. Shortly before Air Force One landed, Terry O'Donnell, the President's Appointments Secretary, came over to me with a worried look. Terry was responsible for researching and then suggesting to the President who should be named in his opening acknowledgements of the host organization and head table notables. He said, "Bob, there are going to be so many top people on the platform, if the President acknowledges all of them, we could be there till Christmas. I don't know where to cut." I looked at the list and suggested "Don't cut any of them. Add a few more and here's the way we'll play it . . ."

An hour later President Ford stood before his audience and began: "Governor Blanton, Governor Carroll, Governor Waller, Governor Holshouser, Governor Rhodes, Governor Busbee, Governor Moore." He took a deep breath, smiled ever so slightly, sighed and continued, "Senator Brock, Senator Baker, Congressman Quillen, Congressman Duncan." A few chuckles as the audience began to anticipate. "Mayor Testerman, distinguished guests, ladies and gentlemen." The President paused for effect and then added: "That concludes my speech. Thank you and good night." Picked up his text and started to leave. Laughter, applause, an awkwardness overcome, an audience put at ease and ready to hear the serious talk that followed. An on-the-spot writer is not a "reward" for the writer—it's an insurance policy for any prudent executive.

***

Let's carry this involvement back to the very genesis of any speech—the invitation to the principal to speak. Most public officials and corporate executives receive many more invitations than they can possibly accept. Unfortunately, it is extremely rare for the writer to be a part of the acceptance process. He or she will have to create the ultimate product, but the forum, date and audience are usually determined before they are brought into the picture.

The problem with this arrangement is that the writer, perhaps more than anyone else involved, knows whether there is really something worthwhile to say to the group. Nothing beats sitting at a keyboard working out the specific problems of a talk to put the subject, approach and audience into very sharp focus. What may seem like an ideal forum may not be. Too many speaking dates are accepted before serious consideration is given to what can or what should be said. This inevitably leads to commencement addresses in which the kids are told the future is theirs—and similar exercises in sterility. Bring the writer into the acceptance process. It's another protection in the executive's insurance policy.

***

Since leaving the White House, I have given speeches and conducted humor workshops for corporate communicators and speakers. By means of instruction and example, I show how humor can be introduced into speeches and then effectively performed. During and after the always lengthy Q.&A. sessions, I've learned a great deal from speechwriters and executives about how they relate to each other. Quite often, they don't.

It is not unusual for the client to accept a speaking date, have an aid turn a writer loose on the project, and not be concerned until the first and, sometimes, the final draft, is delivered. The wordsmith chooses the subject, fashions the style, constructs the approach in a state of splendid isolation from his client. As a result, there are no personal touches, no guidance derived from the greater experience of the executive, and no chance to try out unusual ideas for acceptability. It is the Titanic approach to speechmaking. Some of the icebergs may be missed but one of them will eventually getcha!

I heard the Chairman of the Board of a huge corporation give a speech to a convention in Washington. It wasn't a bad speech but he had obviously only read it over once on the plane coming to the event. The word patterns, the phrases, the rhythms were all strange to him. He was making a statement and the script called for him to say: "This bizarre incident." What he actually said was: "This brassiere incident." It was a few minutes before the audience settled down sufficiently to absorb anything else he had to say. And needless to say, any comment about the speech afterwards contained some reference to the blooper. It did not create the image executives should cultivate.

The further the distance between the speaker and writer, the greater the opportunity for embarrassing moments. Put it down as another variation of Murphy's Law: Whatever can go wrong, will go wrong. A Senator is alleged to have been given his speech and a copy of the press release concerning it. He went out and read the press release. Another speaker performing a text he had never seen before, came to the line: "Which reminds me of a very funny incident." Then he read the incident to the audience. And it was a very funny incident. And he had never heard it before. And he broke up laughing to the point where he couldn't proceed with his speech.

***

Why don't more executive speakers work one-to-one with their writers? The usual answer is time—the crush of other urgent matters and the feeling that this area of communication can be handled without their personal involvement. No one has a more demanding time schedule than the President of the United States. President Ford gave an estimated 1,200 speeches during his term of office, and all were conceived, developed, rewritten, edited and polished based on his direction and guidance received from meetings in the Oval Office.

We usually had two meetings a week with President Ford. One to discuss the concept and content of future speeches and a second to review, page by page, drafts of immediately upcoming speeches. We knew precisely what he liked, what he didn't like, and what he wanted changed. On very important messages, such as the State of the Union, the President might bring in pages of handwritten text to give us the precise wording he wanted on a sensitive point. It was an ideal and very productive relationship.

***

One last thought concerning speakers and their speechwriters: approval and disapproval. The writer is usually made aware of his or her failures—quickly, pungently and in detail. The successes are sometimes not even mentioned. Sure, the writers are paid. Sure, they have a whole package of fringe benefits. Sure, they get a pat on the back at the company picnic. But what about those intensely emotional moments immediately after the great event itself? Days, perhaps weeks of anguish, nail-biting, all-out and all-night effort have resulted in a speech the writer, the speaker and the audience have reason to feel good about. If you're the speaker, share a little of the emotional high you get from a dynamic performance with the writer who contributed to your success. The writer needs to keep that adrenaline pumping too.

Gerald Ford as Congressman, as Vice President and as President, was always there with a phone call, a note, or an invitation to have dinner with him in his cabin on Air Force One, to say thanks for a job well done. When it's three o'clock in the morning and a deadline is near, your brain is numb, your typing fingers paralyzed and you feel you will never be able to write another word again, you remember such appreciation—and you finish the assignment.

But kindness comes in all forms—even in rejection. Years ago, I was retained to do a series of humorous sales letters for a large mail-order concern. On the deadline date I was ushered into a large conference room to show them to the Chairman of the Board. The two of us sat at opposite sides of a mammoth table. He, thoughtfully reading each page while I tried to look interested in the paintings on the walls. Finally, after what seemed like a long weekend, the chairman put my efforts down, looked out the window, sighed—and said, "I'm not discouraged."

I have never been so gently demolished before or since. I couldn't help but laugh. He laughed because I laughed. And then we proceeded to work out the problems—face to face.

Speechwriters, Professional —See MONEY AND SPEECHWRITING

SPICING UP THOSE DULL SPEECHES

I begin my humor workshops for corporate speakers and communicators by saying that a lot of show business terms will be used, explained and demonstrated.

I point out that some members of the group may feel this is inappropriate. The participants are in the world of business, not show business. That's right. But the minute they stand up in front of an audience, they have crossed the line. They *are* in show business and the further they are from that awareness, the less effective they will be.

In today's image-conscious world, the executives

who find themselves much in demand are the effective speakers, the dynamic communicators. Few audiences know much about the inner workings of the John Doe Corp. But, if the chairman of the board, John Doe, appears before them and scores with a speech that holds their attention, provides information and concepts in a well-organized and interesting manner—and yes, even makes them laugh a bit—the John Doe Corp. will have become a more personal and more highly regarded part of their lives. This isn't theory. It is a fact, known to every alert corporate speaker. We make sure that we are completely prepared for an important appointment—even down to the shine on our shoes. We must be equally prepared for an audience—and put a gloss on our words.

***

Humor has often been the key that unlocks an audience's receptivity. The apt, well-timed and confidently executed opening immediately puts listeners at their ease. They realize they are in secure hands and can look forward to hearing a professional communicator.

"Apt" is the operative word. Some top-level executives shy away from humor because they feel it may be undignified. I have found that the distinction between a jokester and an accomplished raconteur lies in the choice of material. To get laughs, the jokester relies on oneliners and stories, some old, some new, but usually irrelevant to the purpose of the event. The raconteur never loses sight of his or her reason for being there. The laughs are supportive or illustrative of the occasion, the audience or the speaker. They show a speaker involved with the listeners and in tune with them. They narrow and eliminate the gulf that so often separates a VIP speaker from an audience.

Where does such apt material come from? Obviously, it can be custom written by specialists in the field. A speechwriter with a feel for humor can research an event, the sponsoring organization, the guest list, the locality, the substance of the speech and the high-visibility aspects of the speaker—and come up with effective audience grabbers. The problem with such special material is the expense. It may only be a page or two of double-spaced items—three or four jokes—but the *right* three or four jokes may have taken up to a week to research and create. Consequently, the professionals in this area charge a few thousand dollars to do it.

***

There is an alternative to custom-written humor, and it has the down-to-earth title of "do-it-yourself." By "do-it-yourself," I am not suggesting that you sit down and try to write professional-level, performable laugh lines. Creating humor is an art form that relatively few writers have mastered and only after years of trial and error. To executive speakers, "do-it-yourself" represents an ongoing commitment to search for the lines, anecdotes and stories that are right for them, their industry and their audiences.

The good news is, there are hundreds of surefire laugh lines that are just perfect for you. They are in the many humor books and services readily available to public speakers. The bad news is, to get them you will have to go through tens of thousands of jokes that you can't use. It is a long, laborious process but frequently the discovery of that one gem, floating in a sea of tedium, makes it all worthwhile.

First, let me caution you not to overdo it. Restrict your reading of any joke book or humor service to no more than fifteen minutes, two or three times a day.

278

You will then be able to judge the material with the fresh outlook necessary to this type of research.

What are your looking for? First, is the item funny? Two, would you feel comfortable saying it? Three, is it performable humor?

***

The reason for the first question is self-evident: If the joke doesn't strike you as funny, that's it. If you are concerned about a piece of material, follow the old adage: "When in doubt, cut it out!"

The second question also involves a critical decision: Would you feel comfortable telling the joke? Many novice speakers hear a joke, think it's funny and use it in a speech without considering whether or not it suits their personality, or the mood of the occasion, or the subject matter of the speech. An inappropriate anecdote dragged in by the heels will invariably make you look like a novice. "To thine own self be true" in all things—even humor.

The third question is just as important: Is it performable humor? If someone tells you a joke, the chances are it is constructed in such a way that it "plays."

Unfortunately, good performable humor sometimes looks rather drab on the printed page. If you read one of the great comedy routines like *Who's On First?*, you may be somewhat disappointed in it. But when you heard it performed by Abbott and Costello, it was hilarious. It often takes a practiced eye to spot the performing values of a joke. You get this practiced eye by going out and doing material in front of an audience. The jokes that work give you the warm feeling of success. The jokes that die eventually give you the practiced eye.

One final consideration in the selection of usable humor: Is the line or story applicable to your business, your area of expertise, or occasions and events you may possibly be concerned with? For example, if you have found some good retirement and leisure time material, is it likely that you will be called upon to speak at a retirement dinner? This final shifting based on the relevancy of the humor will reduce the number of items to be stockpiled to a precious few.

**

The next step is to have the selected jokes and stories put into a file—computer or hard copy—and then classified according to possible use and subject matter. Cross-index liberally. If you have a joke about getting a fruitcake for Christmas that could be used as an opener, file it under *Openers, Christmas, Gifts* and *Food.* As the file grows, you may miss a joke that is ideal for a specific speech unless it is filed under the subject and category you are researching.

The last step in the process is the use of the file itself. When you accept a speaking engagement, make a list of all possible aspects of the occasion—the subject of your talk, the location of the hall (city and state), the audience, who will be introducing you, other head table guests, etc. Turn to your file and look up the categories your list would suggest as relevant and then pull all of the items in those classifications.

In many cases, a natural continuity, linking a few of the jokes, will suggest itself. Or, you may have to write simple bridges to get from one item to another. Keep in mind that in humor, less is always more. One, two or three laughs at most, should be the maximum used before a serious speech. And please keep the whole speech to twenty minutes, for pithy's sake.

Spontaneity —See *Don't Read the Jokes—Tell 'Em!* at DON'TS . . . IF YOU WANT TO GET LAUGHS

STAGE FRIGHT AND HOW TO DEAL WITH IT

I.

You see it frequently. Sometimes as a filler; sometimes as a news story. It's a report of a survey concluding that the Number One fear of people is public speaking.

According to this survey, standing up to "say a few words" represents a greater threat than death, illness, loss of a job or a host of other misfortunes that usually get our attention.

It's a great space-grabber and so it has assumed a life of its own. The survey is an easy beginning for any article on public speaking and as such, will probably appear in print for many years to come.

Pity.

Personally, I have never seen much in the way of detail as to the who, what, when, where and how of this survey. More important, I have never heard of any attempt to replicate the results. I doubt that they ever could be.

Stage fright is a reality. In varying degrees, we all suffer from it. But to list the fear of speaking in public as greater than the fear of death, loss of eyesight, loved ones or job places a tax on our credulity that sorely needs cutting.

***

There is no question that standing up and becoming the focal point of a group's attention is a challenging action. It invites expectation and interest, and if these hopes are not met, it can result in disinterest and disdain. And so, for most, public performance is a difficult, if not an unnatural act.

Rosalind Russell wrote that acting was like "standing up naked and turning around very slowly."

And if you do humor, I would add one more element:

281

That comedy is like "standing up naked and turning around very slowly"—and then asking, "What do you think?"

In my opinion, comedy is the most tension-filled of all the performing arts because it demands an immediate audience reaction.

If you're a singer, you're judged every three or four minutes when you finish a song and the audience is called upon to applaud. If you're an actor or actress in a drama, you're judged when the curtain comes down at the conclusion of each act. But if you do humor, you're judged every time you come to a punch line, and if you work at the pace of Jay Leno, that can be as often as three to five times a minute.

I don't know of any other profession that puts an individual's emotions on the line as frequently or that calls for a reaction that is so indisputable. People can applaud insincerely. It's easy to do. It takes no great skill to slap one's hands together.

***

But laughter is the most honest of emotions. Even professional actors and actresses know the difficulty of producing a staged chuckle or belly laugh that sounds genuine. In real life, we've all heard the strange and strained attempts at laughter on the part of employees who have just heard the boss tell a weak joke.

Perhaps the most poignant comment on the difficulties of causing laughter is found in a book by Don Widener entitled "Lemmon." The book is about Jack Lemmon but in it Widener tells a hard-to-forget story about Edmund Gwenn. When the famed character actor was close to death, he was visited by his friend, movie director George Seaton.

Gwenn, feeling his life coming to an end, said, "It's frightening and I hate it." Seaton, unsure of what to say, ventured, "I guess dying can be very hard."

Gwenn turned this over in his mind for a moment, then looked up at Seaton and said, "Yes, but not as hard as playing comedy."

And so, more than any other aspect of verbal communication, humor produces the most stage fright. But *any* time you stand up to speak and look into a few hundred pairs of judgmental eyes—whether you're providing humor, instruction or inspiration—it can be an intimidating experience.

Clammy hands and stomach flutter are part of any speaker's territory. I can remember standing in a hotel elevator with a top comedy star, on our way down to the ballroom where he was to perform. And as the elevator approached the lower floors, he grew unusually silent. I asked if there was anything wrong. His answer was a shake of the head, a bemused smile and the observation that he had been a performer for forty years and every time he walked onstage, it was like facing a firing squad.

***

So much for the bad news. Now for the good news. What's so wrong with sweaty palms and a racing heartbeat if it means the adrenaline is running and every part of your body is mobilizing to meet a challenge?

I begin to worry when I'm sitting at a head table, waiting to be introduced, and I'm *not* nervous. It invariably means that emotionally I'm in second gear rather than in power drive.

If you're revved up to the point where every nerve ending is sparking and ready to go into action, that's not stage fright—that's the way it should be.

But what do you do if your symptoms go beyond the normal signs of tension? How do you handle the nerves, the anxiety and the sheer panic that can adversely affect performance?

First, let's examine the things you don't do.

You don't wait to the last minute to prepare your

remarks or presentation. Procrastination is the booking agent for stage fright. The more you delay, the more time there will be for fantasies of failure to build in your mind. So get down to the nuts and bolts of what's required as quickly as possible and let your fantasies roam in more pleasurable areas.

You don't pretend the audience doesn't exist. What would you think of a sales person who talked to you without ever looking you in the eye? Would you be at ease with such a person? Would you relate to them? Would you trust them?

Some speakers do just that with an audience. To relieve anxiety, they ignore their listeners and talk to the back wall, the ceiling and the lectern. I'm sure that back wall, ceiling and lectern appreciate this attention, but your audience wants to say hello.

You don't cop out unless it's to set up a joke. You don't say you forgot your glasses, you lost your notes, you didn't have enough time to prepare, you're not feeling well or it's your first time, so please be kind. You gain nothing from it, but you do make the audience more critical of everything that follows. It's a do-it-yourself demotion from pro to amateur.

You don't find relief from stage fright in bottles, pills or prescriptions. The mood-adjustment hour that often precedes an event does far more for audiences than it does for speakers. As one very successful platform personality used to say, "Butterflies are bad enough. Drunken butterflies are even worse."

*****

When tranquilizers first appeared on the market some years ago, they looked as if they might be the answer to the jitters problem. They weren't and they aren't. Before tranquilizers, speakers would worry themselves sick about giving a bad performance. Thanks to tranquilizers, they can still give a bad performance—only now they don't worry.

The latest entry in the coping through chemistry sweepstakes are the beta-blockers. These are drugs that block some of body's normal reaction to stress. In tests, beta-blockers have kept the heartbeat of performers from racing and reduced the sweating and trembling associated with anxiety. But they may also have dangerous side effects for people with certain medical conditions.

But the question I would have to ask is: Why? Why take any drugs, stimulants or depressants just to be able to reach out and communicate with your fellow human beings?

I have read that Robert Anderson, the noted playwright, has a sign on his desk that reads: NOBODY ASKED YOU TO BE A PLAYWRIGHT. Well, in today's world, quite frequently people *are* asked to speak in public even when they are not entirely thrilled with the idea.

But if they eventually say "yes," it means that under all that pile of chicken, there's a little ham in them trying to get out. And that ham doesn't need seasoning with alcohol, tranquilizers or beta-blockers. All it and they really need is a little bit of preparation, rehearsal and experience.

II.

How do you control the trembling hands and sweaty palms? Sometimes it seems as if speakers have cornered 60% of the world's proven reserves of perspiration. If you doubt it, weigh yourself immediately before you given a speech—and immediately after. It could be the basis of a great new reducing program—the Demosthenes Plan.

One of the problems most speakers face is a lack of practice. In show business, they used to talk about the need for places "to be lousy in"—out-of-the-way clubs or resorts where you could try out new material or learn your craft. And if you bombed, who's to know? Scores of comedy clubs throughout the United States and Canada now provide the learning place for comedians. Where do novice speakers go?

As a starting point, I would recommend Toastmasters International. This is a non-profit educational organization founded in 1924. It now has Toastmaster clubs in most cities throughout the world.

How does Toastmasters International work? I'll let their own literature speak for them:

***

A Toastmasters club is a 'learn-by-doing' workshop in which men and women overcome their fear of public speaking in an atmosphere of fellowship and enjoyment. A typical club has 20 to 40 members, who meet weekly or biweekly to learn and practice public speaking techniques. The average club meeting lasts about 1½ hours.

There is no instructor in a Toastmaster club. Instead, the members evaluate one another's oral presentations; this evaluation process is an integral component of the overall educational program. Besides taking turns delivering prepared speeches and evaluating those of other members, Toastmasters have the opportunity to give impromptu talks, develop their listening skills, conduct meetings, learn parliamentary procedure and gain leadership experience by serving as club officers.

You also receive *The Toastmaster,* a monthly magazine featuring articles of interest to speakers. Regional conferences as well as an annual convention provide opportunities to hear leaders in the field.

But in my opinion, one of the greatest benefits of membership is that your local club provides a practice audience. Toastmaster audiences are warm, supportive and invariably constructive in their suggestions for improvement.

Week after week of standing up "to say a few words" in public will work wonders on your stage fright. Speechmaking becomes a routine occurrence rather than a fearsome once- or twice-a-year encounter. In this case, familiarity does not breed contempt—it breeds content.

***

If your job, profession or career calls for speaking in public, I would suggest you start your training process early. Once you attain some stature in your chosen field, the expectation of audiences rises accordingly.

The address of the World Headquarters of Toastmasters International is at P.O. Box 9052, Mission Viejo, CA 92690-7052. Phone: (949) 858-8255. Web site: http://www.toastmasters.org.

Once you get your feet wet in the learning process, another organization to consider joining in the public speaking area is the National Speakers Association, 1500 South Priest Drive, Tempe, AZ 85281, phone (480) 968-2552.

The National Speakers Association holds excellent annual conventions that offer you the opportunity to see scores of top professional speakers in action. They represent a listening and learning experience that can't help but make you a better communicator.

But a brief sidebar regarding hearing other speakers: I've found that you learn a lot more from the bad speakers than the good ones. The good ones make it look too easy. Their platform deportment, words and attitude—all smooth as silk. They're a joy to watch, but the inept speakers are your best instructors. Rather than just wince at the presentation of a bumbler, make notes on what you're reacting to unfavorably. Once home, study the notes and see if you might be guilty of the same mistakes. Sometimes it's a humbling post-mortem.

***

Back to stage fright. Let's talk about the jitters that affect speakers on-site. I've found that most people in the performing arts go through little rituals to psych themselves up for a show. They put on their lucky shoes, or drink exactly 2½ cups of tea, or run in place, or meditate on their mantra. (The best mantra is a dollar sign.)

I'm all for it. Anything—anything that makes you feel more comfortable or better able to deliver the goods—is right. If you have a favorite tie, shirt or suit—wear it. If a rabbit's foot has never missed—don't leave home without it. Anything and everything that supports your feeling of well-being should be used.

On the flip side, anything that might upset you or be a downer should be carefully avoided before a speech. If you're up to your ears in the stock market, don't look at the results of the previous day right before show time. The up days never produce as much sunshine as the down days produce gloom.

***

If you read enough about coping with stage fright you'll see many conflicting opinions. Let me add one more. I've seen it suggested that a speaker should find a quiet place or go to a dressing room and use the peace and quiet to calm down, regroup and focus on the task ahead.

My solution to stage fright is just the opposite. Keep moving, occupied and involved with people right up to your opening words. Don't give yourself the quiet time to concentrate on your fears. Mix, mingle and make friends with your audience. See for yourself that they're not the enemy.

And this above all—act!

Who do you admire most as an accomplished, urbane, knowledgeable and self-confident speaker? Become them. Move out of your own trembling psyche and inhabit theirs. Eat, drink, move and converse as you think they would. Put the mantle of their security around your shoulders.

That may seem a trifle fanciful—but there are a number of top personalities in show business who do not feel comfortable performing as themselves. They only come alive doing a character. They lose their inhibitions and their anxieties in the personality of someone else. If it works for them, why not for you?

But if I had to name the two most important weapons with which to slay the dragon of stage fright, they would be: Know your material and know your audience.

**

Nothing breeds insecurity faster or with better reason than not being properly prepared and rehearsed. If you plan to stand up before an audience of your peers and grope for words, concepts, information and structure, you have every right to expect that you might make a fool of yourself. Panic goes hand-in-sweaty-hand with such an approach.

In public speaking, there is no such thing as being over-prepared. Research, write and rehearse so thoroughly that if you are awakened out of a sound sleep, a spotlight beamed on you and you hear your introduction—you will be able to rise to your feet and do your twenty minutes without a glitch.

The other weapon in the war on stage fright is knowing your audience. Research the history, background and interests of your audience. Know what turns them on and turns them off. If you can reach out before and during your presentation and establish a connection with your listeners, the acceptance you see in their faces will go a long way toward reassuring you.

Author Max Wilk once asked Ed Wynn to identify the most important aspect of his comedy performing. Wynn answered, "In the first thirty seconds I go out and make friends with the audience. After that, I can do anything."

And—you're rarely afraid of friends.

***

Finally, one aspect of the subject that is seldom discussed—post-event stage fright.

Claudette Colbert, a legendary figure in show business, once came to Washington, D.C. to appear in a play. She was then 77 years old with a half-century of stardom behind her. Nevertheless, as reported in *Time* magazine: "Getting up early the next morning to read the *Washington Post*, she was stunned by a savage review, and almost immediately began throwing up."

But that same night she was on the stage once again, giving a delightful performance and receiving a standing ovation from the audience. It was tangible and immediate reassurance.

We need it when things go wrong. They say that if you fall off a horse you should get right back on again. Same thing with speaking. If you have a totally awful experience—the sound system fails, the lights go out, the introduction is wrong, the audience is drunk, your words turn to gibberish, and you fall off your self-esteem—climb right back on again. Go out and do another speech as soon as you can, even if you have to arrange a local freebie.

If stage fright is the ailment—success is the cure.

Standing Ovation

It's always a surprise when you finish a speech and ten people jump to their feet. You're never quite sure if its a standing ovation or their Preparation H has worn off.

Wooden chairs have produced as many standing ovations as talent.

I'm not like some speakers who'll do anything to get a standing ovation—but what makes you so sure you haven't dropped change on the seat of your chair?

In all honesty, I've only received one standing ovation in my life and that was when I spoke at an underwear manufacturers convention—and I think it may have had something to do with their newest product—velcro shorts.

A good speech is one that offers faith, hope and hilarity.

Starting a Speech —See (1) STARTING YOUR SPEECH A WINNER; (2) OPENER: THE FIRST TWO MINUTES OF YOUR SPEECH

STARTING YOUR SPEECH A WINNER

I learned how to tie my shoelaces last year.

Yes, I did learn a method of tieing shoelaces at the proper childhood age. Sometimes the bow stayed intact for an entire day. More often than not, it came undone and had to be retied at least once before the shoes were retired for the night.

Then, about a year ago, I picked up a pair of shoelaces that were packaged with, what I considered to be an unnecessary frill—a set of instructions. And while adding the laces to my shoes, I read the instructions. And it wasn't the way I've been tieing my shoelaces for all these years. So I tried it their way—and, miracle of miracles—they haven't voluntarily come apart since.

So what has all this got to do with speechmaking?

Well, it's quite easy to fall into a habit when preparing and delivering speeches—a pattern that we no longer question or examine. The speeches may come "unstuck" at times, but since this is the way they have always been done, no attempt at change is made. Maybe a quick look at some new instructions is called for.

***

The speech begins the moment you advance to the lectern and speak your first words. Right? Wrong. The performance part of your speech begins the minute you step out of your car in the parking lot. It begins with a friendly smile and "hello" to anyone else you see in that parking lot who might be part of your audience. It continues when you are brought in to the reception or gathering that precedes the event.

The whole idea is to meet, shake hands with and become friends with as many members of that audience as time permits. So you don't remain in a tight circle of the head table elite. Escorted or not, keep moving about the room. Be introduced or, if necessary, introduce yourself. Exchange some small talk. Engage in a little light banter. Drop in a joke. Become more than the visiting speaker to as many people as you can.

The purpose? To establish a cadre of listeners who now relate to you on a personal basis. People who want you to succeed and are emotionally geared to helping you achieve that success. It is no longer a faceless stranger telling that first joke or making that first statement—it is their friend.

I can sense a few people shrugging. How important can a platoon of friendly faces be in an audience numbering in the hundreds or thousands? Never underestimate the impact of a cheering section. Enthusiasm, applause and laughter are contagious. In the old days of radio comedy, studio audiences were salted with "laughers." These were individuals who triggered each joke response with a long, loud and infectious laugh. Six such laughers could lead an audience of 300 down the belly-laugh path. And Milton Berle has described, with pride and affection, the tremendous influence one person alone had on some of his early audiences—his mother. So your first objective at any speaking event should be the subliminal recruiting of your own personal rooting section.

***

Now we move on to the event itself. You're seated at the head table, in easy view of the audience, eating dinner and/or listening to the program that precedes your speech. The question to ask yourself: "If you were a member of the audience watching you during this period of time—would you like you?"

Be assured that if you are the guest speaker, at one time or other during the dinner and program, every member of the group will look you over. The bigger the celebrity, the more and longer the looks. They are trying to assess, long before your speech begins, whether they like you or not.

I believe that many a speech is won or lost during this "sniffing out" period. This is your opportunity to win over the majority of the audience with whom you were not able to make personal contact. If they see you with a grim look on your face, with head in your speech making last minute changes, ignoring your seatmates or what is going on in the program—no sudden burst of charm at the start of your speech is going to turn them on.

On the other hand, if you are a smiling and affable diner, reacting to the other speakers, laughing at the jokes, applauding in the proper places—you're both one of them and someone they'd like to know better. Actors are usually good speakers because they are actors—and actors, in public, are always "on."

There are other advantages to being an alert and reacting member of the head table. Conversations with your fellow head-tablers will give you background information that can be worked into your speech. Look over the table arrangement, the menu, the programs, the room decor—look for anything that is highly visible that might be the peg for an "ad-lib." I recently gave a speech at a lectern that was flanked by two huge funereal sprays of flowers. They just couldn't be ignored. And so it was the most natural thing in the world to look them over and say, "I dunno. I've died in front of many an audience but this is the first time anybody ever sent flowers."

***

The big moment arrives and you're being introduced. The introduction is short, sharp and to the point—because you have written it and provided it for the toastmaster. Your seat is pushed back a foot or two so that you can stand and head toward the lectern without looking like Quasimodo.

Now for a suggestion that sounds a little bit like science-fiction. As you hear yourself being introduced, imagine the conclusion of your speech. In your mind's eye, see it as the most fabulous success in the history of the spoken word. See a standing ovation, cheers, shouts of unrestrained joy—whatever turns you on. The introducer arrives at your name, the audience applauds and you approach the lectern in a posture of success. A posture an audience recognizes and responds to. Sounds crazy—but it works.

Now you're at the lectern. You don't test the microphone. You don't drink from the glass of water. You don't arrange your notes. You've walked up to the lectern with vigor and there should be no pauses, no hesitation. You're off and running with your best relevant joke or your strongest audience grabber.

You're confident in the knowledge that fifty or more people in the audience now call you by your first name, are friends and are pulling for you. And it's more than likely that the rest of the audience will follow their lead.

You're starting your speech a winner.

Staying Power of Humor —See KINDER, GENTLER COMEDY

Stop Signs to Observe in Planning a Roast —See *Preparing the Roast* at ROASTS

STORIES: WHERE DO THEY COME FROM?

During a recent dinner in Washington, the conversation turned to a discussion of the understated humor of the United Kingdom. One of the group said that he had recently visited London and as part of some casual banter, a British acquaintance looked him over, fingered the lapel of his jacket, then sighed and said, "Well, why pay more?"

Last year a friend of mine told me of an incident that involved her husband. He had spent a few weeks in New York City giving a short course in his specialty at one of the universities. A dedicated jogger, on his first day in town he set off on his usual daily run.

An hour later, he decided it was time to return to the school. The question was, "Which way?" In this new territory, his sense of direction had deserted him. So he jogged up to a young man standing on a corner and asked how to get back to the university. The man's answer was to pull out a knife while saying, "Gimmee your wallet."

The jogger said, "Look, all I've got on is this T-shirt, shorts and shoes. I don't have a wallet. All I have is 35 cents!" And he fished in a pocket and held out two coins. The mugger looked him over and then, in obvious frustration, smashed the coins out of his outstretched hand, growling, "Get outta here!"

With no hesitation, the jogger sprinted some 50 feet, when he suddenly heard the mugger yell, "Hey!" His heart pounding and fearing the worst, he turned to look back at his assailant—who was standing with his arm outstretched saying, "It's three blocks down and two blocks over."

***

I was an acquaintance of Harold Gary, a Tony Award winner and a successful Broadway character actor for many years. Harold told me that at one point in his career, it was suggested that he wasn't doing enough for himself in a public relations sense. The advice was to do more interviews, cultivate the media—and above all, make the rounds of the television talk shows. I got the impression that the whole idea was rather distasteful to Harold, but he reluctantly agreed to give it a try.

An appearance on a Philadelphia talk show was duly arranged, and a few hours before the taping of the show, Harold Gary showed up for the pre-interview interview. The guest is met by a researcher or talent coordinator, subject matter determined, and a page of questions developed for the talk show host. This interview was the beginning of the end of Harold's talk show career.

As he told it, he was ushered into an office to meet a 23-year-old talent coordinator with his feet on the desk and smoking a huge cigar. With an imperious wave of the stogie, he indicated a chair for Harold to sit in, took a quick glance at Gary's considerable bio on the desk, looked at his watch and said, "Well, Mr. Gary, in the interest of time, why don't you just tell me what you've done." And Harold Gary answered, "I'll tell you what, son. Why don't you tell me what you've done. It'll be much shorter."

***

Now what do these three stories have in common? They are true, they are funny, and they are performable.

During my years as a comedy writer, I have often been asked during interviews, "Where do stories come from? Who writes the stories and anecdotes that are suddenly on the lips of every joke-teller from New York City to Melbourne, Australia?"

I have long felt that, overwhelmingly, one-liners are written. Somebody sits down, thinks about the subject to be humorized, and then grinds them out. On the other hand, I believe that stories evolve. Quite often they are based on a comedic true happening that is then sharpened and refined by telling and retelling and retelling.

I have heard millions and millions of jokes in my lifetime and people are sometimes inhibited when telling me a joke. They feel I've heard them all—and, to some extent, I have. But I will never cut someone off in mid-joke because of its familiarity. Somewhere in the telling, there may be a twist, a nuance, or an improvement that makes a much more effective joke out of the original version. Most stories are almost human in their development—they are born, grow, expand, mature, and then die.

I've found that real life can be our best joke writer if we just raise our comedic antenna. There are two principal criteria by which to judge a true story: Is it funny? Is it retellable? The fact that it is true tends to make it relevant to your business, community or social scene. But true, semi-true or pure fiction—most stories should be told as truth. They should sound as if they just happened and within a framework of people and places your listeners can relate to. Never preface a story by saying it's true. This raises an element of doubt. The way you set up a story should imply its authenticity.

***

Let's examine the two criteria you're going to apply to real life humor. Is it funny? This is an easy one. If it made you laugh, chances are others would find it laughable as well. Is it retellable? There's the rub.

Good stories, true or otherwise, require an attention-grabbing premise, an interesting development, and a punch line or finish that snaps. It's the lack of this explosive definitive ending that puts much of real-life humor into the "you had to be there" category.

By way of example, a few years ago I was in a plane on my way to give a speech. I was reviewing some new material while sipping from an ice-cube-filled drink that sat on the armrest. The pilot announced a scenic attraction that could be seen from the other side of the plane and I half stood up to see it. As I did so and without my realizing it, the glass tipped over and the ice cubes tumbled out and onto my seat.

Having satisfied my curiosity, I dropped back into my seat and resumed my reading—for about ten seconds. Then I slowly began to feel the strangest sensation—an increasingly cold dampness in the seat of my pants. I jumped up with only a moderately restrained yelp and discovered that I had been sitting on an ice-cube cushion.

Now if this little incident had been observed or filmed by someone across the aisle, it would have had all the essentials of a Three Stooges bit. The unexpected tipping over of the glass; the anticipation of what's going to happen next as I confidently resumed my seat; the slow take of confusion as the ice cubes began to make their presence known; and the less-than-dignified jumping to my feet—all would have seemed very funny to another person watching it. But it is not a retellable story. Why? No finish. There is no definitive punch line to trigger an audience's laughter.

Most funny true life incidents can be ruled out as platform humor because of this weakness—no finish. But a surprising amount do qualify. Or, if the build or premise of an incident is that unusual or amusing, it might be worthwhile to concoct a finish. I would guess that most of the "true" anecdotes and stories told about famous personalities, past and present, have been liberally fixed, fudged and fictionalized. If it makes the story work, by all means book passage on the next flight of fancy.

***

Where do you find these true life gems? Obviously, your own eyes, ears and comedic instincts are your best resources. We all witness fun incidents in our jobs, community, and private lives that are all too often enjoyed—and then forgotten. My suggestion is: write them down. Preserve and cherish them as you would anything else that's precious.

You can also seek out and draw on the fun experiences of others. I always urge writers to interview their clients, as well as the associates, employees and families of their clients, with a view toward discovering these real-life funny anecdotes. It takes a lot of digging but the nugget found may be pure gold. The relevant story or anecdote that has the ring of "real" to it, will often outscore the most expertly crafted joke.

In addition to personal interviews, I also suggest that writers scan company bulletin boards, trade publications and, if possible, the contents of suggestion boxes—with a view to finding the laughter that is sometimes buried within.

Finally, don't overlook the mail room. A rich vein of humor can be mined from the thousands of letters every company or organization receives in the course of a year.

When I was at the White House, the mail room would occasionally send me some of the funny and some of the touching letters received. Letters from children are always winners and entire books have been made from them. One of my favorite letters, however, came from an adult. He was commenting on one of President Ford's Bicentennial speeches and took particular exception to the fact that the President had not made any reference to "our foundling fathers." For obvious reasons, this letter was never used in a speech.

But another one was—and it sums up all that a good true story should contain. It began with a letter to the President but it was the envelope that got our attention. It said: "To President Gerald R. Ford, or Vice President Nelson Rockefeller, or Secretary of State Henry Kissinger, or just plain anybody who will listen."

It was real. It was funny. It was retellable. And we did.

"Storm Warnings" for a Speech About to Sink —See LESSONS I LEARNED FROM LOWELL THOMAS

Substitute Speaker —See Introduction to a Substitute Speaker

Suggestions for Overcoming Writer's Block —See WRITER'S BLOCK AND HOW TO GET AROUND IT

Suggestions for Speakers Who Are Uncomfortable with Humor But Are Determined to Give It a Try —See USING HUMOR WHEN YOU'RE AFRAID TO USE HUMOR

Surprise Element in Demand-Laugh Jokes —See *Demand-Laugh Jokes* at OPENER: THE FIRST TWO• MINUTES OF YOUR SPEECH

Symposium

The word SYMPOSIUM comes from the ancient Greek and literally means "drinking together." And it's always a pleasure to be in the company of so many who retain and revere this classical tradition. And it's also so reassuring to know that when you make your unsteady appearance back home and your wife asks you where you've been, your thick but truthful tongue can answer: "To a symposium, my dear, to a symposium."

T

Tanking —See THE USES AND LIMITS OF HUMOR

TAPING: After the Applause Has Ended

The program is over. The audience files out. Compliments are extended—and the event comes to its predictable conclusion.

Well, maybe not all that predictable. There is the often-told story of a speaker who ended his presentation and was approached by the program chairperson, honorarium in hand. Still aloft on a performer's high, the speaker magnanimously gave the check back to the organization. He said, "I'm sure you can put it to good use." The program chairperson said, "That's very kind of you. We'll add it to the Special Fund." The speaker asked, "And what's the Special Fund for?" The program chairperson answered, "To get better speakers."

Most speakers, better and worse, tend to put all of their effort into the time leading up to their speech. When the speech is done, their focus of concentration moves on to the next one. Postmortems are usually brief, emotional or nonexistent. But there is much to be learned and much to be done after your speech has ended.

First, upon returning to your seat, assume that you and your speech have been winners. That may seem like an odd suggestion, but I have found that the person in the spotlight is usually the least efficient judge of how the performance was received. If the audience reaction deviates from expectations in any way, the performer immediately feels the mantle of failure closing about his or her shoulders.

***

I have seen speakers and performers show up at post-event receptions in advanced stages of despondency, babbling apologies when in reality, their presentation had been well received and congratulations were in order. Audiences are like fingerprints—no two are alike. Some audiences are demonstrative. They laugh out loud; they applaud on cue; they beam at the speaker. Others smile; nod their heads in agreement and listen intently. The sound level will be nil, but they may be enjoying your presentation every bit as much as the more outgoing group.

The best guidance I have ever received on this point was given to me by Jack Paar while I was a writer on his prime-time TV hour. We taped the show before a live audience, and with most shows the audience reaction was overwhelmingly enthusiastic. One time it seemed to me that it wasn't. And so, at a far too early hour the next morning, I phoned Jack Paar and did a non-stop monologue on how to "save" the episode in question.

Jack, in his quiet way, always considerate of others, heard me out. Then he said, "Bob, let me tell you something. If I've learned anything from the business, it's this: nothing is ever as bad as it first seems." And sure enough, he was right. When I later watched the show on my TV screen at home, in a more relaxed and objective mood, it was apparent that while it wasn't one of our better shows, it wasn't the disaster I had envisioned either.

Since then, I have shared Jack Paar's wisdom with many speakers and performers who were too quick and too wrong in mind-reading an audience's reaction. We are often our own worst and most erroneous critics—and so some outside help is called for.

The most effective help can be a tape recording of your speech. I believe that speakers should record *all* of their speeches as an invaluable guide to self-improvement and as an indisputable reference file.

***

Let's talk about self-improvement. Many a snap judgment is made by speakers in the car, plane or hotel room after a speech. They wince at the joke that died. They preen at an unexpected burst of applause. Editorial decisions are then made as to what will be used in or deleted from future speeches.

Quite often these decisions, based on visceral recollection rather than fact, are counterproductive. Listen to the tape a week later, and you may find that the joke you thought bombed got a small but appreciative laugh. On the other hand, the burst of applause you remembered as thunderous was merely a waiter hitting the bottom of a bottle of ketchup.

The tape must always be listened to with the realization that it is not a professionally produced product. The tape recorder is either on the lectern or directed at the speaker and does not fully reflect the audience's laughter and applause. But taking this into account, it is usually a much more accurate record of response than the emotion-laden memory of the speaker.

Audiotapes and videotapes are excellent do-it-yourself tools for self-improvement. They provide indisputable demonstrations of all the things we are doing wrong: the things we readily recognize in others but don't see in ourselves until we are confronted by ourselves on tape.

If you are addicted to repetitive word patterns, your speech notes won't reveal them. But an audiotape will allow you to count the number of "uhs," "you knows" and "okays" you are sliding into your speech as an often unconscious device to bridge paragraphs, sentences and phrases. There is nothing like a heartfelt, "Did I say that?" as the first step to making sure you don't say it again.

Studying audio- and videotapes of your presentation is also a very effective way to diagnose and to eliminate nervous performing habits. Years ago I was called in to write for an up-and-coming comedian. I watched and taped two of his shows, and then we sat down to discuss what material was needed. In discussing a specific joke, I asked him why he clucked his tongue after punch lines. He said, "I don't do that." I said, "Sure you do. After any big laugh, you cluck your tongue." He just stared at me. I finally had to play the tape and demonstrate when and where he was doing it. The performer was totally unaware of this nervous reaction that added nothing but distraction to his act.

***

Videotapes will go a long way toward acquainting you with just how many times you push your glasses up on your nose, scratch your ear, or look grim when you should be looking friendly. Recognition of the problem is the first step toward removal of the problem.

A tape library of your speeches can help in many other ways. If you use a speechwriter, a one-on-one relationship will produce the best results. Sometimes this isn't possible. But by listening to your tapes, a writer can get a working sense of your speaking style, phrasing and delivery.

If the speechwriter does not accompany the speaker to the event, a tape becomes even more important. Without the means to analyze what was right and what was wrong with a speech, there is no chance for improvement. Mistakes will be repeated. Clues to areas that should be built upon will be missed. Wheel-spinning replaces movement.

Perhaps the best reason for taping speeches is that

tapes provide a letter-perfect record of what was actually said. Most speakers tend to retain their lectern speech pages as the document of record. As we all know, there is many a slip and many a change twixt the written text and what the audience actually hears.

Jokes are cut, paragraphs are paraphrased, humorous and serious ad-libs are inserted. Quite often the speech as given is radically different from the speech as written. But what do we tend to put into the archives? The speech text once removed from reality. As a result, a year later, in talking to the same group, you eliminate one of your best jokes or rhetorical conclusions because, according to your previous text, you already did it. A tape might indicate otherwise. It may have been cut in actual performance because of time considerations or to make room for another more topical example.

***

A speech tape can also be a safety net to retrieve ad-libbed gems of humor or rhetoric. All too often, speakers return to their seat and try to reconstruct a chance remark that pulled a good laugh and/or applause. But the exact words or their order have slipped away. A tape restores what your memory erases.

I believe that all speech tapes should be reviewed so that all new, effective ad-libs can be transcribed and added to a working file of usable humor and speech material. These spontaneous chunks are particularly valuable because they are already audience-tested. They also tend to be in everyday language rather than the highfalutin convoluted sentences most of us construct when putting words on paper.

The final reason for taping and filing all speeches is to be able to analyze improvement or deterioration in your performing style and material. We usually look upon improvement as a given: If we do the jokes and the text enough times, we obviously improve in the process. Not necessarily.

There is usually a learning curve that *does* result in speaking improvement. A speaker becomes comfortable with material—refines it, polishes the rough spots—and a performing peak is achieved. But then a corresponding descent seems to take place.

Performers become bored with repetition. Consciously or unconsciously, they begin to substitute other words and phrases and give different readings to tried-and-true material. It keeps their interest in the speech alive, and it all seems like rather minor alternations until a point is reached where the big joke is no longer getting a laugh—and the big conclusion is no longer getting spontaneous applause.

Speakers then shake their heads in puzzlement. They say, "But I'm doing it the way I always have. Why, suddenly, doesn't it work?"

Tapes can come to the rescue. A review of the tapes may reveal a year or two of tinkering with style and content that has produced a far less effective vehicle.

The old tapes will also bring to front and center the good jokes, speech points and nuances that have fallen by the wayside. They're dropped out of one speech for a good and valid reason, aren't put back into the next speech, and eventually are forgotten. Even the most effective jokes, if not used, will fall into the wastebin of memory.

***

I once knew a comedian who kept his jokes on scraps of paper in an old shoe box. Not the entire joke, just the punch line, just enough to jog his memory, because these jokes he'd *never* forget! Some years later he sheepishly admitted to me that his shoe box was still filled with those punch lines, but he had forgotten most of the set-ups that made the tag lines work. So, in addition to letting your fingers do the walking, let your tapes do the remembering. *All* of the remembering.

Then again, at some speeches, things happen that

you would prefer not to remember. It has been written that a minister once ended his sermon, and at the conclusion of the service, a member of the congregation was ecstatic about it. The parishioner said, "Reverend, that was one of the most inspiring sermons I have ever heard. Tell me, will it be published?" The minister smiled shyly and said, "Oh, I don't know—perhaps someday it will be published posthumously." Whereupon the parishioner said, "Good. And the sooner the better!"

Taping in Rehearsal —See REHEARSING YOUR SPEECH

Television and Audiences —See ASSESSING YOUR AUDIENCE

Telling Something About Yourself in Your Speech —See LESSONS I LEARNED FROM LOWELL THOMAS

Tension Relief Through Humor —See "WHY HUMOR?"

Testimonials / Testimonial Dinners

First, I want to pay tribute to the leader of our organization. A man who has mastered all of the skills and demonstrated all of the talents necessary to being a great Chair Person—folding and stacking.

I love testimonial dinners. They're like an ego massage parlor.

Even if you'd like to believe yours is otherwise, testimonials are like cotton candy—sweet, sticky and mostly air.

Responding to a Testimonial: Right now I feel like a sled dog in Alaska. It's a lot of mush but I like it.

I want you to know there is one thing in particular about this dinner that has brought a lump to my throat. I think it was the gravy.

I have an idea that could cut the length of most testimonial dinners in half. Put the speakers under oath.

A testimonial dinner is a little like fertilizing your lawn—you have to be careful not to spread it on too thick.

Testing Your Material —See ADVICE—AND HOW TO IGNORE IT

Thanks

First, I want to thank the Arrangements Committee for this wonderful dinner—which will forever have a special place in my heartburn.

I'd like to thank all those who helped to make this such a warm and relaxed occasion—the Program Committee, the master of ceremonies, the bartender.

Thank you for that very fine speech. I'm sure those thoughts, like the chicken cacciatore, will stay with us for a long, long time.

Thank you. If kind words were money, that introduction alone would put me in a higher bracket.

"Thank You and Nice to Be Here" —See OPENER: THE FIRST TWO MINUTES OF YOUR SPEECH

Therapeutic Use of Humor —See (1) "WHY HUMOR?"; (2) THE USES AND LIMITS OF HUMOR

Throat Clearing —See ADVICE—AND HOW TO IGNORE IT

Time Limits and Roasts —See *Preparing the Roast* at ROASTS

Timidity —See *Don't Preface* at DON'TS . . . IF YOU WANT TO GET LAUGHS

Timing Your Speech —See PREPARING FOR YOUR SPEECH

Toastmaster

I'm your toastmaster for tonight and so, not to raise your expectations, let me tell you what a toastmaster is. A toastmaster is like an AWACS plane. He doesn't do anything himself—he just tells you what's coming.

Toastmasters International —See STAGE FRIGHT AND HOW TO DEAL WITH IT

Tone of a Roast —See *Delivering the Roast* at ROASTS

TOPICAL HUMOR: THE CUTTING EDGE
When I speak on the uses of humor in business communication, I pay tribute to humor and its ability to soothe, heal, build, or destroy. Laughter has had a good press in recent years. Articles praise its curative

powers. The business world is adding humor to its speeches, advertising, and training efforts. It is now generally accepted that mirth motivates and laughter can lift productivity and morale.

As a result, my audiences tend to focus on the positive aspects of humor. They hear the "soothe, heal, and build" part of my tribute. Humor's capacity to destroy is rarely considered. It's much more pleasurable to bask in the warmth of comedic sunshine. But humor can, and does, have the ability to destroy or play a significant part in adding fuel to a destructive fire.

People love topical humor—humor that springs from this morning's headlines. Audiences place a higher value on kidding the topics of the moment and tend to feel such humor is harder to create. In actuality, the reverse is true.

With most jokes you have to set a scene and establish the characters before you can get to a punch line. Topical jokes require far less set-up. All you have to do is mention the subject or the people involved. The audience immediately has the total picture in mind and all you have to do is give it the comedic twist.

Are the jokes fair? Of course not. Topical humor is almost always one-sided in its approach. It tends to take the easy, popular, readily comprehended and accepted approach to any subject. Topical humor is the fast food of comedy. As such, it is greedily consumed, the content rarely questioned, and people continue to come back for more.

***

Current jokes, particularly one-liners, are easy to accept, easy to remember, easy to tell, easy to pass on to others—and so, they are. Thanks to the telephone and the Internet, an apt topical joke is being told, heard or read across the continent and the world within hours of its creation. The impact can be enormous.

311

How do you cope with a comedic assault? You lay down a foundation of goodwill and acceptance long before the first shots are fired. I feel that Ronald Reagan would never have been threatened with impeachment if he had been President during the Watergate incident. He would have been criticized, dumped on, joked about, but, basically, the public and the media liked him, and they would not have gone for the jugular. Richard Nixon was an aloof, humorless loner, and he was ripe to be picked on.

But if a public personality has created a basic aura of goodwill to begin with, when the jokes start coming his or her way, humor is the best and frequently the only defense. No one did this better than Ronald Reagan. Whenever he was attacked or criticized on any issue or any shortcoming, he immediately led the comedic charge by doing jokes about himself. Today his faults and gaffes are mostly forgotten. His positive image lives on.

**

Given all that, humor is still a two-edged sword and one must be very careful in how it is handled. Some years ago I was doing a radio interview and the host of the show asked me if there were any special problems in writing humor for a President of the United States. I said, "The biggest problem is that you can't go for the cheap, easy laugh. For instance, a President can't do jokes about the water in Mexico."

Three days later, Jimmy Carter traveled south of the border, made his famous Montezuma's Revenge remark—and proved that a President can't do jokes about the water in Mexico.

When reaching for the laugh, we can never lose sight of the downside risk. The ill-timed and ill-considered joke can live on for years in the memories of an individual, or a group, or a nation. Before you fire off any comedic salvos, put yourself in the position of the target. Is it good-humored funny—or is it hurtful, below-the-belt, and likely to have a long shelf-life of resentment? If so, there's an old adage that goes: A closed mouth gathers no feet.

Treasurer

Being treasurer of an organization does affect your outlook on life. Frankly, I never really thought that it would until one day a Brinks truck went by—and I found myself holding my hat over my heart.

In introducing our Treasurer, the good news is— he's honest as the day is long. The bad news is— for the last five years he's been working the night shift.

I don't want to cast any aspersions on our Treasurer, but who takes out an I.R.A. in Brazil?

Tripping, Dropping Something, or Injuring Yourself on Your Way to the Lectern or at the Lectern

My name is _____ and I'll be your designated klutz for the evening.

If You Drop Something: As you can see, what I may lack in coordination, I more than make up for in clumsiness.

If You Trip: That was for all those who say I don't have a leg to stand on.

313

If You Injure Yourself: Well, that proves it. You always hurt the one you love.

True Stories as Humor —See (1) USING HUMOR WHEN YOU'RE AFRAID TO USE HUMOR; (2) STORIES: WHERE DO THEY COME FROM?

U

Unexpected Request to Speak

Well, as you might have guessed, I'd like to start out—by wishing I was ending up.

Unexpected Situations (and how to anticipate them)
—See CONTROLLING YOUR AUDIENCE

Unique Attitude / Approach —See MISTAKES

Upbeat Humor —See KINDER, GENTLER COMEDY

USES AND LIMITS OF HUMOR, THE

I.

It was the spring of 1974. I was in Charleston, South Carolina, waiting for an event to begin and making small talk with Senator Ernest "Fritz" Hollings. The Senator often has a very keen comedic view of current events.

We were discussing Watergate and the Nixon tapes. Each morning's headlines were spotlighting new and more damaging revelations found in the tapes. These secret recordings had become a key factor in linking Nixon to the Watergate cover-up. Talk of impeachment was growing louder. A question frequently asked was, "Why hadn't Nixon destroyed the tapes?"

Senator Hollings said, "You know, this mess never would have happened to Lyndon Johnson." I asked, "How so?" Hollings said, "The day after the tapes became public knowledge, L.B.J. would have gone on national TV. He would have been sitting behind his desk in the Oval Office with all the tapes piled up in front of him. And then he would have said, 'Mah felluh Amuricans. Ah caught 'em! Ah caught 'em red-handed! You know what they was doing? You see these here tapes? They was listenin' to everything Ah said. They was listenin' to me talkin' to you—and they was listenin' to you talkin' to me. And they're not gonna get away with it! You see that big ole fahrplace over there?' And L.B.J. would have picked up the tapes, and on network TV, burned them to ashes—live from the Oval Office."

It has been written that many a true word is said in jest—and chances are, if Nixon had followed Senator Hollings' comedic scenario, he probably would have been able to survive the hearings in progress and serve out the rest of his term in office. The tapes were the irrefutable evidence that brought about his resignation.

For humor to work, it has to cut to the heart of an issue or problem. It covers a kernel of truth, or perceived truth, with a coating of laughter. Humor often points the way to go—or the way to be avoided. This predictive power is a useful tool, but one rarely used.

* * *

I have sometimes felt that any President of the United States would benefit by adding one more person to the Cabinet—a Secretary of Humor.

What would a Secretary of Humor do? By keeping in

316

touch and in tune with the jokes being told throughout America, he or she would be a more reliable pollster than most. Humor springs from gut feelings. If the jokes being told overwhelmingly reflect one position, attitude, or viewpoint—it's a message that can't be ignored.

In a similar vein, a Secretary of Humor could be influential in preventing the ridicule that often greets ill-advised actions. How? By assessing the comedic response to an action before it is taken.

The White House, Congress, and corporate headquarters function in a rarified atmosphere that is sometimes out of touch with the real world. The result can be statements and programs so out of step with everyday thinking that they invite derision. To identify and eliminate these potential gaffes before they happen would be a valuable contribution by the Secretary of Humor.

A small example: President Carter, at a senior staff meeting, said he had been fishing when what looked like a rabid rabbit came swimming in a straight line toward his boat. He then grabbed his oar and stood up, prepared to defend himself against the rabbit. Apparently, Carter had told the story a couple of times before, but this time it got to the press. A Humor Secretary could have predicted the reaction.

The first time he heard the story, he would have quietly taken the President aside and suggested that he never, but never, tell that story again. No way was the President of the United States going to look heroic standing up in a boat with a paddle battling a killer rabbit! A ton of jokes and cartoons could have been avoided.

David Richards of the *Washington Post*, wrote in a theater review: "Words are feelers, sent out into the world to do reconnaissance work." Jokes perform the same function. They can make an instant analysis of a situation and determine how it will play. Maybe not a Secretary of Humor—but every private and public organization could benefit by including a humor-damage-control analysis of proposed actions and policies.

***

Another very valuable use of humor is the role it plays in helping us all to deal with the inevitable or the unchangeable. Humor helps us to cope. Humor goes to the normality in a situation. Seeing the humor in our own trials and troubles is a way of cutting them down to a size that can be handled.

My thoughts go back to a time when my books first became popular with comedy performers. I frequently received letters asking questions about performing techniques and choice of material. One letter asked some rather involved questions. I wrote back with some brief answers and suggested that the writer phone me for additional information.

No phone call, but a few weeks later, another letter with more questions. Once again, I answered with a few paragraphs and suggested a phone call. No phone call. This went on for a few more letters until the writer explained why he had not called.

He was deaf. He had lost his hearing in his adult years. He could speak but he couldn't hear any responses. A phone call would have been pointless. He then went on to explain that he was part of a hearing-impaired theatrical group that performed before audiences that were also hearing-impaired. As the comedian of the show, he was trying to find ways to adapt the verbal material in my books to performable sight gags. It was a formidable challenge.

We exchanged letters on the subject and then he invited me to attend one of their shows. I went and I will always be grateful for the learning experience it provided.

An audience of a few hundred—a dozen or so performers onstage—all hearing-impaired. The first lesson learned was that in the company of those who could not hear, my being able to hear was no advantage. They were able to communicate quite well by a combination of signing and lip-reading. I had to resort to paper and pencil for anything more complex than "yes" or "no" or "thank you."

At one point, the ability to sign was a distinct advantage over the ability to hear: My host had to communicate an instruction to someone who was onstage—about 60 feet away. Once he got the person's attention, he delivered this long-distance message by signing. If I had shouted the instructions to a hearing person 60 feet away, I doubt if they would have been heard over the background noise in the hall.

I was also struck by the vivacity and expressiveness of the facial and body movement that accompanied the signing. Statements and questions were frequently supplemented by a little bit of pantomime, often humorous, that underscored the meaning. It occurred to me that communicators who can hear can learn a lot from communicators who can't. Most speakers rely totally on their voice to carry the message. The hearing-impaired show us that a blend of the verbal and nonverbal makes for a more effective mix.

The show began and, as in any variety show, comedy played an important part. The subject matter and attitude of the jokes and sketches reflected the news and interests of the time. Signing and pantomime carried the humor to the audience as effectively as the spoken words of any verbal performer. It was also evident how comfortable both the cast and the audience were with hearing impairment.

It was a condition they acknowledged but with no indication that they considered it a handicap. Jokes about deafness were plentiful. In a sketch, one performer signed a straight line. His partner mimed not being able to hear him. The first performer then repeated the line but with greatly exaggerated signing—causing his partner to recoil and cover his ears in a "not so loud" gesture.

The underlying message of their humor: Hearing impairment is a part of our lives—and it's being dealt with.

When I think back to that evening, one additional memory comes to mind. My host was halfway through his stand-up comedy routine when I noticed a man at a table close to the stage stand up and begin signing. A woman beside him pulled him back into his seat. A few minutes later he stood up again and began signing at the performer. Once again the woman pulled him down into his seat. And it was only then that I recognized what was happening: He was a hearing-impaired heckler—and he was signing his heckling.

The condition of not being able to hear was not going to impair or inhibit the lives of anyone in that room and their humor showed it.

To paraphrase the immortal words of Pogo: They have met the enemy and he's no big deal!

II.

Humor is its own therapy. The healing power of laughter has been known throughout the centuries. The Ancient Greeks established a medical center in Epidaurus, and comedies were performed in its theater. In the 13th century, hospitals in Egypt used storytellers to boost the spirits of patients. Today, some hospitals have laughter rooms stocked with joke books and comedy videotapes—new techniques to further a very old concept.

Humor is also a vital ingredient in self-help situations. People who come together to battle alcoholism, drug abuse, obesity, smoking, or other addictions—recognize the equal value of tears and laughter. Humor can put a spotlight on the emotional truth of behavior. Even more important, humor can present this truth in a way more likely to be accepted. To paraphrase Mary Poppins: "A little bit of laughter makes the medicine go down."

***

Self-deception is a key element in all addictions. The first step to a cure is acknowledging the fact that there is a problem. A funny true anecdote is often the mirror that shows a troubled person just how transparent his or her behavior has become.

A friend of mine, a member of Alcoholics Anonymous, gave me this example. An alcoholic went into a liquor store every morning to buy three half-pints of booze—for her purse, for her desk, and for her car. And in an attempt to keep the clerk from thinking she had a drinking problem—every day she had them gift-wrapped.

Can't you just hear the burst of sympathetic laughter that must have greeted this story—and see the nods of recognition from other members relating it to their own feeble attempts at concealing their addiction? Humor opens the door and humor can define the problem. My friend said he attended his first AA meeting at a location miles away from his home. He said, "I wasn't ashamed to be seen drunk around my neighborhood, but I was ashamed to be seen sober at an AA meeting. That's the insanity of our disease."

***

Think of what life would be without laughter. Think of all the times anger, confusion, fear, and embarrassment were instantaneously assuaged or eliminated by a timely quip. And why not? There is the thinnest of lines

321

between the deadly serious and the intensely comic at any given moment.

Take that classic moment in horror movies we've seen so many times. An eerie castle in Transylvania. Lightning is flashing, thunder is crashing, and Dracula has sunk his fangs into the neck of an innocent young victim. Remember how you might even have been frightened the first time you saw this often-played scene?

But as Dracula is sucking up the blood, what if we added the sound effect of a gas station pump dinging off the gallons? In a microsecond the threat would be gone and laughter would take over.

***

Many times in our everyday lives, we're offered this same choice—tears, fright, anger, or laughter? Frequently, laughter is the better and more effective way to go.

By way of example, my wife and I attended a recent World's Fair. As is true of all successful expositions, the lines of people waiting to get into the exhibition buildings were enormous. Two-hour waits to see 15-minute shows were not unusual. Feet grew tired, legs grew weary, some grew impatient—but not many. Instead, there was an infectious good humor about a shared situation. People joked about the length of the lines, facetious ways to beat the system, whether the attraction was worth the wait. A steady stream of banter and humorous small talk made the minutes fly by. Laughter stepped in and pushed irritation aside.

This infectious good humor was picked up and echoed by the attendants in the exhibition buildings. Because of the long waits, a chance to sit down was of prime interest to most attendees. And so, a laugh and a thunderous round of applause were given the attendant who announced, "There will be a four-minute slide show—followed by a fifteen-minute film—in a theater with real—I repeat, real—seats!" This one light-hearted remark gave both information and conveyed a sympathetic understanding of what the audience had endured to see the show.

The humor varied but the impact was always positive. As we entered the Australian pavilion, an attendant said, "You can sit on the floor, but please don't sit by the doors or people will walk on you—and, unless you're a carpet, you won't enjoy it."

As we left another building, we received the following instructions: "Please be sure to take all of your personal belongings—everything you brought in with you—especially your kids." The reminder was delivered and, with a smile or a laugh, the audience gathered up its possessions and offspring and left.

***

The soothing use of humor is also very evident in the airline industry. Flying is also associated with long waits, unexplained delays, and the normal anxieties of sitting in a 20-ton metal tube being propelled through the air by three king-sized blowtorches. Sometimes air travel provides you with a lot more anxiety than peanuts. Tension-breaking humor often helps.

I recall once being in a plane waiting to take off. The pilot had kept us informed of how many planes were ahead of us and also that he felt sure he would be able to make up this lost time. His last announcement was made just as we turned onto the runway. He said, "Here we go. Now everybody pedal real hard!"

Cabin attendants have also mastered the art of the informational joke. On a recent flight, I heard one of them deliver this: "Once again, this is Flight 333 going to Chicago. If you are not going to Chicago, now is the time to panic."

Meal service on planes has frequently inspired jokes—and called for them. One cabin attendant said, "Once we are under way we will be serving you the beverage of your choice—and the meal of *our* choice."

One of my favorites was heard during a very short flight. The stewardess announced that there would be beverage service but they didn't have much time and she didn't have much change. So if people could give her the exact amount, she'd be very grateful. And if anybody paid for a drink with a $20 bill, she'd be even more grateful—for the biggest tip she ever got.

***

I know that some airlines frown on this sort of freelance stand-up routine, but if done with taste and sensitivity, I think it's a real plus. There are very few situations that cannot be helped by an infusion of laughter. When a company, organization, or individual has problems that are known and cannot be ignored—jokes will inevitably surface concerning them. Smart public relations is when you do the jokes first. You have an embarrassment? A crisis? You've made a terrible mistake? If you're the first to do the jokes about it, chances are it will diminish or defuse the other slings, arrows, and one-liners that may follow.

More often than not, when I research a speech for a corporate executive or political figure—a subject or incident will be mentioned and they'll immediately say, "Well we can't use that. That's too sensitive." My response is that, with few exceptions, they *must* refer to it. If they don't, others will—and usually in a way that's harmful and beyond control. If you try to ignore the obvious, you become even more the butt of the joke.

The mere mention of the sensitive subject is a plus. It indicates that the speaker is aware of the audience's interest or concern. It also indicates that he or she is strong enough and secure enough not to try to hide the obvious. It's like saying to the audience, "Let's talk about it." And an interesting thing happens. Just by putting the subject on the table, the audience is allowed to draw any conclusions it wishes. Some will see in the jokes a tacit apology. Others will interpret them as an indicator that a change of heart or direction is taking place. And still others will greet them sympathetically as the human side of a warm and self-confident personality.

***

The humorous airing of problems, embarrassments and vulnerabilities is an ideal way to command a sympathetic ear. George Bush, a less than great communicator, used it in his acceptance speech at the 1988 Republican Convention. He said he would try to hold his charisma in check. It got a good reaction and the positive carryover indicated he might have even created a little glimmer of real charisma.

At the same year's Democratic Convention, the then governor of Arkansas, Bill Clinton, delivered a snoozer of a nominating speech. Thirty-two minutes in length, it was far too long and far too dull. The audience, his fellow Democrats, hooted, waved white handkerchieves as a sign of surrender, or ignored him totally by talking to each other. It was an intensely humiliating experience witnessed by tens of millions on network TV. Overnight, Bill Clinton's speech became *the* national joke. It was the stuff that could put you out of politics.

But then, with one wave of a comedic wand, Clinton turned it all around. He accepted an invitation to appear on the Johnny Carson TV show. Carson talked

325

about the speech and did a few jokes about it—but Clinton did even more jokes about it. He kidded himself relentlessly. He said the Democrat nominee, Michael Dukakis, called him next day, said there were no hard feelings, and asked if he would consider doing the nominating speech for George Bush (his Republican opponent) the following month.

When Johnny Carson asked how such a long, wrong speech had come about, Clinton said he did it on purpose—he always wanted to be on the Johnny Carson show. It was a delightful parade of funny self-deprecation and it worked. When it was over, Clinton left a total winner—a folk hero.

Once again, the bottom line is that when something is so big you can't ignore it—don't. When life hands you a lemon, make lemonade. When life hands you a mishap, make jokes. And the mishaps don't have to be monumental ones.

Joe Griffith is a very popular and successful speaker. While he was delivering a banquet speech, a waitress came up to the head table near the lectern and began clearing dishes. All eyes went to her. It was a situation that couldn't be ignored. Joe Griffith smiled, gestured to the waitress, and then said to the audience, "You all, of course, have met my wife."

The speaker was back in control.

III.

Humor effectively done is almost a narcotic: you can't get enough of it. To have a few hundred people erupt in appreciative laughter at something you have said is a heady experience. I think back to one of my favorite heart-warming memories. A prominent CEO had just finished an extraordinarily well-received humorous presentation. He came down from the stage and, with the applause still filling the hall, leaned over to me and whispered, "I wish I could go back and do it all over again."

When humor works, it delivers a natural high to both speaker and audience. Humor has many uses. It can delight, divert, defend, and defame. Humor can derail conflict and defuse tension. It has become a necessary and highly-regarded management resource. A timely joke is valued for its ability to break the tension of an emotional gridlock or frightening situation. But there are limits—and it is prudent to know the limits.

I use the analogy of people flying in a three engine plane. If one engine quits, any tension-breaking joke would work because the plane can fly on two engines and the passengers probably would feel they are not in danger. If a second engine quits, a tension-breaking joke still might work if the passengers had some amount of hope that they could limp in on one engine. But if that last engine quits and the plane is going down—even the most inspired joke would not get a reaction. When the unhappy or undesired reality of a situation is too overwhelming, chances are that humor will be either unwelcome or unrecognized.

***

I have always believed this, and then, a few years ago, the theory became actuality. I was in an airliner flying from New York to Washington, D.C. As we were making our final approach to Washington's National Airport I heard an unfamiliar screeching of metal. Shortly after, we started to gain altitude, and a few minutes later I looked down and saw that we were somewhere near Baltimore.

At that time, "stacking"—planes circling airports waiting for clearance to land—was not all that uncommon. Most of the passengers paid no attention to the delay. We circled for another ten minutes or so and then the pilot announced that they were having problems with the nose landing gear. It had not gone down automatically. They had then cranked it down manually but a cabin control light, indicating the landing gear was locked in place, had not lit up. They weren't sure the nose gear would hold when it hit the runway. They were working on the problem.

More circling. A round of nervous joking spread throughout the plane. Each heretofore silent group of three passengers, elbow to elbow in coach, became convivial. Bad jokes got good reactions. A few people looked concerned—some because of the potential danger, others because they would be late for appointments—but generally there was an almost festive, "we're all in this together," atmosphere in the cabin.

Now the pilot made another announcement. He said he thought the landing gear was locked in place, but he couldn't be sure, so we were going to land at Dulles Airport which has a longer runway than National. This is true. But I am sure that I wasn't the only one who mulled over the fact that Dulles had far fewer flights at that time than National. If we piled up at Dulles, it would create a much smaller traffic problem for the Washington area. I heard a few jokes on this theme but the humor level was rapidly dropping.

We were now heading for Dulles Airport, and the cabin attendants were getting the passengers ready for an emergency landing. With ample amounts of reassurance that all would be well, we were shown the exit doors and stronger passengers were placed beside them and given instructions as to when and how to open them.

Attaché cases and carry-on bags under the seats were collected together with anything else that could get in the way of a fast exit. Any personal items with pointed edges or corners were also collected from the passengers, put into big plastic bags and stored in the lavatories. One cabin attendant tried to take my eyeglasses but I refused. I figured if I was going to meet my Maker, at least I wanted to see what He—or She—looked like.

***

We were now descending toward Dulles Airport. Once again the captain gave us words of reassurance and outlined the procedures that would be followed in this emergency landing. As an additional bit of comfort, he said that all of the airline's pilots were required to go to their headquarters' training facility twice a year to practice emergency landings and, by coincidence, he had just gone through this training procedure the week before. Then, after a perfect comedic pause, he added, "And I think I remember most of it."

I still don't know if this was intended or unintended humor. In either case, no one laughed. The psychological third engine of my analogy had cut out. Passengers were just plain scared and no humor was going to penetrate the fear.

Our plane was now making its final approach to Dulles Airport. We had been instructed to tighten our seat belts as much as possible, to assume a semifetal position, and to clasp our hands over the backs of our heads. Now there were no jokes, no comments, no talk at all.

But as I crouched in this strange position, I could see one of the cabin attendants running down the aisle to get to her seat. I raised my hand and beckoned to her. She asked, "What do you need?" I said, "Things haven't been going all that well for me lately—so could I ask one small favor?" She said, "What's that?" I said, "Could I move up to first class? It'd look so good in the obituary."

She put her hand on my arm and said, "Relax. It's going to be all right." She continued to her seat and that's when *my* fear started to grow. She hadn't recognized this out-and-out joke—which meant to me that in spite of the pilot's calmness and attempts to make it all sound routine, and in spite of her very professional, not-to-worry reassurance, in actuality, her psychological third engine had quit as well.

The ending of this story is pure anticlimax. The plane touched down. The nose gear held. It had locked into place, but the panel light that should have indicated this had malfunctioned. But the instant it was apparent we had made a safe landing, the jokes began again. A level of comfort had been reached that allowed for the tension-breaking use of humor.

***

My three-engine theory has a reverse corollary. We don't laugh if we feel ourselves to be seriously endangered. We also don't laugh when someone we perceive to be seriously endangered or vulnerable attempts humor. Our concern for the safety and well-being of the individual blots out everything else.

For example, picture a clown high-wire act in the circus. He's 50 feet above the ground, no net, doing comedic gymnastics. His verbal jokes are well received, not just because they're funny, but they also ease the anxiety the audience feels for his safety.

Suppose he slips? Not a phony slip that's part of the act—but a real one. Suddenly he's teetering on the wire in serious trouble, and a chill goes through the arena. Would the same jokes (still as funny as before) work? Hardly. An audience must be at ease with itself and the performer before laughter can take hold.

***

It doesn't have to be a life-or-death situation. When I was a writer on the Red Skelton TV show, Red did a sketch as one of his most popular characters, Freddie the Freeloader. Freddie was supposed to jump into a barrel and hide from someone chasing him. When the pursuer left, Freddie was to get out of the barrel and continue with the scene. This was all performed before a studio audience.

The cameras were rolling. The audience was laughing. Red jumped into the barrel. Some bits of comedic business followed and then Red was to climb out of the barrel. But he didn't. Instead, still in character as Freddie the Freeloader, Red delivered the rest of his lines from the barrel as the other cast members improvised around this new staging. The scene ended. The curtain came down. The audience loved it.

In back of the curtain, Red Skelton was motioning to stagehands to help him out of the barrel. There had been props in the bottom of the barrel. When Red jumped into it, one ankle hit the side of a prop and doubled over. The pain was sharp and immediate. Red thought he had broken his ankle. He also knew that if the studio audience had any inkling that he was in trouble, they would stop laughing. Red also knew he couldn't stand, much less walk—so he finished the scene in the barrel and the laughs rolled on.

During my six years on the show, I can't recall Red Skelton ever missing a show. But there were a few occasions when he arrived with a 24-hour virus that was so severe, it wasn't certain that he would be able to go on. In each instance, with a doctor and nurse in attendance backstage, he decided to give it a try.

I can still remember Red coming to center stage to begin the monologue so weak he was almost reeling in place. His face was flushed. He was sweating. His voice was strained. But the audience did not notice, nor would Red let it notice, his illness. With a lifetime of performing know-how to draw upon, he masked and glossed over every hint of the effects of the virus.

And then an interesting thing happened. As the monologue progressed, Red was hearing the audience response—the giggles, the belly laughs, and the roars. You could see him standing more steadily. Then he did the sketch and the audience was really hot. With every succeeding laugh, the sweat of the virus receded and the glow of the artist returned. By the time he did the Silent Spot, the pantomime sketch that closed the show, the doctor and nurse could have been sent home. The audience couldn't have been more responsive to Red—and Red couldn't have been more responsive to them.

Red had been given the best prescription any comedian can ask for—the plasma of laughter. The 24-hour virus notwithstanding, when the show ended Red had regained so much of his strength that he stayed on to do 20 minutes of his nightclub act as his way of saying "thanks."

Humor has its limitations but its benefits cannot be denied for long.

IV.

Humor has become a key ingredient in modern communication and the creation of a favorable image—for a cause, a product, or a person. But there are pitfalls in humor of which any prudent speaker should be aware.

Let's start with the premise that most humor is unfair. There can be no equivocation if a joke is to work. The joke is either for something or against it. Humor always takes a position—and the stronger the position, the more effective the humor becomes.

In this sense, humor is unlike real life. In the real world, true black or white is a rarity. Every position, action, or person is made up of varying shades of gray. Almost everything is a crazy quilt of good and bad, true and false, yes and no. Fairness calls for looking at all aspects of an issue. A joke can't do that. An effective joke assumes a "take no prisoners" view of life.

Picture a roast. The person being roasted is an avid golfer and the audience knows it. The roaster smiles benignly at his target and says, "I won't comment on his golf game, but it's the first time I ever saw anyone pick up his club, step up to the tee, take a mighty swing— and bunt."

An obvious falsehood. The golfer may not be another Jack Nicklaus, but he also isn't the complete wipeout the joke implies. On the other hand, it would be impossible to make a fairer assessment of his golfing talent and still have the joke work. So humor is unfair. Jokes are unfair. And in telling one, the joke-teller may be assuming and identifying with a position or attitude that is unfair. Enter danger.

***

All political leaders and corporate executives have to make an assessment of humor and its suitability to their positions. I urge business speakers to apply humor to ticklish or highly-charged issues—but *only* if they are bringing an acceptable—implied or actual— solution to the problem. If there is no reasonable light at the end of the tunnel, jokes will seem callous and will certainly be counterproductive.

Does this mean that humor should not be attempted by the principal in a volatile situation without an apparent happy ending? Probably. Only one comedic approach might work if adroitly done. If, over a period of time, the speaker has developed a basic rapport of goodwill with his audience, "woe is me" type self-deprecating humor might help.

Without ever referring directly to the controversy, the speaker could humorously relate the anguish and travail it has brought into his life. An observation like: "I won't comment on the events of the last few weeks but I'll tell you one thing—when I go into the office each morning, I no longer ask, 'What's new?'" It says that he or she is hurting and is as concerned as the listeners— and that could be the start of some bonding between the two.

Nowadays professional comedians can do or say virtually anything without repercussions. This is a luxury not afforded to business and political speakers. The sensitivity factor and the emotional response of an audience have to be carefully considered.

There is a basic underlying sense of fair play that always tempers the public's reaction to humor. The right joke delivered by the wrong person isn't appreciated. The right jokes, but too many of them for too long a period of time, can also produce a backlash. It is the comedic equivalent of "piling on," and almost as if by an invisible signal, the subject dries up as a humor peg. Jay Leno and David Letterman tell their writers, "Enough already." Speakers may see audience reaction to the same joke or jokes go from enthusiastic to quiet to hostile.

Humor is a two-edged sword. You should know what you're doing before taking it out of its sheath.

Uses of Humor —See THE USES AND LIMITS OF HUMOR

USING HUMOR WHEN YOU'RE AFRAID TO USE HUMOR

Many years ago, on one of my first trips to Washington to do some political writing, I was taken to a restaurant on Capitol Hill for dinner. The atmosphere was warm and convivial. I was introduced to a number of senators, congressmen, and White House officials.

There was a great deal of banter and easy conversation about the political topics of the day.

I was very impressed, and as dinner drew to a close, I remarked to my host how warm and friendly the political figures we had talked to had been. He gave the remaining wine in his glass a long thoughtful look that slowly turned into a smile. He said, "That's right. It is very warm and friendly. We work together. We dine together. We play golf together. We see each other socially. And when one of us stumbles and is hurt—we eat him!"

I once had a fascinating talk with a magician who specialized in mind-reading effects. The tricks were puzzling and dramatic, but he was up front with his audience that they were just tricks. Clairvoyance, mysticism, and psychic phenomena had nothing to do with it. In fact, he cast a rather jaundiced eye at the claims of all psychics.

One time a TV talk show had him and a leading astrologist as guests. The astrologist was well-known for making scattershot predictions of things to come and attributing the information to divine guidance. That was the last straw for the magician. He said to the astrologist, "You know, I wish you wouldn't keep saying you get all these predictions from God." She said, "Why?" He said, "Well, you've been wrong so many times, you make God look bad."

A group of Russians were touring the U.S. Two of them, a popular playwright and a top-ranked actress, found themselves at a party surrounded by interested American guests.

The actress was a woman of imposing proportions—not quite five by five, but certainly eligible for Weight Watchers. At one point she was asked what plays she had appeared in. She mentioned a few of the classics but explained that many of the plays would not be known outside of Russia. "For instance," she said, "one of the most popular plays was about the peasant revolt against the tyranny of the Tsars." Someone asked, "What part did you play in that?" She said, "A tank."

***

Why am I telling you these wonderful stories? First, because they actually happened, and that always adds a special luster to any anecdote. Second, they are performable stories with a beginning, middle, and snapper of an ending. And third, they each contain an insight, viewpoint or attitude that can be expanded. This qualifies these stories as possible introductory anecdotes to a speech or a segment of a speech.

Most important of all to the premise of this piece— "Using Humor When You're Afraid to Use Humor"—they are funny, true stories that happened to and involved *other* people.

Humor is risk-taking. Whenever we tell a joke to one or one thousand people, we are asking for a reaction. In the process, we are putting ourselves uniquely on the line. Most verbal communication does not demand a response, as does humor, that so immediately reflects the success or failure of the communicator. A joke never bombs alone. The joker is always perceived as having bombed with it. Many speakers are reluctant to take the risk.

There are two ways to cope with this challenge and potential trauma. The first is avoidance. Don't attempt humor at all. But humor has become so important a communicating tool and so expected by audiences, avoidance now carries its own risks.

The safer approach, when timid about humor, is to shift the responsibility for it to other people. The speaker becomes a reporter rather than a humorist. You recount relevant, funny stories in which you are not the key factor. If the anecdotes involved high-visibility personalities, or people and situations the audience is close to, the likelihood of acceptance is high. But your personal and emotional investment in telling the story is low. After relating the incident, in effect you join the audience as an onlooker, a bystander. If the story doesn't get a reaction, it is much easier to continue as if it was an illustrative anecdote rather than a joke.

***

Each of the stories I began with are ideal speech openers because they are funny and also embody a thought or a punch line that can be expanded.

"We eat him" is an easy introduction into a discussion of the stress and fluid loyalties of politics.

The astrologist story might be a good start if you have made a high-visibility error or wrong move and want to recant.

"A tank" is a delightful little example of honest humor that can create an atmosphere conducive to further communication and understanding.

It is usually possible to find a reasonable bridge from the punch line of an anecdote to the substance of a speech. This connective thought then validates the inclusion of the anecdote. It introduces an agenda or a theme springboarding from the anecdote. The opening becomes more than a joke for a joke's sake.

Interestingly, audiences are less judgmental of this secondhand approach to humor. They are not challenged and confronted by someone overtly trying to be funny and so are frequently more relaxed and supportive in their response.

***

The artful use of short, funny quotations is another way to enter the humor arena without putting too much of yourself on the line. To quote Mark Twain or Woody Allen or Sam Goldwyn or Yogi Berra is a surefire way to add lightness to your presentation while putting the burden of the quote's success or failure on the celebrity being quoted.

You can help to insure a good reaction by signaling to the audience that now it might be fun time. If you're using a funny quote, always set it up in a playful manner: "As one of America's greatest philosophers, W. C. Fields, once said . . ." and then the real and actual quote.

***

One last suggestion. Nothing makes a humorist, timid or confident, feel better than hearing and seeing that first laugh. To stack the cards in favor of this happening, before the program begins study some of the people nearby in your audience. Spot someone who seems to be a good listener and an easy smiler and laugher.

When you step up to the lectern, give this person your own best smile. Then do most of your opening joke directly to them—particularly the punch line. The chances are overwhelming that your attentions will be rewarded with a laugh. Even if this person turns out to be the only laugher, for the moment you won't be aware of it. Self-confidence is frequently built on such fragile support as this.

Once again, these are suggestions for speakers who are uncomfortable with humor but who are determined to give it a try. Experienced speakers will always try to have eye contact with and involve as many in their audience as possible. Focusing on one laugher is just a small confidence-building step along the way.

But I have to warn you, there is no such thing as certainty in this world. I think back to my very first public speech years ago. I found my friendly face—a jolly woman who laughed and laughed and laughed. So every time I needed a quick fix of reassurance, I looked over in her direction and there she was—laughing and laughing and laughing. Until, halfway through my speech, I once again looked over at her and there she was, head thrown back, almost facing the ceiling—snoring and snoring and snoring.

Assessing an audience is not an exact science.

Using Other Speakers (to make you a better speaker)
—See (1) STAGE FRIGHT AND HOW TO DEAL WITH IT; (2) THE HARD WORK OF HUMOR

V

Values and Humor —See KINDER, GENTLER COMEDY

Verbose Person —See Advice to the Verbose

Videotaping Your Performance —See TAPING

Vote Call / Voting

If there is no further discussion, let's take a vote. All in favor . . . All opposed. . . All who'd rather be home watching *(TV show)*. . . .

It did get a little confusing at times. If you saw a delegate raising his arm, you could never be quite sure if he was voting his conscience or testing his arthritis.

There's a reason why it was possible to create the world in only six days—no roll-call votes.

To speed up the roll call, would all those who are absent, please raise your hands.

When Something Is Being Railroaded Through: I won't say how that vote was handled but it's obvious the Chairman is a member of the National Stifle Association.

W

Wardrobe —See ADVICE—AND HOW TO IGNORE IT

Water (consumed at the lectern) —See THE HARD WORK OF HUMOR

Weak Applause —See Applause

Weak Introductions and Openings —See OPENER: THE FIRST TWO MINUTES OF YOUR SPEECH

When a Joke Dies —See A Joke Dies

"When in Doubt, Cut It Out" —See SPICING UP THOSE DULL SPEECHES

When People Leave in a Conspicuous Way

To Anyone Leaving the Room: Sir, I'm taking an exit poll. Why are you exiting?

If People Get Up and Leave: Look at that. A moving standing ovation!

When Someone Leaves During Your Talk: Did you know there's a substantial penalty for early withdrawal?

When the Speakers Start to Repeat

Cloning is nothing new. I've heard speakers who repeat themselves.

When to Pull the Plug on a Speech —See ASSESSING YOUR AUDIENCE

When You Address a Small Crowd

Now you can rely on this because I firmly believe that it's a sin to tell a lie—to such a small crowd.

When You Misspeak or Make a Mistake —See (1) MIS-TAKES; (2) Mistakes and Misspeaking

Where Do Jokes / Stories Come From? —See STO-RIES: WHERE DO THEY COME FROM?

"Which Reminds Me of an Old Story" —See *Don't Preface* at DON'TS . . . IF YOU WANT TO GET LAUGHS

Who Should Be the Object of a Roast (and who should not) —See *Preparing the Roast* at ROASTS

"WHY HUMOR?"

I.

The most unusual question I've ever been asked during the Q.&A. period following a speech was at a small college in Texas. After the usual run of questions concerned with how I got started in the humor-writing business and how others should go about getting started, a student raised his hand—and deadly serious—asked me how I justified my way of making a living.

It stopped me cold. How do I justify a lifetime of creating laughter? I mulled over a choice of answers—some straight and others facetious—but then a long-ago memory came into my consciousness. I saw myself as an eight-year-old in 1935 in the midst of the Great

Depression. My family had lost the assets it had in the 1929 stock market crash and the economic stagnation that followed. Paying the rent was a once-a-month crisis. Putting adequate food on the table was an everyday challenge. The anxieties, the tensions, the fears this created haunted the adults and in spite of their best efforts, spilled over into the awareness of this eight-year-old.

But, on Saturday mornings, all these economic concerns and survival fears were forgotten. With a hard-to-come-by dime in my hand I'd be standing in a long line of kids waiting to get into the first Saturday morning show at the local movie house. For ten cents we would see a cartoon, a short subject, an episode of a serial, and two feature films. It was three full hours of adventure, thrills, excitement—but mostly laughter. Donald Duck, Goofy, Mickey Mouse, Laurel and Hardy, the Three Stooges, and the always good-natured, light-hearted banter of the Fred Astair–Ginger Rogers musicals—all combined to provide a refuge of laughter from the threatening realities outside. An eight-year-old laughed and momentarily forgot.

***

This flash of memory became my answer to the student's question but, even as I was speaking, I realized that the need for and the benefits to be derived from humor go far beyond the escape factor. In America, a sense of humor has generally been regarded as a valuable component of a person's psychological make-up. We like to be around people who make us feel good. But the recognized importance of a sense of humor has now taken a front-and-center position in business, politics, medicine, teaching and communication. Laughter is in.

It is now generally recognized that humor is one of the best devices to enhance the image of a person, product, or philosophy. Effective humor carries a message that's very hard to debate. If a point or claim or charge is made via a joke, it can only be countered by a better joke. Rebutting humor with facts, figures and counter-charges only leaves you open to the question, "What's the matter? Can't you take a joke?"

Business executives and political leaders have embraced humor because humor works. Humor enhances and projects a favorable image, eases tensions, influences thinking and attitudes, helps reassert control, reduces the embarrassment of mistakes and awkward moments, serves as a useful teaching tool, is a potent and hard-to-defend-against weapon, usually conveys goodwill, and, perhaps most important of all—humor makes your listeners feel better.

In the early 1970s, when I first began speaking and holding workshops on the uses of humor in business and politics, the concept seemed to many to be frivolous and of back-burner importance. When, in 1972, I suggested somewhat facetiously that a new corporate position be created—the Staff Jester—it was picked up by the wire services, circulated throughout the world, and in London's *Daily Mirror* presented as "another daffy idea from America."

Well, the corporate position of staff jester may have been daffy, as it was intended to be, but the underlying principle of using humor as a healing, communicating, and influencing tool was not. Today, the worlds of business, politics, health care and education are all in hot pursuit of the benefits to be derived from this old, but always new, communicating device—humor.

***

Americans, in particular, have always taken to people with a sense of humor. Humor is a happy communication between equals. Master and slave do not laugh together. The well-placed joke or the apt bit of fun is an instantaneous leveler. A shared laugh can temporarily erase all differences of position, power and outlook between the funner and funnee. And, if properly nurtured, the goodwill and the good feeling can live on long after the fun has ended. If you can laugh together—you can work together.

Consider our recent American presidents. If you were to list those you most approved of and those you least approved of, chances are the leaders who used humor the most would fall into the first category; those who used humor the least would be in the second group. Consider your friends, relatives, neighbors and business associates. More often than not, wouldn't they also fall into the same categories?

Humor has become such an effective image-enhancer that it has affected every aspect of our lives. The clergy leaven their sermons with humor. Products are sold on TV using humor. Teachers hold their students' attention by humor. Politicians and lovers reach their goals via humor.

Humor is associated with youth, vigor, intelligence and being "with it." The broad smile and light remark are welcome guests at any gathering. Without really saying it, they say, "I want to be friends." It makes for instant win-overs, but, having said all this, on occasion it still surprises me when I'm confronted with humor's effectiveness in unusual situations.

***

A few years ago I was privileged to meet the Dalai Lama of Tibet at a Washington reception. We exchanged a few minutes of small talk. I don't know what I was expecting—probably a conversation halfway between *Lost Horizon* and a *National Geographic* documentary. What I got was a fascinating exchange of comments I could only describe as banter. What can I tell you? He came, he charmed, he conquered.

One of the reasons we respond to people with a

sense of humor is that humor implies control and command of a situation. If there is a crisis, an emergency, a time of challenge—and a leader can joke in the face of it—it implies that a solution has been found, the right path to follow has been determined. Humor is the ultimate expression of being cool, calm, and collected. In 1944, the German army had the 101st Airborne Division surrounded and trapped at Bastogne. When the German commander presented an ultimatum to surrender to General McAuliffe, he gave a one word answer: "Nuts!" It brought a smile to Allied faces throughout the world and a new resolve to the men of the 101st to break out of the ring and move on to win—and they did.

***

Humor enhances an image, humor motivates, but humor also creates reality.

We all know that hundreds of people who were ruined by the stock market crash of 1929 hurled themselves out of high windows. But did they? Kenneth Galbraith in his definitive book *The Great Crash* says no. Why do we think they did? Because cartoonists then and ever since have pictured 1929 by showing brokers and their customers leaping from Wall Street ledges.

How many celebrities and public figures do most of us know personally? For the most part, personalities in the news are strangers to us. Nevertheless, we all have formed strong opinions about their characters, abilities, foibles, strengths, and weaknesses. How do we do this? The facts come from newspapers, magazines, TV and books. The translation of those facts into feelings is substantially the work of our humorists. The jokes, stories, and cartoons that immediately encase every public figure and event in large part become the basis of our personal perceptions. Humor creates its own consensus.

There is no doubt in my mind that if you gathered

the leading comedians, comedy writers and cartoonists together—chose a public figure at random and invented a completely false and fictitious event or characteristic concerning that public figure—and sent this army of humorists out with the order to do a ton of jokes and cartoons based on this fabrication—within a month the falsehood would be indisputably accepted as fact.

Why humor? Why not humor? I'd rather it be my ally than my enemy.

II.

Humor has always been a second-class citizen in the arts. The comedies of Shakespeare are less highly regarded than the tragedies. The skills of comedians have been recognized and rewarded, but never with the same respect and admiration that has been heaped on serious dramatic actors. Woody Allen summed it up best with the observation, "When you do comedy, you are not sitting at the grownups' table."

The most memorable putdown of the comic art I have ever seen was contained in a short news item in *The Times-Picayune* of New Orleans. A Boston radio station had appointed a 12-year-old girl as its sports director—perhaps the youngest sports director in the nation. So far, so good. But what really hurt was the follow-up sentence: "The girl had been a comedy writer for the morning 'Joe and Andy' show, and the appointment is seen as a step up."

Oh, punch line—where is thy sting?

***

Throughout the centuries, the attitude towards humor has been ambivalent. We have treasured it but we haven't honored it. We have considered it frivolous and of little consequence—but then reached for it first in bookstores, theaters and life. But to come right out and

347

admit to enjoying enjoyment is something the human species has rarely done. Up until now.

In the last ten years there has been a sea change in the attitude of the establishment towards humor. A Pentagon study of the U.S. Military Academy at West Point listed a pervasive lack of humor as one of the institution's ongoing problems.

Anatomy of an Illness as Perceived by the Patient, a best-selling book by Norman Cousins, was a fascinating account of his belief that he was cured of a terminal illness through the application of humor therapy. Researchers in a variety of medical disciplines are now investigating the uses of humor in the healing process.

Astute business and political leaders are salting, peppering and thyming their speeches with relevant topical humor that audiences appreciate, remember, and quote. The apt, well-chosen joke—no savvy speaker leaves home without it.

***

Humor helps to create and enhance your personal image and that of your organization—but humor can and should serve many purposes beyond that. What about those embarrassing mistakes and awkward moments that tend to turn the victim into a red-faced, confused babbler? The right riposte can sometimes make for an instantaneous recovery.

Louis Armstrong, the legendary master of the trumpet, had signed an exclusive contract with a recording company. At one point during the term of the contract, the recording company heard Armstrong's strong and distinctive horn on another label. They called him in for a meeting and presented their case. Louis Armstrong then proved himself to be an equal master of comedic reconciliation. He said, "I didn't do it—and I'll never do it again." Both sides leveled with the other but laughter allowed the relationship to continue.

Humor can also ease tension in more stressful situations. A minister once told me that when conducting a funeral service, he always tries to include in the eulogy the favorite joke of the deceased. It serves as a temporary respite from grief and also brings back warm memories of happier times with the loved one.

Quite often, humor not only eases a stressful confrontation but also reasserts the user's control of the situation. One of my favorites examples of this dual effect was described by John Costello in *Nation's Business*. Frederick R. Kappel, then chairman and CEO of the American Telephone and Telegraph Co., was conducting its annual shareholders' meeting.

The meeting, a volatile one, was now in its fourth hour. Kappel had fielded many tough questions, the hour was late, the large audience ready to go home. But a woman who had made a specialty of attending corporate annual meetings, had still another question to ask. She was unhappy with the magnitude of corporate contributions to good causes.

"Mr. Chairman," she asked, "how much did AT&T give to charity?" "Ten million dollars last year," Kappel answered. The woman said mockingly, "I think I'm going to faint." Kappel said, "That would be very helpful." Laughter and applause from the audience. Control was back with the speaker. Humor scores again!

***

One of the most important attributes of humor is its ability to influence thinking and attitudes. E. B. White wrote: "A despot doesn't fear eloquent writers preaching freedom—he fears a drunken poet who may crack a joke that will take hold." I don't know if it calls for a drunken poet, but once an image-building or image-destroying joke takes hold, it's almost impossible to turn the effect around.

President Reagan was extraordinarily adroit and

effective in his use of humor as an influencing device. In his race for the Presidency in 1980, it was evident that his age could be an issue and a problem. So at every opportunity he kidded himself about his age. Whenever he referred to an historical event or something that had happened in the distant past—he'd comment, "Seems like only yesterday,"—or imply that he was there. In short order, Ronald Reagan's age became old news because he had taken the high and funny ground first. Age never became a factor in the 1980 election.

Humor again saved the day for Ronald Reagan in 1984, and it also had to do with the age issue. In his first debate with Walter Mondale, the Democratic challenger, President Reagan looked nothing like the Great Communicator. He bumbled through answers, seemed disoriented, and rambled through a long closing anecdote that he never got to finish because time ran out. Suddenly the age and senility question dominated the attention of the media.

Cartoonists, satirists, columnists and editorial writers all addressed the over-the-hill issue. A negative image roll had begun. Even though the polls still showed the President to be well ahead, the White House couldn't have been comforted by Mark Russell saying, "The consensus is that even though Reagan appeared to be hesitant, nervous, confused and incoherent—as long as he keeps remembering to put on his trousers, he'll be re-elected."

Who knows how far all this could have gone? But it stopped on a dime two-thirds of the way through the second Reagan-Mondale debate. Predictably, one of the questions addressed to the President was concerned with age and his ability to do the job. As the question was being asked, you could almost see Ronald Reagan's eyes lighting up with anticipation. He said, "I am not going to make age an issue in this campaign. I am not going to exploit for political purposes my opponent's youth and inexperience."

It was all over. The audience roared, even Mondale laughed, and age never again surfaced as an issue in that campaign.

***

In recent years political figures have paid close attention to the slings and arrows of outrageous humorists. They know all too well the power of a widely circulated joke—or, worse, a barrage of jokes making the same point. The common wisdom in Washington is that when Jay Leno and David Letterman repeatedly attack a political personality on a single subject—it's the beginning of the end. There is a herd instinct in humor. As soon as the route is made clear, the bandwagon never lacks for passengers.

In addition to Leno and Letterman, political cartoonists are frequently the ones to get the bandwagon rolling. Politicians are well aware of this. *Washingtonian* magazine referred to "HHF" as an acronym sometimes heard in the office of the Secretary of Defense. It stands for "High Herblock Factor." Herblock is the Pulitzer Prize-winning editorial cartoonist of *The Washington Post*, and the acronym indicates that the Pentagon doesn't want to do anything to rouse Herblock's very pointed pen.

This sensitivity to ridicule enters into the very highest halls of government. A daily news summary is published by the White House to keep the President and his staff aware of national media coverage and concerns. A representative sampling of TV news programs, newspaper editorials and magazine features are boiled down to essentials for quick reading. But cartoons, comic strips and humor columns are also included to give the White House reader a sense of the emotional response to programs and policies.

The humor factor is also a concern of the business community. Through the years I have occasionally been called in by advertising agencies in the process of preparing a major media campaign for a new or existing product. I'm shown the ads, the slogan, the TV storyboards—and then asked to write a few dozen jokes inspired by the advertising approach. Then they analyze the jokes to see if they are positive or negative—supportive or destructive of the sales potential of the product. They feel this gives them a hint as to how other humorists would react when the campaign goes public.

Many years ago, the late Willie Sutton was asked why he robbed banks. His answer was, "That's where the money is."

Why humor? Because that's where the influence, the appeal, the control, the good feeling—and eventually, the money is.

Wine —See Food and Drink

Winter and Cold Places

I won't say what the weather is like, but this morning's "Travelers' Advisory" is DON'T!

We have now entered that fascinating period of the driving year known as "icy roads"—when we have a choice of either going 30 miles on a gallon or 80 yards on a brake pedal.

Nobody wants to come out in weather like this. Nobody! In Minneapolis, three women are now in their 14th month.

And so, as they say in _____: "Let a smile be your umbrella—and you'll wind up with a face full of snow."

"Where are the snows of yester-year?" If you live in _____—right outside your window.

In _____, it's very hard to accept the fact that we were all created in God's image. Somehow I just can't see God with a red nose and blue lips.

I want to thank all those who have braved this weather to be here tonight. This morning the snow was so bad, the only one who got to the office was our bookkeeper—Nanook.

I can tell we're going to have a great evening because you all have that perfect winter coloring on your faces—half Jack Frost and half Jack Daniels.

—See also During a Snowstorm

"With It" Quality of Humor —See "WHY HUMOR?"

Writers —See (1) MONEY AND SPEECHWRITING; (2) SPEECHWRITERS

WRITER'S BLOCK AND HOW TO GET AROUND IT
I.

The most effective cure of writer's block I've ever witnessed occurred while I was a writer on the Jack Paar TV show. I shared an office with another writer on the show. It was a comfortable set-up, except for one thing. Our office was directly across the hall from Jack Paar's office. No problem in itself. But the proximity encouraged Jack to make random visits that usually began with the perfectly reasonable question, "What are you working on?"

Well, as any writer knows, quite often the only truthful answer to such a question is "Nothing." Writers spend a good part of their existence waiting for inspiration to strike, or at least deliver a glancing blow. To their spouses, friends and neighbors, straightening out paperclips may seem like goofing off, but writers know it's working.

And so, one day my fellow writer and I were sitting in our office and nothing was happening. The creative muse was out to lunch. A couple of hours had gone by and neither of us had come up with an idea worthy of being recorded. Silence reigned. In support of Murphy's Law, that was when our boss, Jack Paar, decided to make one of his visits.

As Jack came through the doorway, I self-consciously said "Hi!"—and continued to stare at my keyboard. But at that moment my fellow writer erupted into a fire-storm of creativity. His face lit up and little gurgles of excited laughter came from his lips as they silently formed words of obvious hilarity. Fingers that had not touched a keyboard all morning were now a blur in their frenzy to capture these gems on paper.

Jack Paar, not one to foolishly turn off the torrent of inspiration that was pouring forth, smiled encouragingly at my colleague, nodded at me, and left. The story would have ended there if, a few minutes later, my fellow writer hadn't visited the washroom. Out of curiosity, I went over to his typewriter to see what gems he had come up with. I, and millions of others, will never forget the words that he had written: "The quick brown fox jumps over the lazy dog. The quick brown fox jumps over the lazy dog. The quick brown fox jumps over the lazy dog."

***

Writer's block. It's what keeps the profession of putting words to paper from being paradise on earth. To get up from a full day at the keyboard, look at the two pages you've written, and then consign them to the wastebasket is an exquisite agony known only to writers, composers, and other masochists.

The most accurate emotional profile of a writer I have ever heard was in a play and subsequent movie called *Tribute.* It starred Jack Lemmon, and as I recall it, in the opening scene, a new-found acquaintance asked him what he did for a living. Lemmon said, "I'm a writer." The acquaintance asked, "Do you like writing?" And Lemmon answered, "No, but I like being a writer."

How many of us feel that way! We enjoy having written, but the act of writing is often a fine agony. I sometimes start off my speechwriting workshops with a little bit of inspiration. I tell the group what a crummy business writing is and that they ought to reconsider their mother's advice to become a pharmacist.

Writing is frequently a frustrating, exasperating, low-paying, highly stressful, lonely and anonymous way of spending a lifetime. A friend of mine, a hugely successful but unsung TV writer, once said he had the modus operandi for the perfect crime. You commit the crime—get a job writing for television—and you will never be heard of again.

But of all the afflictions that rain down upon word-pushers—writer's block has to be the worst. It's an occupational hazard unique to the creative professions. If you're a bus driver, when you go into work in the morning, you know the route, what's expected of you, and there's no doubt in your mind that you can and will do it. That same certainty applies to most jobs—butchers, bakers, candlestick makers. But not writers.

No matter how long a writer has been a writer—no matter how acclaimed, well paid and motivated a writer may be—a little bit of self-doubt hangs over every pen, pencil, computer and word processor. No one really knows where inspiration comes from. We only hope it knows our address. But when we don't hear that knock on our inner door, it doesn't take long for panic, despond and writer's block to appear.

How to cope? How to get past the desert of a blank screen or sheet of paper and into the oasis of creativity once again? When I speak to writers, that's one of the questions I'm most frequently asked. We are all looking for a magic solution to the problem. As a result, some writers are less than satisfied with one of the answers I give.

***

During the sixties, when I was one of eight writers on the Red Skelton TV show, I was sometimes asked to speak to radio and TV writing classes at local colleges. I would outline the procedures we followed—throw in a few funny anecdotes to keep the audience interested— but I would also underscore what a stressful and de- manding job it was. Fun and games alone did not produce the 90-page script that was required by this once-a-week comedy-variety show.

The hard-work aspect of comedy writing frequently led to this question during the Q.&A. period: "You talked about how difficult it is and how much tension is involved in writing TV comedy. Why do you do it? What motivates you?" I always had the feeling that these young writers were looking for something inspi- rational. Something like: "I do it because I want to bring a little joy, happiness and laughter to a troubled world."

That was never the answer I gave them. I always said that TV comedy writers have two motivations—fear and greed. Greed, because it is a very well-paid busi- ness and it doesn't take long to adjust your lifestyle to it. And fear, because if you don't deliver the goods, you will no longer have the job that leads to the purchase of these earthly delights.

"Well, what if you don't feel funny or just run out of ideas? What then?" My answer was that you always had the option of going to the star of the show and saying, "I'm sorry. I just couldn't think of anything this week." Yes, you could do it. But, in the immortal words of Richard Nixon, it would be wrong. Very soon the show would find someone who could come up with something, and the right something, on a weekly basis—and you would find yourself with more time to contemplate the maintenance bills for your swimming pool. What we're talking about here is industrial-strength motivation.

***

But the reality of writer's block is recognized. In the days when TV comedy-variety shows were popular, each show would average eight writers. Today, situation comedies tend to be written by individuals or teams of two—while the late-night comedy/talk shows still rely on a much larger staff of writers. This is a practical solution to the problem that inspiration does flag, and so the expectation is that while some of the writers are running cold—others are running hot. Even with teams of two, the pattern seems to be that one is sparking and the other is transcribing—and then, like a comedic square dance, they change places.

But team writing, while common in television, is rarely the case elsewhere. Writers tend to fly solo, and the very loneliness of the occupation may lead to dry periods. I once had the theory that most comedy writers were overweight. My own problems with the scale led to this somewhat dubious belief.

The scenario goes something like this: The phone rings and a client says he needs three minutes of opening humor by 3:00 p.m. Tuesday. I say, "Today is Tuesday." He says, "That's right." A pause—and then, "It's a real tough audience so it's really got to be boffo. But we know you can do it." CLICK.

Now another bit of inspiration I give to fledgling writers is that it doesn't get better with age, experience, expertise or accomplishment. Whenever I hang up after receiving a phone call like that—I look at my watch, I look at my typewriter, and then my mind goes completely, totally, irreversibly blank.

It is moments like these that junk food was made for. I walk. I do not run. I walk to the nearest source of such comfort, stuff myself with whatever non-nutritional goodies I can find, and then waddle back to the task at hand.

I look at the blank sheet of paper, say to myself, "You've been doing this for 50 years. You can do it one more time"—and somehow it gets done. There is nothing like the imminence of a fast-approaching no-nonsense deadline to get the creative juices flowing.

II.

A blank piece of paper and a mind to match is a writer's idea of hell.

One of my favorite memories of Fred Allen goes back to an incident that happened while he had one of the top-rated comedy shows on radio. If comedy writers ever needed a patron saint, Fred Allen would be my candidate. A writer himself, Fred always took the part of the creators against the slings and arrows of the network bureaucracy.

One time a network vice president came into Fred's office and proceeded to tear apart the proposed script for an upcoming show. Nothing pleased him. The jokes were weak. The premises were stilted. The subject matter wouldn't be recognized by many listeners. Fred Allen listened patiently to the critique and then, when it finally came to an end, looked at the vice president and said, "Where were you when the pages were blank?"

Fortunately, for most writers most of the time, blank pages are an invitation, a challenge, and are quickly covered with words. But there will always come a time when a creative drought occurs. What to do then?

***

In time, all writers develop strategies to cope with these dry spells. I doubt if my solutions are all that unique, but they have worked for me—and, perhaps, may be helpful to others.

At the top of the list is the driving, energizing, galvanizing power of routine. Few professional writers wait for the muse to appear. They set up a writing routine and stick to it. The schedule may call for a fixed number of hours per day at the keyboard or a certain number of pages or words to be completed. If it is a realistic schedule (taking into account your personality, and normal work habits, and it's based on reasonable expectations), your creative subconscious will usually respond and do its job. If 8 a.m. to noon is your writing time, your psyche knows it's time to roll up its creative sleeves and get to work.

But your psyche should not be trifled with. Failure should never be rewarded. Routine works best when you're absolutely committed to it. If you have set a four-, or six-, or eight-hour writing day and you can't manage to get even a paragraph on paper—don't cut your agony short. Don't reward your block by going out and playing tennis or seeing a movie. If your subconscious knows it really is going to spend the required time writing—or trying to write—with no time off for bad behavior, it is much more likely to get down to business.

The reverse of this is how do you handle a day when you are really sparking—when the right words just seem to be tumbling out and your quota of hours or words has been met? Obviously you ride the wave of inspiration and continue writing. But the instant you feel that wave may be losing its power, pack it in. If your psyche has been promised a finite day or quota, and then it's off to the beach, don't fool with it. It may not believe you the next time.

***

Now, whenever someone mentions things like the subconscious and the psyche, it all begins to sound very metaphysical. We have to determine for ourselves if there are practical ways to unlock our inner creativity. I'm firmly convinced that my subconscious is continually working away at solving the writing problems I face—even when my surface awareness is occupied with something else. For this reason, whenever possible, I like to gather, read, and assimilate the background materials to any writing project I'm working on—and then put it all aside for a few days to let my subconscious join in the effort. If time is short, even just reviewing the problem before going to sleep can produce solutions in the morning.

When it comes to courting creativity, writers are always in search of patterns that sometimes border on the superstitious. If two cups of coffee and a cheese Danish for breakfast are followed by a good day at the word processor, then two cups of coffee and a cheese Danish it is until the magic doesn't work. I'm all in favor of this (particularly the cheese Danish). Who knows what primes the creative pump? If, for the moment, you think that coffee and cheese Danish help—go for it!

The whole idea is to get started—to put something on that fearsome blank page. Some writers get started by putting any words that occur to them on the page. The words may be good, bad, wise, dumb, appropriate or off-the-wall—but they are a start. The logjam of inaction is broken.

But again, we each have to find our own way and that one has never worked for me. It comes back to the premise "don't try to con your psyche." If I start off with something I know doesn't stand a chance of being right or accepted, it reinforces the root cause of writer's block: "Fear of failure." It isn't even fear of failure so much as the fear of not achieving our own expectations. And so, if we begin with something far below those expectations, little is likely to come of it.

**

Then how do we get started? My favorite device has been to leave something on the page. If I am working well, the words are coming easily, and it's near quitting time—I leave it in the machine to be finished the next day. The path has been determined. The writing offers no resistance. It's easy. So the next day I sit down and do it without the normal uncertainties of a new project. It can be an idea, a joke, a paragraph—anything that has been fully thought out and fairly easy to complete. And in the completion, the next day's writing has begun.

I normally write in a straight line—from beginning, to middle, to conclusion. But when writer's block enters the picture, I immediately go for the aspect of the speech, article, or routine that seems to offer the easiest writing and greatest chance of being right. When completed, this frequently provides the momentum and the inspiration to fill in the remaining areas.

In a similar vein, I also tend to tackle the least threatening, least onerous writing tasks first. The list of writing to be done always seems to be made up of fun assignments I can't wait to begin and dreaded commitments I'm sorry I ever accepted. Obviously, deadlines are a factor that can't be ignored. More often than not, deadlines can still be met even though the path of least resistance is followed. The whole idea is to encourage the inner incentive to start working. Further, it's always interesting how the threat factor of the various items on the writing list changes as you complete assignments and others are added. Suddenly the chore that previously loomed as Public Writing Enemy Number One is perceived as a piece of cake, because a new commitment seems far more of a problem in comparison. So the lesser of the two challenges is now tackled without hesitation.

***

Another dynamic, of course, is at work. The temporary avoidance does not eliminate the realization that the writing must be done. Your subconscious is aware of this, but the slight delay allows this inner ally time to work on the problem.

I believe the success of most speeches and articles is determined by something that goes on long before the writing begins. By and large, we all know what subjects, audiences, and speakers we will probably be writing for and about in the months and years ahead. Therefore, the research effort should be a continuous one. Anytime a usable phrase, approach, or bit of information comes our way, we should squirrel it away into a workable file that allows and encourages retrieval at a later date. The smaller your Miscellaneous section, the more helpful your file will be.

When it comes to writing time, the file provides a head start. A good working file can be the ignition that sparks your creative process.

What to do when none of the preceding works? There will inevitably come a time when the creative gas gauge is on empty and forward motion has stopped. What then?

High tech may eventually provide a solution. One of the goals of the computer industry is to perfect machines that automatically convert the spoken word into hard copy. Correspondence will be dictated, the words recognized and stored by a computer, and then reproduced on paper by a printer.

This technology may transform the art of speechwriting. One of the most difficult aspects of speechwriting is putting down words that are acceptable to the ear, as well as to the eye. The minute most writers sit down to a keyboard, their words lose the drive, the naturalness, the spontaneity of spoken language. We tend to use bigger words, longer sentences, stiffer construction. The result is oratory when a natural conversational approach is called for.

***

Speaking the speech into a transcribing computer will be a major breakthrough in solving this problem. But this technology still has a way to go.

Meanwhile, there is the tape recorder. Everything we've just considered can be done by using a tape recorder and then manually transcribing the taped words onto paper. A writer's block rarely turns into a verbal block. While the thoughts, sentences and construction may need further work, they do get the creative ball rolling. When transcribed, editing and rewriting can eliminate awkwardness—but at least there is something solid to work with—a starting point. Since a speech is verbal communication, creating it verbally may be the best way to go.

One last suggestion. I once asked a fellow writer how he coped with writer's block. He said he used two things—a stack of bills to be paid and a mirror. The bills for his rent, electricity, gas, car payments, and groceries were laid out in a neat row along the far edge of his desk with the mirror behind them. "I can understand the bills as a spur to get you to writing, but the mirror?" I asked. He said, "If I don't write, the mirror's the most important part." I said, "What does it do?" He said, "It lets me watch myself slowly starve to death."

Try some of the preceding suggestions first.

Writing Down Criticisms and Observations —See LESSONS I LEARNED FROM LOWELL THOMAS

Writing the Roast —See *Delivering the Roast* at ROASTS

Written Humor vs. Spoken Humor —See (1) *Don't Use Print Language in Verbal Jokes* at DON'TS . . . IF YOU WANT TO GET LAUGHS; (2) REHEARSING YOUR SPEECH

Written Version of Your Speech —See PREPARING FOR YOUR SPEECH

Y

"Yammer" —See OPENER: THE FIRST TWO MINUTES OF YOUR SPEECH

Yawning

When Someone Yawns While You're Speaking:
Why do I feel that I'm talking faster than you're listening?

And now a word for speakers;
Teachers and lecturers too:
Applause is approbation—
A yawn is a silent boo.

Yawns (and other storm warnings for the speaker) —See LESSONS I LEARNED FROM LOWELL THOMAS

"You Had to Be There" —See (1) ADVICE—AND HOW TO IGNORE IT; (2) STORIES: WHERE DO THEY COME FROM?

"You Never Know Who's Out There" —See HOW TO SUCCEED IN HUMOR BY REALLY TRYING